# THE UNAUTHORIZED PRACTICE OF LAW FOR NONLAWYERS

## Concise Video Edition

**M. Ellen Murphy**

*Assistant Dean, Wake Forest University School of Law*

**Steve H. Nickles**

*C.C. Hope Chair in Law and Financial Services*
*Wake Forest University Schools of Law and Business*

WEST
ACADEMIC
PUBLISHING

© 2018 LEG, Inc. d/b/a West Academic
444 Cedar Street, Suite 700
St. Paul, MN 55101
1-877-888-1330

West, West Academic Publishing, and West Academic are trademarks of West Publishing Corporation, used under license.

Printed in the United States of America

**ISBN:** 978-1-64242-509-3

*With thanks to Dean Suzanne Reynolds for encouraging and supporting innovation in legal education, and for helping bring law to the world.*

# PREFACE*†

The dramatic changes in the legal profession since the 2008 market crash, from the increase in virtual law practice to the rise of DIY services to clients' increasing demand for efficiencies, have led to a recognition that nonlawyers have an increasingly critical role in the delivery of legal services. While most regulatory bars are not yet sure exactly: (a) what this role should be; or (b) how, if at all, it should be regulated, that a change is coming is certain. In fact recently, Washington State became the first to create a new professional license, the "Limited License Legal Technician," a regulatory breakthrough.

Meanwhile, companies large and small—saddled with increasing regulations but fewer resources—look more frequently to employees in risk management, compliance, and human resources, to name but a few, to exercise legal judgement, decreasing the reliance on traditional inside and outside counsel.

Law schools, desperate to serve the profession, and increase revenues in a buyer's market, have responded by adding masters-level programs designed for non-JD candidates. (These programs are different from LLM's, which require a JD for admission.) There are more than one-hundred of these non-JD masters' programs to date.

The American Bar Association (ABA) created the Commission on the Future of Legal Services, with a goal of using technology and innovation to increase access to justice. In so doing, the ABA President acknowledged that some people see this shift as a "back doorway of disrupting a system that they're comfortable with." All a perfect precursor to the coming regulatory

---

* This book is limited to conduct by lay people and legal professionals who are not fully licensed attorneys. It does not cover unauthorized practice by persons who are or were fully licensed attorneys and therefore excludes, for example, multijurisdictional practice, multidisciplinary practice, and the unauthorized practice of law by suspended or disbarred lawyers.

† The authors gratefully acknowledge the American Bar Association Section on Dispute Resolution for use of the Resolution on Mediation and the Unauthorized Practice of Law as adapted by the Section on February 2, 2002.

challenges for our current restrictions on the unauthorized practice of law.

The debate is getting hotter over what nonlawyers, people or computers, can do without running afoul of unauthorized practice of law restrictions. Recently, the Second Circuit found that document review is not the practice of law (addressing whether the Fair Labor Standards Act applied to document review). Recently, too, LegalZoom and the State of North Carolina settled a $10.5 million antitrust suit that included a provision that the state bar would support proposed legislation clarifying the definition of "unauthorized practice of law." [Legislation was introduced but failed to pass the state legislature.]

This book explores the extent to which people with legal training, but no practice license, can use the law, as a social and economic variable, to better manage risk without fear of prosecution or civil liability. But, the book only reports selected law and generalizes across topics and jurisdictions, without purporting to advise or decide whether specific conduct is allowed or disallowed in any state. UPL varies widely across the country, is always and everywhere highly fact-specific, is riddled with non-uniform, judicial and legislative exceptions, and always is decided on a case-by-case basis.

The book is intended and should be used only for general education about the overall subject of UPL and its main constituent issues, and to provoke informed thinking and useful discussion about UPL's present and future boundaries.

Ellen Murphy
Steve Nickles

Winston-Salem, N.C.

July 2018

# SUMMARY OF CONTENTS

# TABLE OF CONTENTS

# THE UNAUTHORIZED PRACTICE OF LAW FOR NONLAWYERS

## Concise Video Edition

# CHAPTER I

# WHAT IS THE UNAUTHORIZED PRACTICE OF LAW (UPL)?

■ ■ ■

The individual states regulate the practice of law; and, every state separately, independently limits the practice of law to persons who, by terms of local law, are duly admitted and licensed to *practice law*. The *practice of law* by anyone else is unauthorized. In short form definition, therefore, the *unauthorized practice of law (UPL)* is practicing law without a license. The long form definition includes descriptions of conduct amounting to the practice of law that is limited to licensed attorneys and is therefore unauthorized and unlawful for everybody else. These definitions, however, are always non-exclusive.

Typically, the courts in a state define and prohibit UPL in broad terms in court rules and on a case-by-case basis in judicial decisions; and, in many states, the legislature does so, too, by statutes that sometimes use relatively specific, but always non-exclusive, language. UPL thus commonly violates both judge-made and statutory law.

Here, to begin, we explore the long form definition of UPL and see how the states, whether in court decisions or in legislation, grapple with defining the practice of law, which has never been fully defined anywhere and is dynamic (and likely narrowing) everywhere.

Here, too, we note the related prohibition barring corporations from practicing law. This bar has two parts. First, a corporation cannot be licensed to practice law and therefore cannot represent customers, clients, or other persons. Or, put another way, a corporation can sell goods and services but cannot engage in the law business. (Law firms are different.) Second, corporations and other legally-created entities cannot even represent themselves in court, which is a larger subject explored more thoroughly in Chapter V, *infra*.

### RESTATEMENT (THIRD) OF THE LAW GOVERNING LAWYERS § 4

**A person not admitted to practice as a lawyer may not engage in the unauthorized practice of law, and a lawyer may not assist a person to do so.**

Comment:

a.  *Scope and cross-references.* \* \* \* To some, the expression "unauthorized practice of law" by a nonlawyer is incongruous, because it can be taken to imply that nonlawyers may engage in some aspects of law practice, but not others. The phrase has gained near-universal usage in the courts, ethics-committee opinions, and scholarly writing, and it is well understood not to imply any necessary area of permissible practice by a nonlawyer. Moreover, a nonlawyer undoubtedly may engage in some limited forms of law practice, such as self-representation in a civil or criminal matter It thus would not be accurate for the black letter to state flatly that a nonlawyer may not engage in law practice. \* \* \*

A nonlawyer who impermissibly engages in the practice of law may be subject to several sanctions, including injunction, contempt, and conviction for crime.

b.  *Unauthorized practice by a nonlawyer—in general.* Courts, typically as the result of lawsuits brought by bar associations, began in the early part of the 20th century to adapt common-law rules to permit bar associations and lawyer-competitors to seek injunctions against some forms of unauthorized practice by nonlawyers. The courts also played a large role in attempting to define and delineate such practice. The primary justification given for unauthorized practice limitations was that of consumer protection-to protect consumers of unauthorized practitioner services against the significant risk of harm believed to be threatened by the nonlawyer practitioner's incompetence or lack of ethical constraints. Delineating the respective areas of permissible and impermissible activities has often been controversial. Some consumer groups and governmental agencies have criticized some restrictions as over-protective, anti-competitive, and costly to consumers.

In the latter part of the 20th century, unauthorized practice restrictions have lessened, to a greater or lesser extent, in most jurisdictions. In some few jurisdictions, traditional restraints are apparently still enforced through active programs. In other jurisdictions, enforcement has effectively ceased, and large numbers of lay practitioners perform many traditional legal services. Debate continues about the broad public-policy elements of unauthorized-practice restrictions, including the delineation of lawyer-only practice areas. On areas of nonlawyer practice officially permitted, see Comment c hereof.

c.  *Delineation of unauthorized practice.* The definitions and tests employed by courts to delineate unauthorized practice by nonlawyers have been vague or conclusory, while jurisdictions have differed significantly in describing what constitutes unauthorized practice in particular areas.

Certain activities, such as the representation of another person in litigation, are generally proscribed. Even in that area, many jurisdictions recognize exceptions for such matters as small-claims and landlord-tenant tribunals and certain proceedings in administrative agencies. Moreover, many jurisdictions have authorized law students and others not admitted in the state to represent indigent persons or others as part of clinical legal-education programs.

Controversy has surrounded many out-of-court activities such as advising on estate planning by bank trust officers, advising on estate planning by insurance agents, stock brokers, or benefit-plan and similar consultants, filling out or providing guidance on forms for property transactions by real-estate agents, title companies, and closing-service companies, and selling books or individual forms containing instructions on self-help legal services or accompanied by personal, nonlawyer assistance on filling them out in connection with legal procedures such as obtaining a marriage dissolution.

The position of bar associations has traditionally been that nonlawyer provision of such services denies the person served the benefit of such legal measures as the attorney-client privilege, the benefits of such extraordinary duties as that of confidentiality of client information and the protection against conflicts of interest, and the protection of such measures as those regulating lawyer trust accounts and requiring lawyers to supervise nonlawyer personnel. Several jurisdictions recognize that many such services can be provided by nonlawyers without significant risk of incompetent service, that actual experience in several states with extensive nonlawyer provision of traditional legal services indicates no significant risk of harm to consumers of such services, that persons in need of legal services may be significantly aided in obtaining assistance at a much lower price than would be entailed by segregating out a portion of a transaction to be handled by a lawyer for a fee, and that many persons can ill afford, and most persons are at least inconvenienced by, the typically higher cost of lawyer services. In addition, traditional common-law and statutory consumer-protection measures offer significant protection to consumers of such nonlawyer services.

## N.C. GEN. STAT. ANN. § 84–4.
### PERSONS OTHER THAN MEMBERS OF STATE BAR
### PROHIBITED FROM PRACTICING LAW

Except as otherwise permitted by law, it shall be unlawful for any person or association of persons, except active members of the Bar of the State of North Carolina admitted and licensed to practice as attorneys-at-law, to appear as attorney or counselor at law in any action or proceeding before any judicial body, including the North Carolina Industrial Commission, or the Utilities Commission; to maintain, conduct, or defend the same, except in his own behalf as a party thereto; or, by word, sign, letter, or advertisement, to hold out himself, or themselves, as competent or qualified to give legal advice or counsel, or to prepare legal documents, or as being engaged in advising or counseling in law or acting as attorney or counselor-at-law, or in furnishing the services of a lawyer or lawyers; and it shall be unlawful for any person or association of persons except active members of the Bar, for or without a fee or consideration, to give

legal advice or counsel, perform for or furnish to another legal
services, or to prepare directly or through another for another
person, firm or corporation, any will or testamentary disposition,
or instrument of trust, or to organize corporations or prepare for
another person, firm or corporation, any other legal document.
* * *

## N.C. GEN. STAT. ANN. § 84–2.1.
### "PRACTICE LAW" DEFINED

(a)  The phrase "practice law" as used in this Chapter is defined
to be performing any legal service for any other person, firm or
corporation, with or without compensation, specifically
including the preparation or aiding in the preparation of deeds,
mortgages, wills, trust instruments, inventories, accounts or
reports of guardians, trustees, administrators or executors, or
preparing or aiding in the preparation of any petitions or orders
in any probate or court proceeding; abstracting or passing upon
titles, the preparation and filing of petitions for use in any court,
including administrative tribunals and other judicial or quasi-
judicial bodies, or assisting by advice, counsel, or otherwise in
any legal work; and to advise or give opinion upon the legal
rights of any person, firm or corporation: Provided, that the
above reference to particular acts which are specifically included
within the definition of the phrase "practice law" shall not be
construed to limit the foregoing general definition of the term,
but shall be construed to include the foregoing particular acts,
as well as all other acts within the general definition.

(b)  The phrase "practice law" does not encompass:

(1)  the writing of memoranda of understanding or other
mediation summaries by mediators at community
mediation centers authorized by G.S. 7A38.5. . . .

(2)  The selection or completion of a preprinted form by a
real estate broker licensed under Chapter 93A of the
General Statutes, when the broker is acting as an agent in
a real estate transaction and in accordance with rules
adopted by the North Carolina Real Estate Commission, or
the selection or completion of a preprinted residential lease
agreement by any person or Web site provider. Nothing in
this subdivision or in G.S. 84–2.2 shall be construed to

permit any person or Web site provider who is not licensed to practice law in accordance with this Chapter to prepare for any third person any contract or deed conveying any interest in real property, or to abstract or pass upon title to any real property, which is located in this State.

(3) The completion of or assisting a consumer in the completion of various agreements, contracts, forms, and other documents related to the sale or lease of a motor vehicle as defined in G.S. 20–286(10), or of products or services ancillary or related to the sale or lease of a motor vehicle. . . . .

\* \* \*

### HARKNESS V. UNEMPLOYMENT COMP. BD. OF REVIEW
920 A.2d 162 (Pa. 2007)

In this appeal \* \* \* we consider whether an employer may be represented at an unemployment compensation hearing before a referee of the Unemployment Compensation Board of Review by an individual who is not an attorney. A majority of the Commonwealth Court determined that an employer may not be so represented. We respectfully disagree, and thus, for the reasons set forth below, reverse the order of the Commonwealth Court. \* \* \*

The Pennsylvania Constitution vests with our Court the exclusive authority to regulate the practice of law, which includes the power to define what constitutes the practice of law. What constitutes the practice of law, however, is not capable of a comprehensive definition. For this reason, our Court has not attempted to provide an all-encompassing statement of what activities comprise the practice of law. Thus, we have determined what constitutes the practice of law on a case-by-case basis.

While our Court has addressed the question of what constitutes the practice of law on an individualized basis, we have made clear that paramount to the inquiry is consideration of the public interest. Consideration of the public interest has two related aspects: protection of the public and prudent regulation so as not to overburden the public good.

Regarding the protection of the public, then Justice, later Chief Justice Stern perhaps best summarized this aspect of the Court's concern in *Shortz* [Shortz et al. v. Farrell, 327 Pa. 81, 193 A. 20, 21 (1937)],

> "While in order to acquire the education necessary to gain admission to the bar and thereby become eligible to practice law, one is obliged to 'scorn delights, and live laborious days,' the object of the legislation forbidding practice to laymen is not to secure to lawyers a monopoly, however deserved, but, by preventing the intrusion of inexpert and unlearned persons in the practice of law, to assure to the public adequate protection in the pursuit of justice, than which society knows no loftier aim."

While the public interest is certainly served by the protection of the public, it is also achieved by not burdening the public by too broad a definition of the practice of law, resulting in the overregulation of the public's affairs. As stated by our Court in *Dauphin County* [Bar Ass'n v. Mazzacaro, 351 A.2d 229 (Pa. 1978)],

> "The threads of legal consequences often weave their way through even casual contemporary interactions. There are times, of course, when it is clearly within the ken of lay persons to appreciate the legal problems and consequences involved in a given situation and the factors which should influence necessary decisions. No public interest would be advanced by requiring these lay judgments to be made exclusively by lawyers. . . . Each case must turn on a careful analysis of the particular judgment involved and the expertise which must be brought to bear on its exercise."

Thus, our Court, in determining what constitutes the practice of law, must keep the public interest of primary concern, both in terms of the protection of the public as well as in ensuring that the regulation of the practice of law is not so strict that the public good suffers.

When considering the public interest, our Court has focused on the character of the activities at issue. In *Shortz*, our Court set forth three broad categories of activities that may constitute the practice of law:

(1)   the instruction and advising of clients in regard to the law so that they may pursue their affairs and be informed as to their rights and obligations;

(2)   the preparation of documents for clients requiring familiarity with legal principles beyond the ken of ordinary laypersons; and

(3)   the appearance on behalf of clients before public tribunals in order that the attorney may assist the deciding official in the proper interpretation and enforcement of the law.

More recently, our Court expressed that the practice of law is implicated by the holding out of oneself to the public as competent to exercise legal judgment and the implication that he or she has the technical competence to analyze legal problems and the requisite character qualifications to act in a representative capacity. Thus, the character of the actions taken by the individual in question is a significant factor in the determination of what constitutes the practice of law.

Finally, we have cautioned that the tribunal before which the individual is before is not determinative in deciding what comprises the practice of law, viz., "whether or not the tribunal is called a 'court' or the controversy 'litigation'. . . ." Yet, the nature of the proceedings in which the individual is acting is not to be wholly discounted. Indeed, the nature of such proceedings certainly is relevant in determining the needs of the public, both in terms of protection and overregulation.

Cognizant that a determination of the practice of law is made on a case-by-case basis, focusing primarily on protection of the public and the public weal, and in doing so, considering the character of the activities engaged in, as well as the nature of the proceedings at issue, we turn to the facts at issue in this appeal.

First, we find that the activities performed by an employer representative in an unemployment compensation proceeding are largely routine and primarily focus upon creating a factual basis on which a referee will award or deny unemployment compensation benefits. As a general proposition, providers of services such as the management of payroll, tax, and employee benefit operations will also attend unemployment compensation proceedings to provide appropriate personnel records and other documents and assist in the fact-finding process so as to aid the referee in his or her determination. These individuals are more akin to facilitators rather than legal practitioners. The purpose of their presence is not to engage in the analysis of complex and intricate legal problems, but rather as an adjunct to the employer (or claimant) in offering their respective viewpoints concerning the events at issue.

In terms of the three broad categories of activities that our Court has suggested may constitute the practice of law, there is scant advising as to legal rights and responsibilities and few instances of the preparation of documents requiring familiarity with legal principles. Furthermore, while as noted by the Commonwealth Court, non-attorney representatives certainly appear on behalf of an employer before public tribunals, their role in assisting the deciding official in the proper interpretation and enforcement of the law is lacking. As noted above, the role of the non-attorney representative is more as a facilitator rather than an advocate engaging in an analysis of the law.

Second, we take note of the nature of unemployment compensation proceedings. The Unemployment Compensation Law is remedial in nature. The fundamental purpose of the Law is to provide economic security to those unemployed through no fault of their own. * * *

To this end, the unemployment compensation system must operate quickly, simply, and efficiently. The proceedings are "by design, brief and informal in nature." Thus, the claims for benefits are not intended to be intensely litigated. Unemployment compensation proceedings are not trials. The rules of evidence are not mandated; there is no pre-hearing discovery; the parties have no right to a jury trial; indeed, there is no requirement that the referee be a lawyer. Also, and importantly, there are only minimal amounts of money in controversy. Issues arising in these matters are generally questions of fact not requiring complex legal analysis. Requiring employers to be represented by counsel will not only undermine the informal, speedy and low cost nature of these proceedings, it may dissuade many employers from defending claims for benefits leading to the possibility of an unwarranted drain on the system.

Simply stated, the character of the activities performed by representatives at unemployment hearings coupled with the informal nature of these proceedings, the minimal amounts at issue, and the long history of participation by non-lawyer representatives suggest that the public does not need the protection that serves as the basis for classifying certain activities to constitute the practice of law and that indeed, finding non-lawyer representatives to be engaging in the practice of law by acting in unemployment compensation proceedings would impose an unnecessary burden on the public.[5]

Based upon the above considerations, we hold that a non-attorney representing an employer before a referee of the Board is not engaging in the practice of law. * * *

### IN RE MORALES
151 A.3d 333 (Vt. 2016)

This case calls upon us to consider the applicability of the prohibition against the unauthorized practice of law . . . in violation of 4 V.S.A. § 901[*] and Administrative Order No. 41, § 2. * * *

This Court has historically defined the unauthorized practice of law broadly, to include not merely holding oneself out as an attorney, but also providing services that require legal knowledge or skill such as drafting legal documents and giving

---

[5]    These activities and type of proceedings can be contrasted with the situation in *Shortz*, relied upon by the Commonwealth Court in this matter, in which our Court found non-lawyer representation during workers' compensation proceedings to constitute the practice of law. The formality and complexity of workers' compensation proceedings, however, stand in sharp contrast to the informal, straightforward proceedings that serve as the vehicle to determine unemployment compensation benefits. The hallmarks of workers' compensation proceedings include pre-trial investigation and discovery, the filings of pleadings, testimony by experts, and the potentiality of significant benefit amounts at issue. None of these hallmarks, however, are present in unemployment compensation proceedings.

[*]    "Justices of the supreme court shall make, adopt, and publish and may alter or amend rules regulating the admission of attorneys to the practice of law before the courts of this state." [Ed.]

legal advice—at least when one charges a fee for those services. More recent social and legal developments reflect a trend toward a somewhat more purpose-driven approach to defining the scope of the unauthorized practice of law.

In *In re Morse* [98 Vt. 85, 126 A. 550 (1924)], we concluded that an accountant who held himself out as an attorney and signed pleadings and other court filings on behalf of his debt collection business had engaged in the unauthorized practice of law. The defendant ran a debt collection business and regularly issued trustee writs, signed many of them as "attorney" or "acting attorney," brought suits against various parties who were in default, and acted as an attorney before the court in those cases. In our decision, we emphasized that even though justices of the peace and process servers with whom he did business knew that he was not an attorney, the defendant "acted, and held himself out, as an attorney" and signed pleadings and other court filings. On that basis, we adjudged him guilty of contempt of this Court.

We articulated a broader definition of unauthorized practice in *In re Ripley*, 109 Vt. 83, 191 A. 918 (1937). In that case, the defendant also ran a debt collection agency in which, for a fee, he undertook the obligation of enforcing, securing, settling, adjusting, and compromising a civil claim a Mrs. Spaulding had against a Mr. Stone. The defendant also advised a creditor regarding the liability of Mr. Stone, wrote letters to Mr. Stone threatening him with legal action should he fail to pay the defendant a substantial amount then due and owing, and filed a lawsuit against Mr. Stone. We found the defendant in contempt for engaging in the unauthorized practice of law. In so concluding, we explained:

> According to the generally understood definition of the practice of law in this country, it embraces the preparation of pleadings and other papers incident to actions and special proceedings, and the management of such actions and proceedings on behalf of clients before judges and courts, and, in addition, conveyancing, the preparation of legal instruments of all kinds, and, in general, all advice to clients and all action taken for them in matters connected with the law.

Subsequently, in *In re Flint,* [8 A.2d 655(Vt. 1939)], we concluded that a law student who, for a fee, offered an individual advice about an ongoing dispute, and ultimately negotiated a settlement of the case on the individual's behalf, had engaged in the unauthorized practice of law. We emphasized the following facts: (1) the defendant gave advice to a lay person; (2) the advice was of a legal nature and required some legal knowledge; (3) the defendant negotiated and effected a settlement; and (4) he received payment for his advice and services. We further noted that "A person who gives legal advice to clients and transacts business for them in matters connected with the law in the settlement, adjustment, and compromise of claims is engaged in the practice of law." We concluded that, although the defendant may have "started only as [a] friend," he finished as a lawyer.

Over twenty years later, this Court concluded that a defendant who, acting as a financial counselor of sorts, created debt-pooling plans allowing each of three families facing financial difficulties to pay off their debts by assigning various financial interests to the defendant, had engaged in the unauthorized practice of law. *In re Pilini,* 122 Vt. 385, 173 A.2d 828 (1961). In our analysis, we noted that the practice of law "is not confined to performing services in an action or proceeding pending in courts of justice; but in a larger sense includes legal advice and counsel and the preparation of legal instruments and contracts of which legal rights are secured." We elaborated on that statement, noting "practicing as an attorney . . . is the giving of advice or rendition of any sort of service by any person, firm or corporation when the giving of such advice or rendition of such service requires the use of any degree of legal knowledge or skill." Because defendant in this case "invaded the field reserved for duly licensed attorneys," by providing legal advice and receiving compensation for that advice, he had engaged in the unauthorized practice of law.

Finally, we have held that a surveyor who, for a fee, drafted deeds, advised parties with respect to certain rights-of-way created in the deeds, and advised parties "as to the type of estate and manner of holding" that would serve to meet their desires and needs, had engaged in the unauthorized practice of law. *In re Welch,* 123 Vt. 180, 181, 185 A.2d 458, 460 (1962). We explained that the practice of law means "furnish[ing] to another advice or service under circumstances which imply the possession and use of legal knowledge and skill." Elaborating, we said:

> The practice of law includes all advice to clients, and all actions taken for them in matters connected with the law. . . . Practice of law includes the giving of legal advice and counsel, and the preparation of legal instruments and contracts of which legal rights are secured. . . . Where the rendering of services for another involves the use of legal knowledge or skill on his [or her] behalf—where legal advice is required and is availed of or rendered in connection with such services—these services necessarily constitute or include the practice of law.

Although the above caselaw articulates an expansive definition of the practice of law, as the Attorney General has argued in this case, "This decades-old definition does not reflect the reality of practice in Vermont and does not provide sufficient guidance to prosecutors, practitioners, and the public." Notwithstanding the above broad definitions of the unauthorized practice, this Court has allowed nonlawyers to appear in court in certain specified circumstances, as have some administrative agencies. In its prosecutorial role, the Attorney General has likewise taken a narrower view of the unauthorized practice. These legal developments have tempered the breadth of the unauthorized practice prohibition, and reflect a recognition that the unauthorized practice prohibition should be applied consistent with its underlying purposes of public protection.

Most notably, this Court has held that under certain circumstances a nonlawyer may appear in court on behalf of an unincorporated organization where the requirement of counsel would preclude the organization's appearance. *Vt. Agency of Nat. Res. v. Upper Valley Reg'l Landfill Corp.*, 159 Vt. 454, 621 A.2d 225 (1992). In *Upper Valley Regional Landfill*, an unincorporated citizen environmental group was granted intervenor status in an action involving the closure of a landfill, but the Environmental Division ruled that the group must appear through counsel. On interlocutory appeal of that order, we reversed. We explained that "[t]he primary purpose of the 'lawyer-representation' rule is the protection of the public, not the creation of any private advantage for attorneys." We explained that courts generally refuse to permit nonattorneys to represent organizations "because they do not have the ethical responsibilities of attorneys and are not subject to the disciplinary control of the courts." Nonlawyers often draft inarticulate pleadings and promote needlessly multiplicative proceedings, thereby burdening the parties and the court. Nevertheless, we recognized that some courts have made narrow exceptions to the lawyer-representation rule where appearance by a lay representative would not unduly impede the court in the administration of justice. We concluded that the lawyer-representation rule "should not be rigidly enforced in cases where those interests are not threatened and enforcement would preclude appearance by the organization." We accordingly held that courts may permit an organization to appear through a nonattorney representative where:

> (1) the organization cannot afford to hire counsel, nor can it secure counsel on a pro bono basis, (2) the proposed lay representative is authorized to represent the organization, (3) the proposed lay representative demonstrates adequate legal knowledge and skills to represent the organization without unduly burdening the opposing party or the court, and (4) the representative shares a common interest with the organization.

Similarly, this Court has applied a standard articulated by the Legislature in allowing nonattorneys to represent a corporation in court under certain circumstances. See, e.g., *Bandler v. Cohen Rosenthal & Kramer, LLP,* 2015 VT 115, ¶¶ 7, 14, 200 Vt. 333, 131 A.3d 733 (applying standard in 11A V.S.A. § 3.02(1)); 11A V.S.A. § 3.02 (authorizing corporation to appear through nonattorney representative if proposed representative is "authorized to represent the corporation, . . . demonstrates adequate legal knowledge and skills to represent the organization without unduly burdening the opposing party or the court[,] . . . [and] shares a common interest with the corporation").

And, applying another standard articulated by the Legislature, this Court has recognized that nonattorney employees of the Office of Child Support may sign complaints and motions and participate in child support hearings before a magistrate.

Nonlawyers are also permitted to represent certain parties in some state administrative proceedings.

And finally, as noted above, in its prosecutorial capacity, the Attorney General has represented that it does not consider providing "legal advice internally within a company, department or other entity" by an individual not admitted to practice law in Vermont to constitute unauthorized practice.

Collectively, these developments suggest that the general scope of the prohibition against the unauthorized practice of law may not be solely a function of the tasks an individual performs but also reflects a balancing of the risks and benefits to the public of allowing or disallowing such activities. See, e.g., *In re Op. No. 26 of Comm. on Unauthorized Practice of Law,* 139 N.J. 323, 654 A.2d 1344, 1345–46 (1995) ("The question of what constitutes the unauthorized practice of law involves more than an academic analysis of the function of lawyers, more than a determination of what they are uniquely qualified to do. It also involves a determination of whether non-lawyers should be allowed, in the public interest, to engage in activities that may constitute the practice of law."). * * *

### SUSAN B. SCHWAB, BRINGING DOWN THE BAR: ACCOUNTANTS CHALLENGE MEANING OF UNAUTHORIZED PRACTICE
#### 21 Cardozo L. Rev. 1425, 1443–52 (2000)

Currently, courts apply different approaches depending on their jurisdiction and the type of service being considered. Among the factors courts consider are whether the service is one traditionally performed by lawyers; whether the service is incidental to other nonlegal services; and whether the service involves difficult questions of law. This section examines each of these factors and suggests that a combination is preferable to any one individually.

## A. Professional Judgment Approach

The "professional judgment" approach is the most widely accepted method for evaluating when a service constitutes the practice of law. This approach examines "whether the activity in question is one in which a lawyer's presumed special training and skills are relevant." Under this standard, an accountant is practicing law whenever he resolves difficult or doubtful legal questions by giving advice or taking actions on another's behalf. Further, he is practicing law if difficult or doubtful legal questions are involved which, to safeguard the public, reasonably demand the application of a trained legal mind. Presumably, difficult legal questions require "legal skill and a knowledge of the law greater than that possessed by [an accountant]."

The types of legal questions that would be deemed difficult include questions regarding the interpretation or application of statutes, administrative regulations and rulings, court decisions, or general law. These questions frequently arise in the tax, bankruptcy, and corporate fields. In the tax area, it is well established that difficult legal questions often arise during the preparation of income tax returns:

Federal income taxation is founded on statute, elaborated and interpreted by administrative regulations and rulings, and construed by court decisions. Matters in this field, as in other statutory subjects, will at times involve difficult questions of interpretation of statute or court decisions, and the validity of regulations or statute; they will also involve doubtful questions of non-tax law on which the tax issues may depend, and questions of liability for criminal or civil penalties or of statute of limitations or of liability as transferee for the taxes of another. Such questions, in general, are the kind for which lawyers are equipped by training and practice. In the bankruptcy field, difficult legal questions can arise in determining exemptions and dischargeability, as well as in preparing petitions and schedules. In corporate law, difficult legal questions are often involved in preparing charters, bylaws, and other documents of incorporation, as well as more complex financing, merger, and licensing agreements.

Many legal questions are simple and do not require the professional judgment of a lawyer. For example, many estates are straightforward enough that accountants have the necessary training and experience to prepare the Inheritance Tax Return. Similarly, appraisal disputes usually do not involve difficult questions of law because they are initiated by filing a form that only requires the insertion of the disputed property's identity. Some jurisdictions deem proceedings between realtors and titleholders uncomplicated since they involve factual, not legal, issues; they are not governed by the rules of evidence; and, typically, the board members are not attorneys.

The prime advantage of the professional judgment test is that it promotes the public interest by allowing accountants to render services involving elementary questions of law in their area of expertise, subject to their own professional regulation. This approach gives clients the freedom to choose a nonlawyer, who may be cheaper than a lawyer, to resolve their simple legal questions. Furthermore, this method protects clients by prohibiting nonlawyers from rendering services when legal training, skill, or judgment is required to resolve the issue.

The professional judgment approach is problematic, however: nonlawyers cannot ensure that they do not inadvertently engage in the practice of law, since a determination of whether a difficult legal question is involved turns on the specific facts of each situation.

## B.  Incidental Approach

Some courts rely on an "incidental" approach to the practice of law analysis. Those courts consider whether the "activity claimed by a bar association to constitute unauthorized practice is simply an adjunct to a routine in the business or commercial world that is not in itself law practice." Under this standard, an accountant may advise on elementary questions of law if those questions are incidental to the preparation of an income tax return, or work that has been done on an entity's books. However, an accountant may not advise an unrelated party on any questions of law, even elementary ones. For example, an accountant is prohibited from advising an unrelated client about the view tax authorities, and ultimately courts, would take as to the years in which the city's tax claims would be deductible for federal tax purposes.

The rationale for prohibiting accountants from advising unrelated clients on even elementary tax law questions is that any branch of legal practice requires a thorough understanding of basic legal concepts, legal processes, and the interrelation of different parts of the law. Unlike an accountant, who has only an isolated knowledge of a particular area of law, a lawyer has a legal education and training that gives him a broad grounding in law. Although accountants may know more about tax law than do lawyers who are not specialists in the tax field, accountants generally do not have a deep understanding of the complexity of legal issues and how to resolve them within the common law system. Thus, an accountant may not consult or give legal advice to unrelated parties despite his knowledge in a particular field of law.

The incidental analysis is quite liberal because it does not prohibit accountants from resolving legal questions for their clients as part of their ordinary services. This line of demarcation allows the accountant "maximum freedom of action within the accounting field and is the minimum of control necessary to give the public protection when it seeks advice as to tax law." Allowing accountants to assume jurisdiction over incidental legal questions is a "practical, reasonable and proper accommodation to businessmen and the accounting profession." Accounting clients will benefit by only having to retain and pay for one professional—an accountant, as opposed to an accountant and a lawyer—to advise them.

The problem with this approach is that it does not place any limits on an accountant who is confronted with a legal question while rendering accounting services. Since only a generally trained lawyer is competent to analyze difficult problems and determine which laws are involved, limits should be placed on the types of questions that accountants may answer, even when they are incidental.

## C. Traditional Approach

A few courts rely on a "traditional service" approach. These courts define "law practice by looking to traditional areas of law practice." Under this standard, the actual practices in a community are important in defining the scope of unauthorized practice. As one court explained, the practice of law is the performance "of any acts . . . in or out of court, commonly understood to be the practice of law." Traditional analysts believe that lawyers engage in three principal types of professional activity: (1) giving clients advice that informs them of their legal rights and obligations; (2) preparing documents and papers that require knowledge of legal principles; and (3) appearing before tribunals to represent their clients.

The traditional approach provides nonlawyers with a greater degree of predictability than either the professional judgment or incidental approach. This method focuses on the manner in which "lawyers customarily have carried on from day to day through the centuries." Therefore, a nonlawyer ensures that he is not engaging in the unauthorized practice of law by not entering any of the three fields traditionally practiced by lawyers.

This approach is troublesome because it is tautological—it only defines law as that which lawyers do. Furthermore, this definition is overly broad and unworkable because lawyers provide numerous services in the private, commercial, and governmental arenas which could also be provided by other professionals. Therefore, courts rarely rely on this factor to determine whether a nonlawyer is engaging in the unauthorized practice of law. * * *

## GRACE M. GIESEL, CORPORATIONS PRACTICING LAW THROUGH LAWYERS: WHY THE UNAUTHORIZED PRACTICE OF LAW DOCTRINE SHOULD NOT APPLY
### 65 Mo. L. Rev. 151, 172–74 (2000)

The corporate practice of law doctrine states that no corporation can practice law. Writing in 1931, one commentator noted that "this limitation has been regarded as the distinguishing characteristic which makes the practice of law a profession rather than a business." Although some jurisdictions allow corporations to appear for themselves in small claims court and other specific venues without an attorney, generally a corporation cannot appear pro se by way of nonlawyer employees but must always be represented by an attorney. Chief Justice

Marshall long ago stated in Osborn v. United States Bank, "(a) corporation . . . can appear only by attorney, while a natural person may appear for himself."

**In addition, a corporation cannot render legal services to another party.** This prohibition applies even when the corporate employee rendering the legal service is a licensed attorney. The Tennessee Court of Appeals, in *Third National Bank v. Celebrate Yourself Productions, Inc.,* stated: "It is well established that a corporation cannot practice law, nor can it employ a licensed practitioner to practice for it." Many states have statutes that expressly forbid corporations from practicing law. An Arkansas statute specifically notes that the fact that within the corporation whose party renders the legal service is an attorney does not cleanse the act. Other states, in prohibiting the practice of law by corporations, rely on more general statutes that provide that only licensed persons may practice law. Many states also have case law stating the same. (emphasis added).

### Haw. Rev. Stat. Ann. § 605–14.
### Unauthorized Practice
### of Law Prohibited

It shall be unlawful for any person, firm, association, or corporation to engage in or attempt to engage in or to offer to engage in the practice of law, or to do or attempt to do or offer to do any act constituting the practice of law, except and to the extent that the person, firm, or association is licensed or authorized so to do by an appropriate court, agency, or office or by a statute of the State or of the United States. Nothing in sections 605–14 to 605–17 contained shall be construed to prohibit the preparation or use by any party to a transaction of any legal or business form or document used in the transaction.

### Mich. Comp. Laws Ann. § 450.681.
### Practice of Law by Corporations
### or Voluntary Associations Prohibited;
### Exceptions; Penalty

Sec. 1. It shall be unlawful for any corporation or voluntary association to practice or appear as an attorney-at-law for any person other than itself in any court in this state or before any judicial body, or to make it a business to practice as an attorney-at-law, for any person other than itself, in any of said courts or to hold itself out to the public as being entitled to practice law, or render or furnish legal services or advice, or to furnish attorneys or counsel or to render legal services of any kind in actions or proceedings of any nature or in any other way or manner, or in any other manner to assume to be entitled to practice law or to assume, use or advertise the title of lawyer or attorney, attorney-at-law, or equivalent terms in any language in such manner as to convey the impression that it is entitled to practice law, or to furnish legal advice, services or counsel, or to advertise that either alone or together with or by or through any person whether a duly and regularly admitted attorney-at-law, or not, it has, owns, conducts or maintains a law office or an office for the practice of law, or for furnishing legal advice, services or counsel. It shall be unlawful further for any corporation or voluntary association to solicit itself or by or through its officers, agents or employees any claim or demand for the purpose of bringing an action thereon or of representing as attorney-at-law, or for furnishing legal advice, services or counsel to a person sued or about to be sued in any action or proceeding or against whom an action or proceeding has been or is about to be brought, or who may be affected by any action or proceeding which has been or may be instituted in any court or before any judicial body, or for the purpose of so representing any person in the pursuit of any civil remedy. * * *

**This section shall not apply** to any corporation or voluntary association lawfully engaged in a business authorized by the provisions of any existing statute, nor to a corporation or voluntary association lawfully engaged in the examination and insuring of titles of real property, nor shall it prohibit a corporation or voluntary association from employing an attorney or attorneys in and about its own immediate affairs or in any litigation to which it is or may be a party, or from employing an attorney or attorneys to render legal aid without charge to any employees of such corporation or voluntary association, nor shall it apply **to organizations organized for benevolent or charitable purposes, or for the purpose of assisting persons without means in the pursuit of any civil remedy, whose existence, organization or incorporation may be approved by the circuit court of the circuit in which the**

principal office of said corporation or voluntary
**association may be located** (emphasis added). * * *

# Chapter II

# What Are Examples of UPL Boundaries?

■ ■ ■

## A. DOCUMENT REVIEW

### Lola v. Skadden, Arps, Slate, Meagher & Flom LLP
### 620 Fed Appx. 37 (2d Cir. 2015)

Lola, a North Carolina resident, alleges that beginning in April 2012, he worked for Defendants for fifteen months in North Carolina. He conducted document review for Skadden in connection with a multi-district litigation pending in the United States District Court for the Northern District of Ohio. Lola . . . is not admitted to practice law in either North Carolina or the Northern District of Ohio.

Lola alleges that his work was closely supervised by the Defendants, and his "entire responsibility . . . consisted of (a) looking at documents to see what search terms, if any, appeared in the documents, (b) marking those documents into the categories predetermined by Defendants, and (c) at times drawing black boxes to redact portions of certain documents based on specific protocols that Defendants provided." Lola further alleges that Defendants provided him with the documents he reviewed, the search terms he was to use in connection with those documents, and the procedures he was to follow if the search terms appeared. Lola was paid $25 an hour for his work, and worked roughly forty-five to fifty-five hours a week. He was paid at the same rate for any hours he worked in excess of forty hours per week. Lola was told that he was an employee of Tower, but he was also told that he needed to follow any procedures set by Skadden attorneys, and he worked under the supervision of Skadden attorneys. * * *

[The district court found that] Lola was engaged in the practice of law as defined by North Carolina law. . . .

\* \* \* The district court erred in concluding that engaging in document review per se constitutes practicing law in North Carolina. [I]nherent in the definition of "practice of law" in North Carolina is the exercise of at least a modicum of independent legal judgment. \* \* \*

The gravamen of Lola's complaint is that he performed document review under such tight constraints that he exercised no legal judgment whatsoever—he alleges that he used criteria developed by others to simply sort documents into different categories. Accepting those allegations as true, as we must on a motion to dismiss, we find that Lola adequately alleged in his complaint that he failed to exercise any legal judgment in performing his duties for Defendants. A fair reading of the complaint in the light most favorable to Lola is that he provided services that a machine could have provided. The parties themselves agreed at oral argument that an individual who, in the course of reviewing discovery documents, undertakes tasks that could otherwise be performed entirely by a machine cannot be said to engage in the practice of law. We therefore vacate the judgment of the district court and remand for further proceedings consistent with this opinion. \* \* \*

## B. SCRIVENER

### MATTER OF WAGNER

2016 WL 4618954 (Wash. App. 2016),
*rev. den.* 187 Wash. 2d 1013 (2017)

Elizabeth died in 2010. Her daughter, Jill, was appointed personal representative of her estate. Elizabeth's surviving husband, Elmer, disagreed with Jill's distribution of assets and management of the estate. He brought a[n] . . . action to remove Jill and to settle these issues. Jill defended on the grounds that by typing Elizabeth's will, Elmer engaged in the unauthorized practice of law . . . [and she] points to this court's decisions in In re Estate of Marks, 91 Wn. App. 325, 957 P.2d 235 (1998) and In re Estate of Knowles, 135 Wn. App. 351, 143 P.3d 864 (2006). . . .

But, these cases in fact show that Elmer did not act as a lawyer by typing up Elizabeth's will. In *Marks*, the decedent asked the friends with whom she was staying to help her make a will. The trial court found that the decedent's friends engaged in the unauthorized practice of law by selecting a will kit, discussing the decedent's distribution of assets and whether it was fair, obtaining the inventory of investments, typing the will, and arranging for the signing and witnessing of the will. This finding was not challenged on appeal—the Court of Appeals made no holding regarding whether such actions constitute the unauthorized practice of law. The court's holding was simply that the trial court did not err in voiding the portions of the will relating to the decedent's friends.

In *Knowles*, one of Merle's sons, Randy, wrote the material provisions of Merle's will on a will form. The will appointed Randy as personal representative and left him the majority of Merle's assets. After Merle died, his other children argued that Randy was barred from taking under the will because Randy was practicing law when he drafted the will. The *Knowles* court explicitly disagreed with *Marks* to the extent it held that simply completing a will form is the practice of law. Instead, the Court of Appeals noted that a person practices law by directly or indirectly giving advice. And, in *Knowles*, the decedent's son did nothing more than fill in the form as the decedent wished. The court held that this falls short of practicing law.

Here, Elmer's uncontroverted testimony was that he merely typed up the will as Elizabeth instructed. He stated that he did not add or take out a single thing that she did not want. He clarified that Elizabeth used her own form to make her will. Elmer typed the information Elizabeth gave him, and Elizabeth read a printed copy and made edits until she was satisfied with the will.

We hold that merely typing up another person's will does not constitute the unauthorized practice of law. Elmer did not offer advice about the form or contents of Elizabeth's will. There was no evidence at trial that he did anything other than put Elizabeth's wishes into writing. And, to the extent that Jill argues Elmer should have taken Elizabeth to a lawyer rather than assist her himself, we hold that Washington law does not impose a duty on a spouse to ensure the other spouse consults a lawyer about a will. * * *

## FRANKLIN V. CHAVIS
### 640 S.E.2d 873 (S.C. 2007)

We accepted this case in our original jurisdiction to consider whether respondent Ernest Chavis's involvement in drafting a will and other documents for decedent Annie Belle Weiss constituted the unauthorized practice of law.

Petitioners, who are Ms. Weiss's grandnieces, commenced the underlying action contesting her will on grounds of undue influence and lack of capacity. Ms. Weiss was ninety-one years old and in the hospital when she signed this will on July 31, 2004. Petitioners claim Michael Lehman, Ms. Weiss's nephew by marriage, took advantage of her condition to influence her to make this will leaving 60% of her estate to Lehman and only 10% to each of Ms. Weiss's three grandnieces and their mother, Lynn Franklin. Respondent, a former neighbor of Ms. Weiss, drafted this will. The will names respondent as personal representative of Ms. Weiss's estate but he is not a beneficiary.

Respondent also drafted a power of attorney that Ms. Weiss signed along with the July 31 will. This document names respondent as her attorney-in-fact. Respondent used this power of attorney before Ms. Weiss's death to close a real estate transaction on her behalf. Ms. Weiss died on September 27, 2004.

The third document in question is a Renunciation of Administration regarding the estate of Ms. Weiss's daughter, Sara Crossman, who died in May 2004. Ms. Weiss signed this document on September 14, 2004, relinquishing her right to act as personal representative for Sara's estate and nominating respondent to act in that capacity. Ms. Weiss also signed a waiver of bond form for Sara's estate enabling respondent to serve without posting bond.

The action before us seeks a declaration that respondent engaged in the unauthorized practice of law by drafting the July 31 will, the power of attorney, and the two probate forms; a declaration that all these documents are void; an injunction; and restitution. The record is replete with claims of misconduct that are relevant only to issues pending in the underlying action regarding undue influence and lack of capacity. We limit the facts here to those relevant to the claim that respondent engaged in the unauthorized practice of law. * * *

Petitioners assert respondent engaged in the practice of law by giving legal advice and preparing the above-mentioned legal documents on Ms. Weiss's behalf. Respondent contends he acted as a mere scrivener.

a.    Drafting of July 31 will

Respondent testified that he visited Ms. Weiss socially at her home on July 20, 2004. Respondent is an insurance agent by trade and previously had business dealings with Ms. Weiss. During this visit, Ms. Weiss asked respondent, "Can you help me make a will?" Respondent agreed to help her with a simple will. Ms. Weiss told him she wanted "somebody objective" and she directed respondent as to how she wanted her property divided. Respondent used a "Quicken lawyer disk" to generate a generic will on his home computer and he filled in the blanks. He brought the will to Ms. Weiss on July 31 when he went to visit her in the hospital and she signed it.

The preparation of legal documents constitutes the practice of law when such preparation involves the giving of advice, consultation, explanation, or recommendations on matters of law. Even the preparation of standard forms that require no creative drafting may constitute the practice of law if one acts as more than a mere scrivener. The purpose of prohibiting the unauthorized practice of law is to protect the public from incompetence in the preparation of legal documents and prevent harm resulting from inaccurate legal advice.

The novel question here is whether respondent's actions in filling in the blanks in a computer-generated generic will constitute the practice of law. Respondent selected the will form, filled in the information given by Ms. Weiss, and arranged the execution of the will at the hospital. Although these facts are not in themselves conclusive, the omission of facts indicating Ms. Weiss's involvement is significant. There is no evidence Ms. Weiss reviewed the will once it was typed. The will was not typed in her presence and although respondent relates the details of what Ms. Weiss told him to do, there is no indication he contemporaneously recorded her instructions and then simply transferred the information to the form.

We construe the role of "scrivener" in this context to mean someone who does nothing more than record verbatim what the decedent says. We conclude respondent's actions in drafting Ms. Weiss's will exceeded those of a mere scrivener and he engaged in the unauthorized practice of law.

b.   Drafting power of attorney

Respondent drafted a document entitled "General Power of Attorney" for Ms. Weiss naming respondent as her attorney-in-fact allowing him on her behalf to: 1) open, maintain, or close financial accounts including access to safe deposit boxes; 2) sell property; 3) purchase insurance; 4) collect debts and settle claims; 5) enter contracts; 6) exercise stock rights; 7) maintain or operate business; 8) employ professional and business assistance; 9) sell, lease, mortgage and other acts regarding real estate; 10) prepare, sign, and file documents.

Respondent testified at his deposition that he drafted the power of attorney around July 20 because Ms. Weiss asked him to represent her regarding the sale of some of her real estate. Ms. Weiss signed the power of attorney at the hospital on July 31. It was filed on August 4. Respondent used the power of attorney to close the sale of Ms. Weiss's real estate on August 26, about a month before her death.

There are no details regarding respondent's drafting of this document. It uses legal phrasing with two pages of text and is not a simple form with filled-in blanks. The document itself confers wide-ranging legal rights and would clearly require legal advice in its preparation. We conclude respondent engaged in the practice of law in drafting this document.

c.   Probate forms

The Renunciation of Right to Administration and the Statement of Agreement to Waive Bond are probate court forms with handwritten information filled in the blanks. While these forms do have legal implications, they are straight-forward and are provided to the public by the court. These simple forms are clearly distinguishable from the will and power of attorney discussed above. Respondent basically inserted names, addresses, and dates. There is no evidence respondent gave legal advice to Ms. Weiss regarding these forms. We find there is no factual support for the claim that respondent engaged in the practice of law by filling out these forms. *See Shortz v. Farrell,* 327 Pa. 81, 193 A. 20 (1937) (filling in simple forms provided by tribunal not unauthorized practice of law).

### RYAN G. FOLEY, THE RISKY WORLD OF § 110 AND BANKRUPTCY PETITION PREPARERS
36 Am. Bankr. Instit. J. 30 (April 2017)

Despite consumer bankruptcy filings recently decreasing nationwide, more people are seeking help from bankruptcy petition preparers, also called "typing services" or "paralegals." These are nonlawyer typing services that charge a fee to generate your bankruptcy forms. As growth of the bankruptcy petition preparer industry increases, courts have taken certain bankruptcy petition preparers to task for running afoul of 11 U.S.C. § 110, which governs the actions of bankruptcy petition preparers.

### PENALTY FOR PERSONS WHO NEGLIGENTLY OR FRAUDULENTLY PREPARE BANKRUPTCY PETITIONS
11 U.S.C.A. § 110

**(a)** In this section—

**(1)** "bankruptcy petition preparer" means a person, other than an attorney for the debtor or an employee of such attorney under the direct supervision of such attorney, who prepares for compensation a document for filing; and

**(2)** "document for filing" means a petition or any other document prepared for filing by a debtor in a United States bankruptcy court or a United States district court in connection with a case under this title.

**(b)(1)** A bankruptcy petition preparer who prepares a document for filing shall sign the document and print on the document the preparer's name and address. If a bankruptcy petition preparer is not an individual, then an officer, principal, responsible person, or partner of the bankruptcy petition preparer shall be required to—

**(A)** sign the document for filing; and

**(B)** print on the document the name and address of that officer, principal, responsible person, or partner.

**(2)(A)** Before preparing any document for filing or accepting any fees from or on behalf of a debtor, the bankruptcy petition preparer shall provide to the debtor a written notice * * *.

**(B)** The notice under subparagraph (A)—

**(i)** shall inform the debtor in simple language that a bankruptcy petition preparer is not an attorney and may not practice law or give legal advice;

**(ii)** may contain a description of examples of legal advice that a bankruptcy petition preparer is not authorized to give, in addition to any advice that the preparer may not give by reason of subsection (e)(2); and

**(iii)** shall—

**(I)** be signed by the debtor and, under penalty of perjury, by the bankruptcy petition preparer; and

**(II)** be filed with any document for filing.

* * *

**(e)(1)** A bankruptcy petition preparer shall not execute any document on behalf of a debtor.

**(2)(A)** A bankruptcy petition preparer may not offer a potential bankruptcy debtor any legal advice, including any legal advice described in subparagraph (B).

**(B)** The legal advice referred to in subparagraph (A) includes advising the debtor—

**(i)** whether—

**(I)** to file a petition under this title; or

**(II)** commencing a case under chapter 7, 11, 12, or 13 is appropriate;

**(ii)** whether the debtor's debts will be discharged in a case under this title;

**(iii)** whether the debtor will be able to retain the debtor's home, car, or other property after commencing a case under this title;

**(iv)** concerning—

> **(I)** the tax consequences of a case brought under this title; or

> **(II)** the dischargeability of tax claims;

**(v)** whether the debtor may or should promise to repay debts to a creditor or enter into a reaffirmation agreement with a creditor to reaffirm a debt;

**(vi)** concerning how to characterize the nature of the debtor's interests in property or the debtor's debts; or

**(vii)** concerning bankruptcy procedures and rights.

**(f)** A bankruptcy petition preparer shall not use the word "legal" or any similar term in any advertisements, or advertise under any category that includes the word "legal" or any similar term.

**(g)** A bankruptcy petition preparer shall not collect or receive any payment from the debtor or on behalf of the debtor for the court fees in connection with filing the petition.

### BANKRUPTCY PETITION PREPARER GUIDELINES
United States Trustee Central District of California, March 1, 2014

In accordance with its obligation to monitor compliance with 11 U.S.C. § 110, the United States Trustee for Region 16, which encompasses the Central District of California, is providing the following guidelines for non-attorneys who prepare documents for filing in the United States Bankruptcy Court. A non-attorney who prepares bankruptcy documents for compensation, whether paid or agreed to be paid, is subject to the requirements and prohibitions of section 110. Preparers are encouraged to read the provisions of 11 U.S.C. § 110 prior to undertaking the preparation of any bankruptcy documents.

Failure to comply with the bankruptcy code may result in the taking of enforcement actions by the United States Trustee. These guidelines are meant to assist non-attorney preparers and debtors who use them in understanding the provisions of section

110 and actions brought by the United States Trustee under section 110.

1. A bankruptcy petition preparer may only type forms. When a bankruptcy petition preparer provides services that go beyond typing forms, those services can constitute the unauthorized "practice of law."

2. A bankruptcy petition preparer has an obligation to disclose all amounts received from the debtor, or on behalf of the debtor, in the year prior to the filing of the bankruptcy case, and the source of any fee paid. This disclosure should also include all amount owing to the preparer. Under the Bankruptcy Abuse Prevention and Consumer Protection Act of 2005 ("BAPCPA"), such disclosure shall be made on the date the petition is filed with the Bankruptcy Court.

3. A petition preparer has an ongoing responsibility to disclose to the court any fees received or compensation agreement not previously disclosed to the court. Within fourteen (14) days of receiving additional compensation or entering into an agreement with a debtor(s) for additional compensation, the petition preparer shall disclose all additional fees or compensation arrangements to the court.

4. The charge typically allowed in this district for a bankruptcy petition preparer's services is no more than $200, including, but not limited to, any and all expenses such as photocopying, costs of credit reports, gas, messenger, courier charges, postage and telephone charges. This fee does not include the court filing fee. The United States Trustee may object to any fee above $200. A lower fee ceiling may apply to an incomplete bankruptcy filing, if the documents shows limited typing, or where a preparer acts incompetently or illegally. If the reasonableness of a bankruptcy petition preparer's fee is challenged, the burden of showing that the fee is reasonable belongs to the preparer. The Bankruptcy Court determines what fee is reasonable.

5. The Bankruptcy Code provides that the Bankruptcy Court may disallow all fees in instances where a petition preparer violates any provision of 11 U.S.C. § 110.

6.  Debtors have the right to file their bankruptcy documents in person at the Bankruptcy Court or by mailing them to the court, consistent with the court's procedure. A preparer who files, assists with the physical filing of a petition with the court, or charges a debtor for messenger or courier costs, may be subject to fines under 11 U.S.C. § 110(g) for handling the court filing fee. This prohibition includes a preparer's handling of a money order payable to the "U.S. Bankruptcy Court."

7.  A petition preparer may not charge or accept monies from a debtor for the credit counseling or debtor education classes, unless the petition preparer has been approved as a provider by the United States Trustee.

8.  Under BAPCPA, a bankruptcy petition preparer is required to sign, give a copy to the debtor, and file with the Bankruptcy Court the Declaration and Signature of Non-Attorney Bankruptcy Petition Preparer (Official Form 19). Form 19 is to be completed and signed before preparing a bankruptcy petition, schedules and statements (or the first of any other paper if the bankruptcy petition preparer has not prepared the petition), and before accepting any money from the debtor(s).

9.  A bankruptcy petition preparer should use the Official Court Forms to prepare documents. These forms are available for no cost on the Bankruptcy Court's website. Some providers of attorney software, for example, do not include petition preparer signature blocks on certain documents, that are included on the Official Forms.

10. A bankruptcy petition preparer is not an attorney and is not authorized to practice law. As defined by statute and case law, the activities that constitute the practice of law in the bankruptcy court include, but are not limited to, the following:

    A.  Determining when to file bankruptcy or whether to file a bankruptcy petition;

    B.  Explaining the difference between chapters or determining under which chapter of the Bankruptcy Code to file a voluntary petition;

C.  Explaining information necessary to complete the bankruptcy petition;

D.  Advising debtors regarding the claiming of exemptions;

E.  Explaining or determining which debts are priority, secured, or unsecured;

F.  Suggesting or determining where items belong on the petition, based on information provided by a debtor;

G.  Preparing any pleadings other than filling out official forms promulgated by the United States Supreme Court or by the United States Bankruptcy Court of the Central District of California;

H.  Explaining or discussing the impact that a bankruptcy filing may have on an eviction or foreclosure proceeding;

I.  Explaining or discussing the impact that a bankruptcy filing may have on the dischargeability of debts, including outstanding student loans or taxes, or whether a debt will be discharged;

J.  Explaining, discussing, or assisting a debtor with a reaffirmation agreement;

K.  Assisting or appearing with the debtor or on a debtor's behalf at the § 341(a) Meeting of Creditors;

L.  Discussing or assisting a debtor with determining whether a certain debt should be reaffirmed or redeemed; and

M.  Providing advice or guidance to a debtor regarding the actions that may or may not be taken by a creditor, United States Bankruptcy Trustee, United States Bankruptcy Court, United States Bankruptcy Judge, or another third party.

11. Translating documents may not necessarily be considered the practice of law. However, translation services provided to a debtor should not include services listed in paragraph 10 above.

12. Before typing any document whatsoever and before accepting any money from the debtor(s), the bankruptcy petition preparer must provide a copy of these Guidelines to

the debtor(s), which must be signed and dated by the debtor(s)and the bankruptcy petition preparer as provided below. The original signed copy of the Guidelines must be attached to any petition, pleading or other document filed with the court. If these Guidelines are filed with the bankruptcy petition, the U.S. Trustee suggests that it be placed in front of the mailing matrix. * * *

## C.  BUSINESS COMPLETING DOCUMENTS RELATED TO A CUSTOMER TRANSACTION

### CAMPBELL V. ASBURY AUTO., INC.
#### 381 S.W.3d 21 (Ark. 2011)

Charles and Carol Palasack filed a class-action complaint against Asbury, in which they alleged that Asbury "charged Plaintiffs and other similarly situated members of the Plaintiff class, an illegal document preparation fee for preparing the vehicle installment contract (a legal instrument) for the purchase of a vehicle." The Palasacks asserted that the fee itself was illegal, constituting the unauthorized practice of law, and * * * resulting in unjust enrichment. The circuit court granted class certification. . . . In the ensuing litigation, both parties filed motions for summary judgment, and . . . the circuit court granted summary judgment to Campbell, ruling that the documentary fee charged by Asbury "includes compensation for time spent preparing or filling in the blanks on legal documents and therefore constitutes the unauthorized practice of law and is illegal." * * *

Asbury, for its first point on cross-appeal, argues that the circuit court erred in granting summary judgment to Campbell on the class's unauthorized-practice-of-law claim. It asserts that its completion of standardized forms, necessary to the purchase of motor vehicles, did not require the training, skill, or judgment of an attorney and was not the practice of law. It avers that it did not hold itself out as providing legal services and did not give legal advice or counsel. It further states that the public benefited by its completion of the forms and that its charging of a separate fee did not transform completion of the forms into the practice of law.

Campbell responds that the class was properly granted summary judgment because "Asbury's typical, ordinary, and standard practice is that it selects the legal documents used in each transaction, completes the legal documents, reviews and explains the documents to the customer, and generates millions of dollars in revenue for this service." He further asserts that this court's prior decisions clearly prohibit nonlawyer corporations from preparing legal documents for pay, and, for this reason, the circuit court's grant of summary judgment should be affirmed. Having already set forth our standard of review for summary judgment, we turn then to whether the completion of certain forms by Asbury for a fee constituted the unauthorized practice of law. We hold that it did.

The practice of law by a corporation is prohibited by Ark. Code Ann. § 16–22–211 (Repl.1999), which provides, in pertinent part:

> (a) It shall be unlawful for any corporation or voluntary association to practice or appear as an attorney at law for any person in any court in this state or before any judicial body, to make it a business to practice as an attorney at law for any person in any of the courts, to hold itself out to the public as being entitled to practice law, to tender or furnish legal services or advice, to furnish attorneys or counsel, to render legal services of any kind in actions or proceedings of any nature or in any other way or manner, or in any other manner to assume to be entitled to practice law or to assume or advertise the title of lawyer or attorney, attorney at law, or equivalent terms in any language in such a manner as to convey the impression that it is entitled to practice law or to furnish legal advice, service, or counsel or to advertise that either alone or together with or by or through any person, whether a duly and regularly admitted attorney at law or not, it has, owns, conducts, or maintains a law office or any office for the practice of law, or for furnishing legal advice, services, or counsel.

Likewise, this court has observed that "[c]orporations shall not practice law."

With regard to the practice of law, this court has noted that "[i]t is uniformly held that many activities, such as writing and interpreting wills, contracts, trust agreements and the giving of legal advice in general, constitute practicing law." In *Arkansas Bar Ass'n v. Block,* 230 Ark. 430, 323 S.W.2d 912 (1959), *overruled in part by Creekmore v. Izard,* 236 Ark. 558, 367 S.W.2d 419 (1963), we held that the completion "by filling in the blank spaces" of "standardized and approved prepared forms of" instruments constituted the practice of law and included warranty deeds; disclaimer deeds; quitclaim deeds; joint tenancy deeds; options; easements; loan applications; promissory notes; real estate mortgages; deeds of trust; assignments of leases or rentals; contracts of sale of real estate; releases and satisfactions of real estate mortgages; agreements for the sale of real estate; bills of sale; contracts of sale; mortgages; pledges of personal property; notices and declarations of forfeiture; notices requiring strict compliance; releases and discharges of mechanic's and materialmen's liens; printed forms approved by attorneys, including the various forms furnished by title insurance companies to real estate brokers for use by them as agents of title insurance companies; actions as closing agent for mortgage loans and completion by filling in the blanks therein with factual data such instruments as are furnished to brokers and are necessary, incidental, and ancillary to the closing of the transaction between the mortgagee for whom they act as agent and the mortgagor; and leases. In that same vein, this court held, in *Beach Abstract & Guaranty Co. v. Bar Ass'n of Arkansas,* 230 Ark. 494, 326 S.W.2d 900 (1959), that title examination and curative work, when done for another, constituted the practice of law in its strictest sense.

Notwithstanding those holdings, this court, in *Creekmore v. Izard,* 236 Ark. 558, 367 S.W.2d 419 (1963), modified its decision in *Block*

> to provide that a real estate broker, when the person for whom he is acting has declined to employ a lawyer to prepare the necessary instruments and has authorized the real estate broker to do so, may be permitted to fill in the blanks in simple printed standardized real estate forms, which forms must be approved by a lawyer; it

being understood that these forms shall not be used for
other than simple real estate transactions which arise
in the usual course of the broker's business and that
such forms shall be used only in connection with real
estate transactions actually handled by such brokers as
a broker and then without charge for the simple service
of filling in the blanks.

It did so, recognizing public convenience as a factor in its
decision. In *Pope County Bar Ass'n, Inc. v. Suggs,* 274 Ark. 250,
624 S.W.2d 828 (1981), this court again held that it was in the
public interest to permit the limited, outside use of standard,
printed forms "in connection with simple real estate
transactions, provided they had been previously prepared by a
lawyer" and provided:

(1)  That the person for whom the broker is acting has
     declined to employ a lawyer to prepare the
     necessary instruments and has authorized the
     broker to do so; and

(2)  That the forms are approved by a lawyer either
     before or after the blanks are filled in but prior to
     delivery to the person for whom the broker is
     acting; and

(3)  That the forms shall not be used for other than
     simple real estate transactions which arise in the
     usual course of the broker's business; and

(4)  That the forms shall be used only in connection
     with real estate transactions actually handled by
     such brokers as a broker; and

(5)  That the broker shall make no charge for filling in
     the blanks; and

(6)  That the broker shall not give advice or opinions as
     to the legal rights of the parties, as to the legal
     effects of instruments to accomplish specific
     purposes or as to the validity of title to real estate.

The court noted that, standing alone, the completion of the forms
at issue fell readily within the practice of law; but more
importantly, even when examined in the context of the

restrictions set forth, the court regarded "the use and preparation of these instruments as so indigenous to the practice of law that it would be illogical to say they are not." Nonetheless, the court permitted the use of the forms under the restrictions it set forth.

While we are cognizant of the fact that the forms at issue in this case do not involve real-estate matters, it is clear to this court that the restrictions set forth in *Suggs* have equal application to the forms used in the motor-vehicle-sales business. Asbury admits that the forms are legally binding, but avers that such business dealings are common and simply incidental to the motor-vehicle-dealer business. While that may be true, this court has taken such argument into account and has remained steadfast, as in *Creekmore* and *Suggs*, that the completion of forms legal in nature by nonlawyers, while ordinarily the practice of law, may be permitted, but only within very certain, specific parameters.

Accordingly, Asbury was likewise permitted to complete the forms at issue, but was required to do so within the parameters set by this court in *Creekmore* and *Suggs*, which would include

(1) that the person for whom Asbury was acting declined to employ a lawyer to prepare the necessary instruments and authorized Asbury to do so;

(2) that the forms were approved by a lawyer either before or after the blanks were filled in, but prior to delivery to the person for whom Asbury was acting;

(3) that the forms were not used for other than simple retail transactions, which arose in the usual course of Asbury's business;

(4) that the forms were used only in connection with motor-vehicle-sale transactions actually handled by Asbury as a motor-vehicle dealer;

(5) that Asbury did not charge for filling in the blanks; and

(6) that Asbury did not give advice or opinions as to the legal rights of the parties, as to the legal effects of

> instruments to accomplish specific purposes, or as
> to the validity of the contract.

If it did not act within the parameters of *Suggs* and *Creekmore*, Asbury engaged in the unauthorized practice of law.

The question is, then, did Asbury comply with those requirements? The record in this case makes clear that it did not. Indeed, Asbury does not dispute that it charged a documentary fee, nor does it deny that the fee was charged for the filling in of forms. In fact, in its response to Campbell's cross-motion for summary judgment, Asbury plainly states that it was charging a fee for the act of completing or filling in forms:

> The completion of routine, standardized forms necessary to sell a motor vehicle to a retail customer and the charging of an administrative fee to that customer is not the practice of law and is not a deceptive trade practice. While the forms at issue may or may not have some legal significance, Defendants are not practicing law by filling in blanks or charging a fee for what includes services in addition to the completion of certain forms.
>
> . . . .
>
> Defendants are not posing as lawyers and are not purporting to practice law. They are filling in routine, standardized forms to sell cars to the public.
>
> . . . .
>
> Defendants charge the administrative fee to all customers.
>
> . . . .
>
> The paperwork is standard, pre-printed, and routine for each sales transaction. Defendants are selling motor vehicles. By completing these forms, they are not holding themselves out as lawyers or practicing law.
>
> Defendants charge an administrative fee. The administrative fee includes, among other things, the completion of these documents.

Here, it is abundantly clear that Asbury charged a documentary fee in relation to its completion of legal forms. Because it did so, the circuit court was correct in finding that Asbury engaged in the unauthorized practice of law, in contravention of this court's decisions in *Creekmore* and *Suggs*. For this reason, we hold that the circuit court did not err in granting summary judgment to Campbell. * * *

## D. ACCOUNTANT

### ZACHARY C. ZUREK, THE LIMITED POWER OF THE BAR TO PROTECT ITS MONOPOLY
3 St. Mary's J. Legal Mal. & Ethics 242, 255–56 (2013)

At first thought, if asked whether accountants engage in the practice of law in their everyday course of work, one might easily respond, "No, of course not, they just crunch numbers." Upon closer examination, however, Certified Public Accountants (CPAs) do much more than crunch numbers. Today, CPAs work in professional structures similar to attorneys. Like attorneys, CPAs join forces to create firms through Limited Liability Partnerships, Professional Corporations, and Professional Limited Liability Companies. Similar to law firms, CPA firms combine accountants with different skill sets and backgrounds to offer a wide range of services.

Consequently, as these services expand, so does the friction with UPL laws. The more accountants step away from their traditional role of crunching numbers and step into the role of advising and consulting, the more likely they are to find themselves as defendants in a UPL cause of action. The pervasive debate and confusion surrounding an accountant's ability to perform quasi-legal services is understandable considering the lack of a uniform definition for the practice of law among various state UPL laws. * * *

### WAUGH V. KELLEY
555 N.E.2d 857 (Ind. App. 1990)

* * *

Kelley prepared [Waugh's tax] returns and rendered her a bill at . . . [an] hourly rate. He did not bill for some of his services, as a friend of the family, and reduced his bill from $16,000 to

$11,400 for these services. When Waugh refused to pay, Kelley filed suit. * * * Waugh [defended against liability on the basis that Kelly] was not admitted to the practice of law in this state at the time. * * *

This is a case of first impression.

[T]he simple question here is whether or not the preparation and filing of federal and state income tax returns for Indiana residents constitutes the rendition of legal services to be performed only by those persons admitted to the practice of law in this state.

In *Groninger v. Fletcher Trust Co.* (1942), 220 Ind. 202, 41 N.E.2d 140, appellee furnished:

> ... to its customers pamphlets descriptive of tax laws, state and national, with illustrations indicating tax liability under given circumstances, and the proper method of making tax returns. It sometimes acts through its employees who are not lawyers, in arriving at proper computations and agreements with ministerial taxing officers. It cannot seriously be contended that these activities constitute an unlawful practice of law.

> We find nothing in the facts stipulated to justify a conclusion that the appellee is practicing law.

*Groninger,* 41 N.E.2d at 142, citing several cases in support reaching the same conclusion. The preparation and filing of income tax returns involves substantially the same activity, and does not constitute the practice of law.

Also, in *Miller v. Vance* (1984), Ind., 463 N.E.2d 250, the question was whether laymen bank employees engaged in the unlawful practice of law by filling in blanks in real estate mortgages as an integral part of their employers' business. The court answered that question in the negative. It said:

> Our finding here is consistent with the majority of other jurisdictions where this issue has been considered. Our rule here comports with the general rule that the drafting of documents, when it is incidental to the work

of a specific occupation, is not generally considered to be
the practice of law.

*Miller,* 463 N.E.2d at 253. Without doubt, the preparation and
filing of federal and state income tax returns are tasks incidental
to the business of a certified public accountant, as was Kelley
here. * * *

Other jurisdictions also have held the preparation of income tax
returns does not constitute the unauthorized practice of law.
* * *Because the preparation and filing of federal and state
income tax returns as a matter of law does not constitute the
rendition of legal services requiring the preparer to be admitted
to the practice of law in Indiana, the trial court did not err in
entering judgment in favor of Kelley for the services he rendered
Waugh.

## LOWELL BAR ASS'N V. LOEB
### 52 N.E.2d 27 (Mass. 1943)

This is a petition brought by an incorporated association of
members of the bar, to restrain the respondents, who are not
members of the bar, from * * * from engaging in the practice of
law, and from giving legal advice in respect to liability to pay
income taxes and the preparation and execution of income tax
returns. * * * By the final decree, ... respondents were
'permanently enjoined and restrained from * * * engaging in the
making out of income tax returns as a regular occupation and
other than the occasional drafting thereof and from engaging in
the practice of the law in any of its aspects,' and were ordered to
pay costs. From each decree these respondents appealed. * * *

The facts may be summarized as follows: [The unincorporated
American Tax Service is] * * * in a business of making out
income tax returns for wage earners. * * * The respondent Birdie
T. Loeb devotes all her time to the business, and ostensibly is
the proprietor. The respondent Friedman is general manager,
and has his office at the Boston headquarters. The respondent
Koch was manager of the Lowell branch until succeeded by one
Shea. The business has about one hundred employees during the
season for income tax returns. None of them is a member of the
bar. None of them appears to be an accountant, with the
exception of the respondent Friedman.

The American Tax Service does not attempt to make out income tax returns for corporations, partnerships, estates, fiduciaries or business men conducting a business. Its patrons are exclusively persons whose income consists wholly, or almost wholly, of salary or wages. It advertises extensively in newspapers and by signs in its windows. There is little modesty or restraint about its advertising, which is designed to arrest attention and to bring in a large volume of business. * * *

The proposition cannot be maintained, that whenever, for compensation, one person gives to another advice that involves some element of law, or performs for another some service that requires some knowledge of law, or drafts for another some document that has legal effect, he is practising law. All these things are done in the usual course of the work of occupations that are universally recognized as distinct from the practice of law. There is authority for the proposition that the drafting of documents, when merely incidental to the work of a distinct occupation, is not the practice of law, although the documents have legal consequences. * * *

For example, an architect cannot advise a landowner properly, or plan for him intelligently, without an adequate knowledge of the building laws and regulations. In practice, an architect prepares the building contract, and drafts the specifications that accompany it and determine to a great extent the rights and liabilities of the landowner. An insurance agent or broker, in order to be of service, must know the legal effect of different forms of policies and of various provisions in them. Often he is the agent of the insured, and as such drafts riders, to be attached to a policy, which have important legal effect. An appraiser or valuer of property, real or personal, must be acquainted with the principles of value that find acceptance in the courts. An auctioneer or broker often drafts sale notes, receipts and memoranda for his employer which may affect his legal rights. A so called customhouse broker commonly prepares for the importer documents that have important legal effect, and to do so requires considerable knowledge of the law of customs duties.

The work of an accountant necessarily brings him into touch with rules of law which he must understand if his computations and conclusions are to stand the test of possible litigation. He must know the nature and general legal effect of negotiable instruments, patent rights, corporate stock and bonds of different kinds, insurance policies, and other contracts. He must appreciate the distinction between buying goods, and taking them as bailee, agent, broker or factor. He could hardly prepare a correct account for a partnership without a working knowledge of the main principles of the law of partnership. In preparing an account for a trust estate, he must understand the difference between principal and income, and the rules of law governing the allocation of receipts and expenses to the one or the other. Income taxes have produced a flood of judicial decisions and departmental rulings with which he must have adequate acquaintance, even though he merely works with figures and does not draft tax returns. A sharp line cannot be drawn between the field of the lawyer and that of the accountant. Some matters lie in a penumbra. But any service that lies wholly within the practice of law cannot lawfully be performed by an accountant or any other person not a member of the bar.

Plainly the commencement and prosecution for another of legal proceedings in court and the advocacy for another of a cause before a court, in cases relating to taxes as in other cases, are reserved exclusively for members of the bar.[3] Doubtless the examination of statutes, judicial decisions, and departmental rulings, for the purpose of advising upon a question of law relative to taxation, and the rendering to a client of an opinion thereon, are likewise part of the practice of law in which only members of the bar may engage.

When we pass beyond these propositions we enter debatable ground. The present case does not require us to delimit either the practice of law in tax matters or the right of persons not admitted to the bar to engage for compensation in the business of assisting others in such matters. It would be unwise and perhaps unfair to future litigants, to enunciate at this time broad principles not necessary to the decision of the case before us. * * *

---

[3] An exception may exist in 'small claims' procedure in District Courts. G.L.(Ter.Ed.) c. 218, § 21. Rule 12 for Small Claims Procedure, District Courts (1940) and Municipal Court of the City of Boston (1940). McLaughlin v. Municipal Court of Roxbury District of Boston, 308 Mass. 397, 32 N.E.2d 266; American Automobile Association, Inc., v. Merrick, 73 App.D.C. 151, 117 F.2d 23, 25.

[W]e do not decide at this time whether considering, or advising upon, questions of law only so far as they are incidental to the preparation for another of an income tax return may constitute the practice of law where the return is more complicated than were those in the case before us, and the questions of law as well as of accounting are correspondingly more difficult and important.

Confining our decision to the case at bar, we find the respondents engaged in the business of making out income tax returns of the least difficult kind. The blank forms furnished by the tax officials for that class of returns are made simple, and are accompanied by plain printed instructions. The forms may appear formidable to persons unused to mental concentration and to clerical exactness, but they can readily be filled out by any intelligent taxpayer whose income is derived wholly or almost wholly from salary or wages and who has the patience to study the instructions.

We are aware that there has been said to be no difference in principle between the drafting of simple instruments and the drafting of complex ones. But though the difference is one of degree, it may nevertheless be real. There are instruments that no one but a well trained lawyer should ever undertake to draw. But there are others, common in the commercial world, and fraught with substantial legal consequences, that lawyers seldom are employed to draw, and that in the course of recognized occupations other than the practice of law are often drawn by laymen for other laymen, as has already been shown. The actual practices of the community have an important bearing on the scope of the practice of law.

We think that the preparation of the income tax returns in question, though it had to be done with some consideration of the law, did not lie wholly within the field of the practice of law. The final decree should not have enjoined the respondents from preparing such returns. * * *

### THE FLA. BAR V. TOWN
174 So.2d 395 (Fla. 1965)

On petition of The Florida Bar this Court issued its rule directing that the respondent Albert P. Town, who is not a member of The Florida Bar, show cause why he should not be held in contempt of the Integration Rule of The Florida Bar heretofore adopted by this Court.

In its petition The Florida Bar charged that the Respondent in newspaper advertisements held himself out to be a specialist in the incorporation of businesses and offering to handle all details in the formation thereof; that respondent had been previously informed by the Office of the Secretary of State that the formation of a corporation for another for a fee by a person not a lawyer, could be considered a violation of Section 454.23, F.S.A.; nevertheless, respondent did advise and represent one Richard Price and cause a Florida corporation to be formed for him, preparing the corporate charter and related documents. The petition also set forth various alleged errors or inadequacies in the corporate charter which were to the detriment of Mr. Price.

The respondent has filed an answer in which he denied that he had held himself out as a corporation specialist since October, 1963, but admitted that during the months of October, November and December, 1963, he did act as such a specialist on several different occasions. He states that upon learning that his actions might be construed to be the unauthorized practice of law he ceased them and has done nothing further which could be deemed to be practice of law. He says that he is an accountant and any work recently done for corporations has been accounting. He does not allege that his services as a corporation specialist were performed for and under the direction of a member of The Florida Bar.

Respondent points out that this Court has never decided whether the preparation of a corporate charter, and related documents, does or does not constitute the practice of law. He asks us to do so now.

In State ex rel. Florida Bar v. Sperry, Fla.1962, 140 So.2d 587, 591, in an effort to formulate a general definition of conduct which constitutes the practice of law, this Court said:

> It is generally understood that the performance of services in representing another before the courts is the practice of law. But the *practice of law* also *includes the giving of legal advice and counsel* to others as to their

rights and obligations under the law and the preparation of legal instruments, *including contracts, by which legal rights are either obtained, secured or given away*, although such matters may not then or ever be the subject of proceedings in a court.

We think that in determining whether the giving of advice and counsel and the performance of services in legal matters for compensation constitute the practice of law *it is safe to follow the rule that if the giving of such advice and performance of such services affect important rights of a person under the law, and if the reasonable protection of the rights and property of those advised and served requires that the persons giving such advice possess legal skill and a knowledge of the law greater than that possessed by the average citizen, then the giving of such advice and the performance of such services* by one for another as a course of conduct constitutes the practice of law. (Emphasis supplied.)

That a corporate charter constitutes an important contractual document is settled law. The by-laws of the corporation when properly adopted likewise constituted a binding agreement among the stockholders and between the stockholders and the corporation.

For various reasons the corporation has become an increasingly popular form of business organization. Because of its popularity it has been the object of ever greater attention through statutes and regulations of federal taxing authorities. As The Florida Bar contends was the case here, lack of knowledge of the applicable statute, ch. 608, F.S.A., and experience in the design and operation of the corporate form may well result in failure to provide many advantages in flexibility of purposes, number of shares of stock, and other items which could be initially provided at no extra cost to the stockholders. Moreover, the interest of federal taxing authorities in corporate financing makes it unwise to launch even the smallest corporation without resort to the advice of competent trained and experienced experts in the applicable law and regulations. The formation of a corporation necessarily involves the giving of advice relative to the rights and obligations of those involved in the venture.

We are of the view that the preparation of charters, bylaws and other documents necessary to the establishment of a corporation, being the basis of important contractual and legal obligations, comes within the definition of the practice of law as defined in the Sperry case, supra. The reasonable protection of the rights and property of those involved requires that the persons preparing such documents and advising others as to what they should and should not contain possess legal skill and knowledge far in excess of that possessed by the best informed non-lawyer citizen.

Other courts have reached the same conclusion. * * * The respondent has cited no cases holding to the contrary and we have found none.

The respondent has cooperated in seeking the determination made herein and there is nothing to indicate that he has deliberately or contemptuously violated that part of the Integration Rule prohibiting the unauthorized practice of law. Further, he expresses the intention to abide the decision of this Court. We therefore decline to hold him in contempt.

However, by this order we do permanently enjoin the respondent, Albert P. Town, from forming corporations for others, including the preparation of charters, by-laws, resolutions, and other documents incidental to the contractual rights of the corporation, its incorporators, and stockholders, and from advising others in respect thereto. Respondent states that he is an accountant. Therefore, any rights to advise others as to fiscal and accounting matters which he may have as an accountant shall not be impaired by this injunction.

It is so ordered.

## E.  PUBLIC INSURANCE ADJUSTER

### LINDER V. INS. CLAIMS CONSULTANTS, INC.
#### 560 S.E.2d 612 (S.C. 2002)

Insurance adjusting is the business of settling an insurance claim. Black's Law Dictionary defines an "adjuster" as one "appointed to adjust [i.e., settle] a matter; . . . One . . . who makes any adjustment or settlement, or who determines the amount of a claim."

First-party public insurance adjusting involves the situation where "an insured hires a public adjuster to assist the insured in filing a claim of loss with its insurer" and is based on contract law. Specifically, a first-party adjuster is retained to:

> determin[e] the amount of loss recoverable under the policy. The adjuster documents and measures damages, gathers relevant facts, determines repair or replacement costs, and submits the claim to the insurance company. The adjuster then negotiates with the insurance company, or the insurance company's adjuster, to obtain the best settlement for the insured.

In contrast, third-party adjusting involves the situation where a "stranger to the insurance contract" asserts a claim against an insured tortfeasor. "In third-party adjusting, an adjuster represents an injured client in making a claim under a liability insurance contract against an insurance company that insures or indemnifies a third person who is or may be liable for the injury caused to the adjuster's client." Therefore, the third-party adjuster "must determine the extent of the liability, rights, and duties of the parties before attempting to resolve the issue of a settlement amount."

A first-party adjuster is generally considered to be synonymous with the term "public adjuster." * * *

Petitioners ("the Linders") suffered property loss due to a fire at their home in February 1996. While their claim was being adjusted by the insurance company, the Linders had many concerns about how the repairs to their home were being handled. One of the repairmen recommended respondent Insurance Claims Consultants, Inc. ("ICC") to Mrs. Linder. Mrs. Linder called ICC and met with respondent Gerald Moore.

In that initial meeting with Moore, the Linders discussed the fact that the insurance company had rejected their claim for the full value of Mr. Linder's gun collection. According to Mrs. Linder, Moore advised them the guns should be covered under their policy. Moore indicated that he advised the Linders to read their insurance policy and that he and Mr. Linder read the policy together. Respondent Jeffrey Raines states in an affidavit that they "were successful in obtaining payment for Mr. Linder's guns which was originally and erroneously denied by the company."

The Linders entered into a contract with ICC and agreed to pay ICC 10% of the total amount adjusted or otherwise recovered. In addition, they executed a "Notice" to their insurance company which indicated that ICC had been hired for the preparation of their claim and that ICC should be contacted for "any further information and negotiations" concerning their claim. After executing the contract with ICC, the Linders released the lawyer they had retained a couple of weeks before contacting ICC.

ICC communicated directly with the insurance company's adjuster both orally and in writing, as well as with the insurance company's attorney. The majority of the communications reflect that the adjusters concentrated on cost-related issues, such as completing the contents inventory and the sworn statement of proof of loss, as well as discussions on the extent and amount of repairs. Indeed, Raines stated that ICC spent over 300 man hours preparing the detailed inventory of the damaged household contents. According to Raines, ICC was able to obtain an almost $12,000 increase in what the insurance company originally agreed to cover. The Linders approved the claim, but the insurance company delayed payment. Raines stated that he then recommended to Mrs. Linder that she get an attorney. When the attorney settled the claim, the Linders executed a release of all claims.

On a "fact sheet" given to Mrs. Linder by Moore, ICC describes itself as a "professional Loss Consulting Firm" which represents a client's "best interest" while handling a property damage claim. The fact sheet states that ICC will provide, inter alia: an assessment of property loss; a leading law firm to review the insurance policy (at ICC's expense); a complete inventory of damaged contents; engineers, architects, accountants, etc., if required (at ICC's expense); all required documentation to properly project and substantiate additional living expenses and/or business interruption; and assistance in the preparation with the timely filing of the sworn statement of proof of loss. ICC stated that its main goal is to provide the client with an initial comprehensive study of the loss and damages. Finally, the following was printed at the bottom of the fact sheet:

REMEMBER, your insurance company has already appointed a professional to protect THEIR interest. ICC WILL PROTECT YOURS!

\* \* \*

The Linders did not pay ICC the 10% fee, as they had agreed in the contract. ICC brought suit against the Linders for the recovery of this contingency fee. The Linders answered the complaint, asserting, inter alia, that respondents engaged in the unauthorized practice of law and therefore the contract between them is void ab initio. In an amended answer, the Linders added counterclaims for negligence and breach of contract. \* \* \*

### 1.   *Public Insurance Adjusting Does Not Constitute the Unauthorized Practice of Law.*

Under the South Carolina Constitution, this Court has the duty to regulate the practice of law in South Carolina. Our duty to regulate the legal profession is not for the purpose of creating a monopoly for lawyers, or for their economic protection; instead, it is to protect *the public* from the potentially severe economic and emotional consequences which may flow from the erroneous preparation of legal documents or the inaccurate legal advice given by persons untrained in the law. Indeed, protection of the public is our "paramount concern" in these matters.

The practice of law "is not confined to litigation, but extends to activities in other fields which entail specialized legal knowledge and ability. Often, the line between such activities and permissible business conduct by non-attorneys is unclear." Indeed, we have recognized "it is neither practicable nor wise" to attempt to formulate a comprehensive definition of what constitutes the practice of law. Because of this ambiguity, what is, and what is not, the unauthorized practice of law is best decided in the context of an actual case or controversy. Moreover, it is this Court that has the final word on what constitutes the practice of law.

The issue of whether insurance adjusters engage in the unauthorized practice of law is a novel one in South Carolina, but has been entertained by many courts in other jurisdictions.

For example, in *Rhode Island Bar Ass'n v. Lesser,* 68 R.I. 14, 26 A.2d 6 (1942), a man doing business as "Rhode Island Fire Loss Appraisal Bureau," was found to have engaged in the unauthorized practice of law. The Rhode Island Supreme Court held that the adjuster's activities of negotiating and obtaining adjustments of claims for losses under fire insurance policies, which involved, "directly or indirectly, advice or counsel with reference to their claims and rights under the policies," and charging a contingency fee for his services, constituted the unauthorized practice of law. The *Lesser* court found that these activities exceeded a mere "appraisal service." However, in affirming the injunction against the adjuster, the Court noted that the injunction decree expressly reserved to Lesser the right "to solicit from the general public the work of appraising damage caused by fire, making inventory of real and personal property so damaged, appraising the value of such property both prior to and immediately following a fire, and submitting to the owners of the same a complete and itemized statement showing sound value and loss." Thus, the *Lesser* court was primarily concerned with the adjuster's activities of: (1) advising clients on their claims and rights under the policy, (2) negotiating settlements for the claim, and (3) accepting a contingency fee.

The Pennsylvania Supreme Court in *Dauphin County Bar Ass'n v. Mazzacaro,* 465 Pa. 545, 351 A.2d 229 (1976), declared that a "licensed casualty adjuster" who represented clients on their damage claims against tortfeasors or their insurers was correctly enjoined from handling these third-party claims. The court found that pursuant to Pennsylvania's Public Adjuster Act, only first-party adjusting was authorized. In handling third-party claims, Mazzacaro would investigate the accident, estimate the amount of damages sustained, write a demand letter and attempt to negotiate a settlement. He argued that his representation was permissible because his clients' claims were ones in which liability was presumed and the only issue was damages. The Pennsylvania Supreme Court rejected his argument, noting that it "ignore[d] the vital role that legal assessments play in the negotiation process between a victim of an injury and an alleged tortfeasor or insurer." Significantly, the *Mazzacaro* court stated the following:

While the objective valuation of damages may in uncomplicated cases be accomplished by a skilled lay judgment, an assessment of the extent to which that valuation should be compromised in settlement negotiations cannot. Even when liability is not technically 'contested,' an assessment of the likelihood that liability can be established in a court of law is a crucial factor in weighing the strength of one's bargaining position. A negotiator cannot possibly know how large a settlement he can exact unless he can probe the degree of unwillingness of the other side to go to court. Such an assessment, however, involves an understanding of the applicable tort principles . . . , a grasp of the rules of evidence, and an ability to evaluate the strengths and weaknesses of the client's case vis a vis that of the adversary. The acquisition of such knowledge is not within the ability of lay persons but rather involves the application of abstract legal principles to the concrete facts of the given claim. As a consequence, it is inescapable that lay adjusters who undertake to negotiate settlements of the claims of third-party claimants must exercise legal judgment in so doing.

\* \* \*

The Texas Court of Appeals has spoken twice on whether public adjusters engage in the unauthorized practice of law. In *Brown v. Unauthorized Practice of Law Committee*, 742 S.W.2d 34 (Tex.App.1987), *writ denied* (Jan. 27, 1988), the court found the actions of Brown, who apparently handled both first-party and third-party claims, were clearly the unauthorized practice of law. Brown had accepted settlement checks as "Ron Brown, Attorney at Law." The court found he advised clients as to their rights and the advisability of making claims and approved settlements. Furthermore, the court found Brown's course of conduct encouraged litigation. As to Brown's assertion that he handled only "uncontested" claims, the court stated that "because the evidence shows that Brown negotiated, at least on damage issues, we cannot agree that Brown handled only undisputed and uncontested cases." The court held that such negotiation requires "the use of legal skill and knowledge and, thus, constituted the practice of law."

In 1991, the Texas Court of Appeals decided *Unauthorized Practice of Law Committee v. Jansen,* 816 S.W.2d 813 (Tex. App.1991), *writ denied* (Jan. 8, 1992). Jansen was a first-party public adjuster. At the trial level, the trial court found various activities by Jansen constituted the unauthorized practice of law, and enjoined him from, *inter alia:* (1) advising clients on whether to accept an offer from an insurance company, and (2) advising clients of their rights, duties, or privileges under an insurance policy. Jansen did not appeal. The trial court specifically found the following practices did *not* constitute the unauthorized practice of law:

A.  Advising clients to seek the services of a licensed attorney if they have questions relating to their legal rights, duties and privileges under policies of insurance;

B.  Measuring and documenting first party claims under property insurance policies and presenting them to insurance companies on behalf of clients;

C.  Discussing the measurement and documentation presented to the insurance company with representatives of insurance companies;

D.  Advising clients that valuations placed on first party property insurance claims by insurance companies is or is not accurate[.]

The Unauthorized Practice of Law Committee (UPLC) appealed these findings and argued that the measure and documentation of first-party claims, the presentation of these claims to insurance companies, and the discussion of the claims with insurance company adjusters all constitute the unauthorized practice of law. The *Jansen* court disagreed:

> We cannot agree with UPLC's contention that providing an estimate of property damage and filling out the appropriate forms to present a claim constitutes the practice of law. In reality, this is the same procedure any insured is required to follow to collect on an

insurance policy. The fact that appellee is paid for his services and expertise does not convert his actions into the practice of law. Our holding is not to be construed as authorizing discussions or "negotiations" with insurance companies into coverage matters. Nor do we mean to imply that "presenting" a claim to the insurance company by a public insurance adjuster is the same as negotiating a settlement. The former is, in essence, merely delivering necessary paperwork and data while the latter entails the practice of law. Interpretation of insurance contracts would also most likely cross the line into the practice of law. Appellee agrees that if the issue to be submitted to an insurance company involves a coverage dispute, then the services of an attorney are required. We find that the trial court arrived at a suitable accommodation that will not totally eliminate the profession of public insurance adjusting in the State.

The *Jansen* court then distinguished its earlier decision in *Brown*, and held that a public adjuster may have discussions with an insurance company adjuster about competing property-damage valuations, provided that liability under the policy is uncontested. The court found Brown's activities regarding personal injury claims were sufficiently different from Jansen's activities: "An opinion concerning the valuation, whether it be repair cost or replacement cost, of a damaged piece of property hardly equates to counseling a client to settle a claim."

The *Jansen* case therefore represents a somewhat different viewpoint on what is allowable for first-party public adjusters. Although interpreting policies and getting involved in coverage disputes remained a concern for the Jansen court, it was not willing to rule that negotiating on *valuations* of property damage in uncontested cases constitutes the unauthorized practice of law.

In our opinion, the business of public insurance adjusting does not *per se* constitute the practice of law. We note the parties agree that public adjusters may act as appraisers. Since a public adjuster may use his expertise to determine a value, we simply do not see why it would be beyond his expertise to discuss that value, and the insurer's competing value, with the client and the insurer's adjuster. This type of negotiation activity—as long as it is limited to valuations of property and repairs-does not require legal skill and knowledge.

Nonetheless, because the activities of public insurance adjusters may bring them close to the line between permissible business conduct by non-attorneys and the unauthorized practice of law, we must clarify what is and is not appropriate conduct by public adjusters. After analyzing the decisions in other jurisdictions, we are most persuaded by the reasoning expressed by the Texas court in the *Jansen* case. Like the *Jansen* court, we feel that a suitable accommodation may be made to preserve the business of public adjusting, yet protect the public from the dangers of the unauthorized practice of law.

Specifically, we find there is no problem with a public adjuster measuring and documenting insurance claims, and then presenting those valuations to the insurance company. Therefore, we declare the following practices permissible:

A. Providing an estimate of property damage and repair costs, i.e., any purely appraisal-oriented activities by the public adjuster.

B. Preparing the contents inventory and/or sworn statements on proof of loss.

C. Presenting the claim to the insurance company, i.e., delivering the necessary paperwork and data to the insurer.

D. Negotiating with the insurance company, as long as the discussions only involve competing property-damage valuations.

As to what activities are prohibited, we declare that public adjusters shall not:

A. Advise clients of their rights, duties, or privileges under an insurance policy regarding matters requiring legal skill or knowledge, i.e., interpret the policy for clients.

B. Advise clients on whether to accept a settlement offer from an insurance company.

    C.  Become involved, in any way, with a coverage dispute between the client and the insurance company.

    D.  Utilize advertising that would lead clients to believe that public adjusters provide services which require legal skill.

We believe that these guidelines are consistent with South Carolina's recently enacted statute regulating the business of public adjusting. *See, e.g.,* § 38–48–70(h) (a public adjuster shall not "offer or provide advice as to whether the insured's claim is covered by the insured's contract with the insurer."); § 38–48–100 ("All advertising by a public adjuster shall fairly and accurately describe the services to be rendered and shall not misrepresent either the public adjuster or the public adjuster's abilities. . . ."). Although we reiterate that it is the duty of this Court, and not the Legislature, to delineate the practice of law, we note that the statutory scheme regulating public adjusting specifically addresses many of the concerns that are implicated by the issue before the Court today, and, in our opinion, deals with those concerns appropriately.

In sum, the business of public adjusting does not, in and of itself, embody the practice of law. We are confident that the parameters set out above will inform public adjusters of the limits of their occupation.

### 2.   By Some of Their Actions, Respondents Engaged in the Unauthorized Practice of Law.

The question remains whether respondents engaged in the unauthorized practice of law. Although they certainly did not have the benefit of the guidelines we announce today, we nevertheless must decide whether respondents crossed the line into the unauthorized practice of law. Because they advised the Linders on their rights under the insurance policy and became involved with a known coverage dispute, we conclude that they did.

We find from the record before us that respondents advised the Linders on the extent of coverage for Mr. Linder's gun collection, and then subsequently discussed this with the insurance adjuster. While this "advice" may simply have been pointing out the policy language to the Linders, it still constituted counsel on the Linders' rights under the policy. Moreover, Moore knew at the time that the insurer had limited liability on the gun collection based on its interpretation of the policy. It matters not that the insurance company was mistaken. This clearly was a coverage dispute between the Linders and their insurer, and therefore, respondents should not have become involved. Their involvement went beyond an evaluation on the vital question of "how much" the gun collection was worth, and transgressed into an evaluation of whether, and to what extent, the guns should be covered pursuant to the policy language.

The acts of (1) interpreting and advising the clients on the insurance policy, and (2) negotiating with the insurer *on coverage disputes,* require legal knowledge and skill, and therefore are not permitted without a law license. We find that respondents stepped over the line and that these acts constituted the unauthorized practice of law.

## F. BIDDING COMPANY BROKERING MINERAL LEASES

### LENAU V. CO-EXPRISE, INC.
102 A.3d 423 (Pa. Super. Ct. 2014)

In this case involving subsurface mineral rights, Nancy M. Lenau, Daniel T. Lenau, and Kathleen Trishock (collectively, "Appellants"), appeal from the May 1, 2013 order that sustained the preliminary objections of Co-eXprise, Inc. ("Co-eXprise"), and dismissed the Appellants' complaint. For the reasons that follow, we affirm.

The trial court summarized the factual history of this case as follows:

> This litigation arises out of the conduct of [Co-eXprise], which, acting as an intermediary, encouraged property owners in Beaver County, Pennsylvania to pool their interests by joining [Co-eXprise's] "CX MarketPlace." A property owner would join the CX MarketPlace by signing a form agreement prepared by [Co-eXprise] titled "MarketPlace Agreement." The MarketPlace Agreement authorized Co-eXprise to competitively bid

mineral rights on behalf of the aggregated group of property owners for the purpose of obtaining the most favorable lease terms for each individual CX MarketPlace member.

Property owners who entered into [Co-eXprise's] MarketPlace Agreement were organized into groups with each group comprised of landowners within a defined geographical area. [Co-eXprise] then sought bids from energy companies on behalf of each group of landowners, who as a group could command superior bargaining power and obtain more favorable terms in leases of their subsurface mineral rights, thereby maximizing each property owner's bonus and royalty payments. Under the terms of the MarketPlace Agreement, once Co-eXprise obtained a bid from an energy company which contained lease terms that met or exceeded a predetermined threshold amount for bonus and royalty payments, each property owner in the group was obligated to execute a mineral lease with that energy company, which lease would reflect the terms the energy company proposed during the bidding process.

[Co-eXprise] initially promoted the MarketPlace program through mass [ ] advertising and by conducting meetings with groups of property owners during which Co-eXprise representatives solicited participation in the CX MarketPlace by assuring landowners that MarketPlace participants would obtain the best available bonus and royalty payments through the competitive bidding process. Promotional materials were prepared by [Co-eXprise] and provided to prospective MarketPlace members via regular mail, the Internet, and by hand during promotional meetings. Among the materials that [Co-eXprise] supplied [to Appellants], either directly or through [Co-eXprise's] website, was a terms summary, which explained various terms commonly included in oil and gas leases based on [Co-eXprise's] legal opinion. [Co-eXprise] represented in the MarketPlace Agreement that any resulting lease agreement between the landowner and energy company would contain terms substantially similar to those contained within this [Lease Summary]. These terms were more favorable to the landowner than the terms of the standard lease agreements used by the energy companies.

The MarketPlace Agreement provided for [Co-eXprise] to receive five percent of the up-front bonus in consideration for its services. The money would be paid as soon as the landowner and the highest[-]bidding energy company entered into a lease agreement reflecting the terms of the bid.

On the basis of [Co-eXprise's] representations, [Appellants] entered into MarketPlace Agreements with [Co-eXprise] in January 2011. [Co-eXprise] sought bids on behalf of [Appellants] and fellow MarketPlace participants, and, at the conclusion of the bidding process, identified Chesapeake Appalachia, LLC [(Chesapeake),] as the highest bidder. However, the Chesapeake bid for the Lenau['s] group was lower than a bid that would be binding on the MarketPlace members under the provisions of the MarketPlace Agreement. A bid would be binding on the Lenau['s] group only if it provided for no less than a $3,000 per acre bonus, a 17% royalty, and the substantial inclusion of the sample lease terms. The Chesapeake bid provided for a $2,350 per acre bonus and a 15% royalty.

[Co-eXprise] notified the Lenau [Appellants] and the other members of their group of the offer from Chesapeake at a June 28, 2011 meeting, and represented that the terms reflected the best market terms available. These [Appellants] and the other members of the Lenau group received an email correspondence on July 15, 2011 encouraging them to accept the terms of the Chesapeake offer by signing an "Agreement to Accept Lease Offer from Chesapeake" [(Agreement to Accept)]. The Lenau [Appellants] signed the Agreement to Accept on August 1, 2011[.]

> It appears from the record that [Co-eXprise] continued to recruit landowners into the CX MarketPlace and, pursuant to that recruitment effort, notified other landowners in the area that an offer had been tendered by "a major oil and gas exploration and production company," which offer contained favorable lease terms and the best current market price available in the area. These prospective participants were warned that prices may decline, and, in order to take advantage of the offer, landowners should complete the CX MarketPlace and [Agreement to Accept].

> MarketPlace member landowners who elected to accept Chesapeake's offer were directed to attend a lease-signing event where the landowners entered into individual oil and gas leases with Chesapeake.

> Once a landowner signed a mineral lease with Chesapeake, [Co-eXprise] collected its transaction fee—five percent of the landowner's gross, up-front, bonus payment—directly from Chesapeake.

On November 21, 2012, Appellants filed a "Complaint in Civil Act Class Action," which asserted various causes of action against Co-eXprise, including: (1) breach of contract; (2) unauthorized practice of law; (3) violation of the Pennsylvania Unfair Trade Practices and Consumer Protection Law ("UTPCPL"); (4) violation of the Pennsylvania Securities Act of 1972; (5) breach of fiduciary duty; and (6) unjust enrichment/disgorgement. * * *

On April 13, 2013, the [trial] court filed a "Memorandum and Order of Court" sustaining Co-eXprise's preliminary objections and dismissing all of Appellants' claims. * * *

Appellants allege that the trial court erred in dismissing Appellants' claim that Co-eXprise engaged in the unauthorized practice of law. The trial court has provided an excellent summary of the conduct referenced by Appellants in support of their position:

> In support of their position that [Co-eXprise] is practicing law, [Appellants] refer to the following activities: [Co-eXprise] solicited landowners requesting

they participate in its bidding scheme; [Co-eXprise] presented an agreement for the landowners to execute in order for them to receive [Co-eXprise's] services; [Co-eXprise] delivered to the landowners an explanation of the terms of a lease that the winning bidder will be required to use; [Co-eXprise] described to the landowners the terms of the highest bid and recommended that they accept the bid; [Co-eXprise] furnished information to the landowners who accepted the bid as to documents that would need to be brought to the mass signing and other relevant information; and the bidder and the landowner[s] were required to sign the lease agreement provided by [Co-eXprise] which included protections to the landowners that are not typically included in the form leases of the energy company.

Thus, Appellants allege that Co-eXprise engaged in the unauthorized practice of law. We disagree.

The unauthorized practice of law is prohibited in Pennsylvania, and such conduct is criminalized. *See* 42 Pa.C.S.A. § 2524(a). Additionally, Section 2524(c) creates a private civil cause of action in connection with the unauthorized practice of law. * * *

The Supreme Court of Pennsylvania has thoroughly discussed what constitutes "the practice of law":

The Pennsylvania Constitution vests with our [Supreme] Court the exclusive authority to regulate the practice of law, which includes the power to define what constitutes the practice of law. What constitutes the practice of law, however, is not capable of a comprehensive definition. For this reason, [the Supreme] Court has not attempted to provide an all-encompassing statement of what activities comprise the practice of law. *Shortz et al. v. Farrell* [327 Pa. 81], 193 A. 20, 21 (Pa.1937). Thus, we have determined what constitutes the practice of law on a case-by-case basis.

While our Court has addressed the question of what constitutes the practice of law on an individualized basis, we have made clear that paramount to the inquiry is consideration of the public interest. Consideration of the public interest has two related aspects: protection of the public and prudent regulation so as not to overburden the public good.

Regarding the protection of the public, then Justice, later Chief Justice Stern perhaps best summarized this aspect of the Court's concern in *Shortz*[:]

> While in order to acquire the education necessary to gain admission to the bar and thereby become eligible to practice law, one is obliged to "scorn delights, and live laborious days," the object of the legislation forbidding practice to laymen is not to secure lawyers a monopoly, however deserved, but, by preventing the intrusion of inexpert and unlearned persons in the practice of law, to assure to the public adequate protection in the pursuit of justice, than which society knows no loftier aim.
> * * *

When considering the public interest, our [Supreme] Court has focused on the character of the activities at issue. In *Shortz,* our [Supreme] Court set forth three broad categories of activities that may constitute the practice of law: (1) the instruction and advising of clients in regard to the law so that they may pursue their affairs and be informed as to their rights and obligations; (2) the preparation of documents for clients requiring familiarity with legal principles beyond the ken of ordinary laypersons; and (3) the appearance on behalf of clients before public tribunals in order that the attorney may assist the deciding official in the proper interpretation and enforcement of the law. More recently, our [Supreme] Court expressed that the practice of law is implicated by the holding out of oneself to the public as competent to exercise legal judgment and the implication that he or she has the technical competence to analyze legal problems and the requisite character qualifications to act in a representative capacity. Thus, the character of the actions taken by the individual in question is a significant factor in the determination of what constitutes the practice of law.

*Harkness v. Unemployment Comp. Bd. of Review,* 591 Pa. 543, 920 A.2d 162, 166–67 (2007). "Cognizant that a determination of the practice of law is made on a case-by-case basis, focusing primarily on protection of the public and the public weal, and in doing so, considering the character of the activities . . . , we turn to the facts at issue in this appeal."

Appellants argue that Co-eXprise's actions "directly satisf[y] our Supreme Court's definition of the practice of law because this conduct require [d] abstract understanding of legal principals [*sic*] and refined skill for their concrete application." Specifically, Appellants allege that Co-eXprise's actions:

> required an understanding of each landowner's property rights, encumbrances on the property, liens, easements, and certain environmental issues. The transactions contemplated require[d] an understanding of the legal principals [*sic*] implicated by contract law and real property law. Oil, gas and mineral rights law is itself a specialty in Pennsylvania. There are a variety of concepts including surface rights for drilling, surface rights for pipelines, rights to natural gas storage, concerns related to environmental pollution, just to name a few.

While Appellants urge that Co-eXprise's actions constitute the practice of law, we agree with the trial court's apt assertion that the mere fact that a company utilizes documents prepared by lawyers, and relies upon the opinions of lawyers in conducting its business, does not, ipso facto, indicate that a company is practicing law:

> [W]hat [Appellants] describe is a bidding company conducting its business. There is no explanation by [Appellants] as to which of the activities described above constitute the practice of law.
>
> Lawyers are frequently involved in drafting the writings that the more sophisticated party to a transaction will use. The **drafting** of the writings may

be the practice of law. But the **use** of those writings has nothing to do with the practice of law.

Assuming, *arguendo,* that Co-eXprise's actions touched upon matters that are typically handled by lawyers, our Supreme Court has specifically endorsed such actions in the limited context of business transactions:

> There can be no objection to the preparation of deeds and mortgages or other contracts by such brokers **so long as the papers involved pertain to and grow out of their business transactions and are intimately connected therewith.** The drafting and execution of legal instruments is a necessary concomitant of many businesses, and cannot be considered unlawful. Such practice only falls within the prohibition ... when the documents are drawn in relation to matters in no matter connected with the immediate business of the person preparing them, and when the person so drafting them is not a member of the bar and holds himself out as specially qualified and competent to do that type of work.

*Childs v. Smeltzer,* 315 Pa. 9, 171 A. 883, 885–86 (1934). Instantly, Co-eXprise's actions were limited solely to the subject matter of securing leases for natural gas exploitation on Appellants' respective properties. Appellants have not alleged that Co-eXprise held itself out as a legal actor in any way beyond Co-eXprise's immediate business interests.

Ultimately, we agree with the trial court's conclusion that Appellants have failed to allege any facts that, if proved at trial, would lead to a conclusion that Co-eXprise was engaged in the unauthorized practice of law. While our Supreme Court has clearly stated that we should guard against unauthorized legal practice, that Court also has cautioned against unnecessarily expanding our definition of what constitutes such practice:

> While the public interest is certainly served by the protection of the public, it is also achieved by not burdening the public by too broad a definition of the practice of law, resulting in the overregulation of the

public's affairs. As stated by our [Supreme] Court
* * * [:]

> The threads of legal consequences often weave their
> way through even casual contemporary
> interactions. There are times, of course, when it is
> clearly within the ken of lay persons to appreciate
> the legal problems and consequences involved in a
> given situation and the factors which should
> influence necessary decisions. No public interest
> would be advanced by requiring these lay
> judgments to be made exclusively by lawyers. . . .

Based upon the foregoing discussion, we conclude that the trial
court did not err in dismissing Appellants' claim that Co-eXprise
engaged in the unauthorized practice of law. Appellants were
not pursuing legal representation through Co-eXprise. Rather,
Appellants engaged in contract negotiations regarding their
mineral rights with Co-eXprise, negotiations which Co-eXprise
is authorized to undertake as a matter of Pennsylvania law. * * *

## G.  REPRESENTATION IN
## ARBITRATION PROCEEDINGS

### NISHA, LLC v. TRIBUILT CONSTR. GROUP, LLC
388 S.W.3d 444 (Ark. 2012)

The issue in this case is whether a corporate officer, director, or
employee, who is not a licensed attorney, engages in the
unauthorized practice of law by representing the corporation in
arbitration proceedings. We hold that such a person is so
engaged, and we reverse the circuit court on this point. In
addition, we reverse the circuit court's determination that an
arbitrator, rather than the court, should determine issues
regarding legal representation during arbitration proceedings.

This case began as a dispute over construction costs between
TriBuilt Construction Group, LLC (TriBuilt), the appellee
herein, and NISHA, LLC (NISHA) and Centennial Bank
(formerly known as Community Bank) (Centennial), the
appellants. TriBuilt was the general contractor hired by NISHA
to build the Country Inn & Suites in Conway. Centennial
entered into a Construction Loan and Security Agreement with

NISHA, which assigned its interest in the construction contract with TriBuilt to Centennial as security for Centennial's entering into a construction mortgage for the project. After the project was completed, TriBuilt filed suit in the Sebastian County Circuit Court against NISHA and Centennial and asserted that when the project was completed, they refused to pay TriBuilt the $666,462.12 balance owed, defamed TriBuilt, and intentionally interfered with TriBuilt's ability to get bonding for the project.

NISHA moved to compel arbitration and contended that the contract with TriBuilt compelled the parties to arbitrate all disputes relating to the contract. Contemporaneously with this motion, NISHA moved to stay proceedings pending arbitration. * * * On January 12, 2010, the circuit court entered an order granting the motion to compel arbitration in part and denying it in part. The circuit court granted the motion to compel arbitration and stay proceedings with regard to TriBuilt's claims for breach of contract, quantum meruit, tortious interference with the contract, and conversion against Centennial and NISHA.

On January 26, 2011, the circuit court entered a second order permitting TriBuilt's counsel to withdraw from the case. TriBuilt's attorney subsequently withdrew from the arbitration proceedings as well. Rather than obtain new counsel to represent it in the arbitration proceedings, TriBuilt through its President, Alan Harrison, notified NISHA and Centennial that it intended to represent itself. Harrison, a nonlawyer, would present TriBuilt's case in the arbitration proceedings. On March 31, 2011, NISHA and Centennial filed a "Joint Petition for Permanent Injunction," seeking to prevent Harrison from representing TriBuilt in either the circuit court case or in the arbitration proceedings. In support of its petition, NISHA and Centennial contended that a corporate entity cannot represent itself in litigation and litigation-related matters through agents who are not licensed attorneys. They requested that the circuit court permanently enjoin TriBuilt from permitting, authorizing, or condoning Harrison, or any other officer, director, or employee, from engaging in the unauthorized practice of law by representing TriBuilt in the circuit court proceedings or in the court-ordered arbitration proceedings.

On April 13, 2011, International Fidelity Insurance Company (IFIC) filed a response to the joint petition for permanent injunction. IFIC claimed that TriBuilt was not prohibited by law from representing itself in an arbitration proceeding and that the representation in such a proceeding did not constitute the unauthorized practice of law. It maintained that under the American Arbitration Association (AAA) rules, which governed the arbitration proceeding at issue, any party could be represented by counsel, pro se, or "by any other representative of that party's choosing." IFIC claimed further that no Arkansas law prohibited a corporation from representing itself in arbitration proceedings.

On May 16, 2011, the circuit court entered an order granting NISHA and Centennial's joint petition so far as it pertained to proceedings before the circuit court but denying their petition for a permanent stay so far as it pertained to the arbitration proceedings for two reasons: (1) the circuit court did not agree that nonlawyer representation in an arbitration proceeding constituted the practice of law, and (2) the arbitration panel should decide that issue. NISHA and Centennial filed an interlocutory appeal to this court. . . .

NISHA and Centennial raise two points in their brief on appeal: (1) this court should reverse the circuit court's finding that nonlawyer representation in arbitration proceedings does not constitute the unauthorized practice of law, and (2) that this court should reverse the circuit court's finding that the arbitrator should decide who can represent a party in arbitration proceedings. TriBuilt has not filed a brief in response in this appeal.

\* \* \*

Although NISHA and Centennial present this as their second point for reversal, the question of whether the arbitrator or this court has the power to determine if a nonlawyer can represent a corporation during arbitration proceedings is jurisdictional and must be addressed first. The circuit court concluded that the arbitration body is entitled to determine what parties and representatives may participate in arbitration proceedings, as well as what rules apply in the process. That is in error. This court has the exclusive authority to regulate the practice of law.

Likewise, the unauthorized practice of law falls within this court's constitutional authority to control and govern the practice of law. Because the issue is whether representation of a corporation by a nonlawyer during arbitration proceedings constitutes the unauthorized practice of law, the issue falls squarely within the ambit of this court's constitutional powers and may not be decided by an arbitration body. We reverse the circuit court on this point.

NISHA and Centennial's second argument is that a corporate entity cannot represent itself during arbitration proceedings because that constitutes the unauthorized practice of law. They cite this court to *Arkansas Bar Association v. Union National Bank,* 224 Ark. 48, 273 S.W.2d 408 (1954), to support this contention.

In *Union National Bank,* the Arkansas Bar Association sought to enjoin a bank from engaging in the unauthorized practice of law. That opinion addressed the authority of the bank, as fiduciary, to prepare and present petitions and precedents for orders in the probate and chancery courts without representation by an attorney. In our opinion, this court made five broad conclusions regarding the practice of law in Arkansas:

- Corporations are prohibited from practicing law in this state and a corporate employee, officer, or director who is not a licensed attorney cannot hold himself or herself out as being entitled to practice law.

- An individual can practice law for himself or herself, but a corporation can only represent itself in connection with its own business or affairs in the courts of this state through a licensed attorney.

- A trustee or personal representative does not act on his or her own behalf and a person who is not a licensed attorney and who is acting as an administrator, executor, or guardian cannot practice law in matters relating to his trusteeship.

- When one appears before a court of record for the purpose of transacting business with the court in connection with any pending litigation or when any person seeks to invoke the processes of the court in any matter pending before it, that person is engaging in the practice of law.

- The practice of law is regulated by the judiciary.

While the *Union National Bank* case is helpful in outlining the basic principles governing the practice of law in this state, it does not address the specific issue before this court, which, again, is, whether a corporate officer's representation of that corporation in arbitration proceedings constitutes the practice of law.

NISHA and Centennial claim that arbitration invokes the processes of the courts, is quasi-judicial in nature, and, thus, constitutes the practice of law. They adduce *Union National Bank* as authority for this conclusion. We begin our analysis by noting that Arkansas is among the states that have adopted the 1955 version of the Uniform Arbitration Act. We further recognize that as a matter of public policy, arbitration is strongly favored in Arkansas and is looked upon with approval by our courts as a less expensive and more expeditious means of settling litigation and relieving docket congestion.

There is no doubt that under Arkansas's arbitration statutes, the circuit court remains involved to a degree in arbitration proceedings. Although arbitration proceedings can be initiated without court action, a court can compel parties to proceed to arbitration or stay already existing arbitration proceedings upon application of a party. The court may also send some claims to arbitration, while retaining other claims. Likewise, in some circumstances the court can appoint the arbitrator, if the parties have not agreed on a method for appointment or the agreed method fails or the arbitrator cannot continue.

In addition, a circuit court may, on request, direct the arbitrator to conduct a hearing promptly and render a timely decision. Plus, after a party to an arbitration proceeding receives notice of an award, that party may move the court for an order confirming the award, at which time the court shall issue a confirming order unless the award is modified, corrected, or is vacated. Except in certain limited situations, a valid and final award by an arbitrator has the same effect under the rules of res judicata as a judgment of a court. On appeal, this court will vacate an arbitration award only upon statutory grounds or a finding that the award violates a strong public policy. Based on this statutory scheme and this court's holding that arbitration awards have the same res judicata effect as a judgment of a court, NISHA and Centennial conclude that the courts of this state remain "actively involved" in arbitration and that it is an ancillary court process.

Although this court has never held that a nonlawyer's pro se representation of a corporation in arbitration proceedings constitutes the unauthorized practice of law, courts in other jurisdictions have so held. * * *

This court has never formulated an all-encompassing definition for what constitutes the practice of law. In fact, we have specifically recognized the difficulty in creating a satisfactory definition. We have said, however:

> [W]hen one appears before a court of record for the purpose of transacting business with the court in connection with any pending litigation or when any person seeks to invoke the processes of the court in any matter pending before it, that person is engaging in the practice of law. . . . [A]ny one who assumes the role of assisting the court in its process or invokes the use of its mechanism is considered to be engaged in the practice of law. . . . We make it clear at this point that we are not holding that other activities aside from appearing in court do not constitute practicing law. It is uniformly held that many activities, such as writing and interpreting wills, contracts, trust agreements and the giving of legal advice in general, constitute practicing law.

Similarly, this court has stated that the practice of law is not confined to services by an attorney in a court of justice; it also includes any service of a legal nature rendered outside of courts and unrelated to matters pending in the courts. Finally, our statutory law provides in relevant part:

> It shall be unlawful for any corporation or voluntary association to practice or appear as an attorney at law for any person in any court in this state or before any

judicial body, to make it a business to practice as an attorney at law for any person in any of the courts, to hold itself out to the public as being entitled to practice law, *to tender or furnish legal services or advice,* to furnish attorneys or counsel, to *render legal services of any kind in actions or proceedings of any nature or in any other way or manner,* or in any other manner to assume to be entitled to practice law or to assume or advertise the title of lawyer or attorney, attorney at law, or equivalent terms in any language in such a manner as to convey the impression that it is entitled to practice law or to furnish legal advice, service, or counsel or to advertise that either alone or together with or by or through any person, whether a duly and regularly admitted attorney at law or not, it has, owns, conducts, or maintains a law office or any office for the practice of law or for furnishing legal advice, services, or counsel.

Ark. Code Ann. § 16–22–211(a). * * *

Though this court has never decided whether legal representation in an arbitration proceeding constitutes the practice of law in Arkansas, we have noted, as already referenced, that arbitration is designed to be a "less expensive and more expeditious means of settling litigation," and to relieve "docket congestion." We have also said that "[a]rbitration hearings are not analogous to trial proceedings." Those statements, though, do not decide the issue.

In reaching a decision on this matter, we are influenced by the fact that this court has been resolute in strictly enforcing the rule that a corporation through its nonlawyer officers cannot engage in the practice of law. We are further influenced by the fact that arbitration proceedings bear significant indicia of legal proceedings under the Uniform Arbitration Act, which has been adopted by this state. As already noted, if a hearing is held during arbitration, the parties have the right to be heard, present evidence material to the controversy, and cross-examine witnesses appearing at the hearing.

Bearing in mind the role of an advocate in arbitration proceedings, as just described, we are hard pressed to say that services of a legal nature are not being provided on behalf of the party in arbitration; in this case, TriBuilt. Accordingly, we reverse the decision of the circuit court on this point and hold that a nonlawyer's representation of a corporation in arbitration proceedings constitutes the unauthorized practice of law. * * *

### IN RE TOWN OF LITTLE COMPTON
37 A.3d 85 (R.I. 2012)

On July 8, 2010, the Unauthorized Practice of Law Committee (committee) conducted an investigational hearing in connection with a complaint filed with it by the Town of Little Compton (the town) against the Little Compton Firefighters Local 3957 (the union). In its complaint, the town contended that the union, or its representative, had engaged in the unauthorized practice of law, in violation of G.L.1956 § 11–27–2,2 when the union allowed its nonlawyer business agent to represent it at a labor arbitration hearing. The committee's report to this Court ultimately concluded that the union representative's actions on behalf of the union constituted a "technical violation" of the statute governing the unauthorized practice of law. Mindful that this type of lay representation of unions in labor arbitrations is a common practice in Rhode Island, the committee petitioned this Court for guidance on how to proceed. After reviewing the committee record, the parties' written submissions and oral arguments, and the many amicus briefs filed with the Court, we decline to limit this particular practice at this point in time for the reasons that follow. * * *

Like Rhode Island, most other states have not considered whether nonlawyer representation in labor arbitration is the unauthorized practice of law. However, those states that have addressed this issue have generally permitted the practice.

For example, the Board on the Unauthorized Practice of Law of the Supreme Court of Ohio recently determined in an advisory opinion that "[a] nonlawyer labor consultant, employed by a union, may represent a local bargaining unit in an arbitration process dictated by a collective bargaining agreement, as long as he/she do[es] not engage in those activities that equate to the practice of law." The Ohio Board acknowledged that arbitration, while still an adversarial process, "does not rely on the strict use of formal rules of civil procedure or rules of evidence." Likewise, a 1975 report of the Committee on Labor and Social Security Legislation of the Association of the Bar of the City of New York concluded "that representation of a party in an arbitration proceeding by a nonlawyer * * * is not the unauthorized practice of law."

Other jurisdictions have expressly permitted nonlawyer representation in arbitrations under specific statutes or court rules governing the practice of law. For example, the court rules of Connecticut, Utah, and Washington explicitly permit nonlawyers to participate in labor arbitrations without determining whether or not the act constitutes the practice of law. California's Code of Civil Procedure dictates that while a party to an arbitration has the right to be represented by an attorney, "any party to an arbitration arising under collective bargaining agreements * * * may be represented in * * * those proceedings by any person, regardless of whether that person is licensed to practice law in this state." Although these relatively few states hardly indicate a conclusive trend, it is notable that neither we nor the parties herein were able to uncover any jurisdiction that has specifically declared that nonlawyer representation in labor arbitrations constitutes the unauthorized practice of law. * * *

Although the use of nonlawyer representation in labor arbitrations is commonplace in Rhode Island, this factor alone does not provide the necessary basis for this Court to authorize this practice. Keeping the public welfare at the forefront of our considerations, we must also weigh the public policy interests involved with lay representation in labor arbitrations.

In assessing the benefits of allowing nonlawyer representation in labor disputes, we note that "arbitration usually is not equivalent to judicial factfinding. The record of the arbitration proceedings is not as complete; the usual rules of evidence do not apply." Indeed, "[a] basic incentive for the use of arbitration is to provide the parties with a mode of dispute resolution that is expeditious, inexpensive, and informal."

Further, in contrast to other types of disputes, labor disputes are unique in that the "law of the shop" rather than strict adherence to legal principles typically controls. Union representatives are often particularly qualified to represent a union based on their familiarity with the multilevel grievance process, their knowledge of the operating procedures, equipment, and training, and their understanding of the formation and evolution of the applicable collective-bargaining agreement. This is not to say that licensed attorneys do not have, or are not able to acquire, such knowledge of, or familiarity with, these matters, but simply to acknowledge why union employees often represent unions in arbitrations.

Moreover, prohibiting this practice and requiring both the labor union and management to retain a lawyer may formalize an arbitration proceeding, delay its conclusion, and raise the cost for both parties. Committee Report, 30 Record of the Association of the Bar of the City of New York, at 427–28 (suggesting that requiring lawyer representation will "greatly diminish the informality, flexibility, speed, efficiency and economy which are the hallmarks of the grievance resolution process").

It is also deserving of mention that this Court and the General Assembly have permitted nonlawyer representation to occur in other settings. In *Department of Workers' Compensation* [Unauthorized Practice of Law Comm. v. State, 543 A.2d 662 (1988)], a majority of the Court held that two statutes enacted by the General Assembly, authorizing employee assistants to aid injured employees in informal hearings before the Department of Workers' Compensation, did not violate this Court's exclusive authority to regulate the practice of law. Acknowledging that the actions of the nonlawyer employee assistants would generally fall within the definition of the practice of law, this Court nonetheless authorized this conduct after recognizing the public need and deferring to the Legislature's assessment of the statutes' necessity.

Additionally, in accordance with G.L.1956 § 28–7–9(a), the Rhode Island State Labor Relations Board's General Rules and Regulations allow nonlawyers to represent unions and employers in unfair labor practice proceedings. *See* 16–020–001 R.I.Code R. § 5.01.2(b) ("Business managers, field agents, union stewards, or any other member(s) of a labor organization, may represent a union or an individual complainant in any proceeding before the Board.").

Juxtaposed to these policy arguments are the various factors indicating that Mr. Andriole's actions in the arbitration hearing did, in fact, constitute the unauthorized practice of law. First, we look to the committee's thorough investigation and report on the matter. The committee report noted that § 11–27–2 defines, without limitation, an activity that constitutes the practice of law as "the doing of any act for another person usually done by attorneys at law in the course of their profession, and, without limiting the generality of the definitions in this section, includes the following * * *." Section 11–27–2 then sets forth an exhaustive list of settings and actions where a person doing an act for another qualifies as the practice of law. Although an arbitration hearing is not specifically identified in § 11–27–2(1) as a forum before which nonlawyers are prohibited from appearing on behalf of another party, the non-limiting language emphasized above appears to preclude nonlawyers from engaging in attorney-like activities in any context, even an alternative dispute resolution hearing.

The committee, relying on § 11–27–2, also found that "Mr. Andriole engaged in a number of activities that are 'usually done by attorneys at law in the course of their profession.'" Specifically, Mr. Andriole presented arguments, examined and cross-examined witnesses, submitted evidence to the arbitrator, and objected to evidence and arguments presented by the town. In so doing, Mr. Andriole represented the union in a proceeding that would determine the specific rights and duties of the parties to a legally binding contract. In the process, Mr. Andriole acted in ways normally attributed to the practice of law.

We also note that although § 11–27–11 specifically allows nonlawyers to participate in particular practices that would otherwise fall within the definition of the practice of law, nonlawyer representation in labor arbitrations is not among them.

As is evident from the credible arguments on both sides of the issue, we find this an exquisitely close case. Considering the foregoing factors, as well as the unique facts of the case at bar, the participating members of this Court are reluctant to disturb the status quo at this time. * * *

Accordingly, although the conduct involved in this case may be the practice of law pursuant to the language of § 11–27–2, because of the long-standing involvement of nonlawyer union employees at public grievance arbitrations, we will not limit this involvement at this time. * * *

# H. MEDIATION

## JOSHUA R. SCHWARTZ, LAYMEN CANNOT LAWYER, BUT IS MEDIATION THE PRACTICE OF LAW?
### 20 Cardozo L. Rev. 1715, 1728–36 (1999)

## II. Defining Mediation

* * *

Mediation is defined as "a process in which an impartial third party, who lacks authority to impose a solution, helps others resolve a dispute or plan a transaction." The optimal result of mediation is creation of an agreement suited to the needs of all the parties. The agreement usually is memorialized in contract form and is enforceable according to the rules of contract law. Since the mediator is not a judge, he may not force an agreement upon the parties. The mediator's role is to induce the parties to reach their own agreement.

In contrast to mediation, litigation is premised on the concept of "right versus wrong," which suggests that only one party will receive the positive rewards resulting from the resolution of a conflict. The legal system follows a win-lose model of dispute resolution, which promotes one winner and one loser. Mediation, however, advances a win-win model of dispute resolution.

The typical mediation session begins with introductory comments by the mediator about the process of mediation and the ground rules of the session (for example, no interrupting, who will speak first, and so forth). Next, each party is given the opportunity to discuss all matters of concern. The mediator listens attentively to spot issues for future discussion and to extract potential proposals for resolution of the different issues. After all the parties have had an opportunity to discuss their concerns, the mediator identifies the different issues and sets an agenda for further discussion of each issue. The mediator encourages the parties to listen to each other and helps the parties search for common ground by rephrasing statements in neutral language.

Occasionally, a mediator caucuses individually with each party to elicit information that the mediator does not believe can be acquired in joint session. The caucus is an excellent opportunity to elicit confidential information, such as financial matters, that the parties might not disclose to the other side directly. Further, the mediator has the opportunity in caucus to challenge questionable assertions without jeopardizing neutrality.

Throughout the entire mediation session, the mediator encourages both parties to understand their "BATNA"—Best Alternative to a Negotiated Agreement—by challenging the parties to look critically at their own claims and question what would happen if no agreement were reached at the conclusion of the mediation session. If the parties successfully reach an agreement about the matters in controversy, the parties have the option of having the mediator memorialize the agreement in a written form. This agreement may be a court enforceable contract.

A surprising amount of activities fall within the broad, generally accepted definition of mediation based on the varying approaches that mediators implement when assisting parties to reach an agreement. When parties and their attorneys enter a mediation session, many do not know what to expect—a mediator with an evaluative or facilitative orientation. Although practitioners understand that mediation is a process whereby a neutral third party helps others resolve a conflict or plan a transaction, generalizations about mediation are not very helpful because the goals and methods of facilitative and evaluative mediation orientations vary so greatly in actual mediation sessions. The sections that follow analyze and distinguish the two mediation models.

## A. Facilitative Mediation

Facilitative mediators assist conflicting parties in reaching negotiated resolutions of their differences. Facilitative mediators are neutral third parties who do not proffer opinions regarding the disputed issues. Hence, the mediators do not prescribe solutions to the conflicts, but rather encourage the parties to resolve the conflicts on their own and guide the process to achieve that end.

Facilitative mediation is designed to encourage parties to analyze accurately and realistically their needs, interests, and priorities so as to determine the best methods of meeting them. This process improves the quality of decisionmaking because the conflicting parties are empowered to take responsibility for their own problems, urged to communicate openly to reconcile their concerns, and encouraged to reach a mutually acceptable resolution to their conflicts.

A facilitative mediator's duties include controlling the flow of information and encouraging conduct that is likely to result in an effective negotiation. In this model of mediation, the ultimate authority to resolve the dispute resides with the conflicting parties. The mediator does not impose an agreement upon the parties because the mediation process empowers the parties to exercise self-determination to reach their own solution.

A facilitative mediator ensures that the conflicting parties hear and understand each other by restating proposals in neutral language; however, the mediator does not manifest approval of one party's suggestions for resolving the conflict relative to those of the other. The facilitative mediator neither doles out legal advice nor voices a personal opinion regarding the parties' opposing arguments. While parties involved in a facilitative mediation customarily begin the process "in a hostile and adversarial stance, the mediator seeks to shift them towards a collaborative posture in which they jointly construct a win-win solution."

Bonnie Kleiman, an attorney who is the Alternative Dispute Resolution ("ADR") Coordinator for the Superior Court of Arizona, has stated that legal advice is not given and the law does not enter into facilitative mediation. The design of facilitative mediation is solely to assist the parties in reaching a negotiated settlement. In preserving a facilitative orientation, the mediator aids the parties to negotiate a resolution in a positive manner without counseling the parties as individuals.

Facilitative mediation is the only ADR process that does not evaluate the conflicting arguments of disputing parties. A facilitative mediator helps the disputing parties evaluate, assess, and decide for themselves how best to resolve the matters in controversy. The mediator aids the participants in estimating the strengths and weaknesses of their cases by asking provocative questions intended to highlight arguably weak positions. By using these techniques, the facilitative mediator opens the door to evaluation by the participants themselves.

It is evident that many disputes cannot be settled "without the thundering velvet hand or well-respected legal analysis and opinion of a neutral third party." Despite the fact that the majority of civil suits filed do not make it to trial, there will always be disputing parties that want expert legal analysis or prefer a negotiated settlement based on the lawyers' analysis of the legal merits of claims and defenses in an effort to assess blame and memorialize fault. However, these are evaluative techniques and, by definition, should not be used by a facilitative mediator. Various processes such as litigation, arbitration, early neutral evaluation, summary jury trial, and evaluative mediation are all options for disputing parties that want those opinions and/or decisions. For these reasons, although it is a valuable tool, facilitative mediation may not always be the proper forum for all disputes.

## B.   Evaluative Mediation

Many aspects of evaluative and facilitative mediation are identical. Both processes begin with introductory comments by the mediator, followed by each party having the opportunity to voice all matters of concern. Both the evaluative and facilitative mediators listen for issues and then set an agenda for discussion of the different issues.

The difference between the two processes, however, is that, as part of their role in the parties' negotiation, evaluative mediators give advice, assess arguments, and express their own opinions about the disputing parties' claims. Evaluative mediators assist disputants in reaching agreements by making predictions about likely court outcomes and proposing equitable resolutions to the issues in dispute. The dispute often involves legal questions, and the mediators' prognosis or evaluation of the legal merits of the parties' arguments or likely outcomes of subsequent litigation is sometimes necessary to help reach an agreement.

A danger inherent in the evaluative mediation model is that the mediator's opinion has the potential to overwhelm the parties and their negotiation, and thereby undermine self-determination. The effect of this phenomenon is that the mediator's opinion becomes determinative itself. Once the mediator begins to act in an advisory capacity, it is difficult to leave that role. The evaluative mediator becomes the decisionmaker rather than a facilitator helping the disputing parties reach their own solution. "[I]f the mediator provides the information, he risks confusing his role, deflecting energy from mediation to what is more like counseling, and becoming too directive."

The evaluative roles of finding facts, applying law or custom, and rendering an opinion deflect the mediator away from facilitation and may compromise the mediator's neutrality. Neutrality is jeopardized because the mediator's evaluation usually favors one party. Since disputing parties disagree, the mediator's evaluation will often be seen as favoring one party and disfavoring the other.

A great deal of confusion regarding the different models of mediation stems from the fact that both facilitative and evaluative mediation are labeled "mediation." The models must be clearly labeled and distinguished so that each process's qualities can be understood and appreciated. Because some parties need an outside opinion to generate movement to lead to a resolution of their conflict, evaluative mediation is valuable for many people who are looking to base their resolution, in part, on the opinion of an impartial third party. * * * *

### RESOLUTION ON MEDIATION AND THE UNAUTHORIZED PRACTICE OF LAW

ABA Section of Dispute Resolution
Adopted by the Section on February 2, 2002

The ABA Section of Dispute Resolution has noted the wide range of views expressed by scholars, mediators, and regulators concerning the question of whether mediation constitutes the practice of law. The Section believes that both the public interest and the practice of mediation would benefit from greater clarity with respect to this issue in the statutes and regulations governing the unauthorized practice of law ("UPL"). The Section believes that such statutes and regulations should be interpreted and applied in such a manner as to permit all individuals, regardless of whether they are lawyers, to serve as mediators. The enforcement of such statutes and regulations should be informed by the following principles:

**Mediation is not the practice of law.** Mediation is a process in which an impartial individual assists the parties in reaching a voluntary settlement. Such assistance does not constitute the practice of law. The parties to the mediation are not represented by the mediator.

**Mediators' discussion of legal issues.** In disputes where the parties' legal rights or obligations are at issue, the mediator's discussions with the parties may involve legal issues. Such discussions do not create an attorney-client relationship, and do not constitute legal advice, whether or not the mediator is an attorney.

**Drafting settlement agreements.** When an agreement is reached in a mediation, the parties often request assistance from the mediator in memorializing their agreement. The preparation of a memorandum of understanding or settlement agreement by a mediator, incorporating the terms of settlement specified by the parties, does not constitute the practice of law. If the mediator drafts an agreement that goes beyond the terms specified by the parties, he or she may be engaged in the practice of law. However, in such a case, a mediator shall not be engaged in the practice of law if (a) all parties are represented by counsel and (b) the mediator discloses that any proposal that he or she makes with respect to the terms of settlement is informational as opposed to the practice of law, and that the parties should not view or rely upon such proposals as advice of counsel, but merely consider them in consultation with their own attorneys.

**Mediators' responsibilities.** Mediators have a responsibility to inform the parties in a mediation about the nature of the mediator's role in the process and the limits of that role. Mediators should inform the parties: (a) that the mediator's role is not to provide them with legal representation, but rather to

assist them in reaching a voluntary agreement; (b) that a
settlement agreement may affect the parties' legal rights; and
(c) that each of the parties has the right to seek the advice of
independent legal counsel throughout the mediation process and
should seek such counsel before signing a settlement agreement.

## Comments

1. *Mediation and the practice of law.* There is a growing
   consensus in the ethical opinions addressing this issue that
   mediation is not the practice of law. *See, e.g.,* Maine Bar
   Rule 3.4(h)(4) ("The role of mediator does not create a
   lawyer-client relationship with any of the parties and does
   not constitute representation of them."); Kentucky Bar
   Association Ethics Opinion 377 (1995) ("Mediation is not the
   practice of law."); Indiana Ethics Opinion 5 (1992) (same);
   Washington State Bar Association, Committee to Define the
   Practice of Law, Final Report (July 1999), adopted by
   Washington State Bar Association Board of Governors,
   September 1999 (same). *But see* New Jersey Supreme Court
   Advisory Committee on Professional Ethics, Opinion No.
   676 (1994) (holding that when a lawyer serves as a third
   party neutral, he or she "is acting as a lawyer"). Essential to
   most of the common definitions of the practice of law is the
   existence of an attorney-client relationship. Because
   mediators do not establish an attorney-client relationship,
   they are not engaged in the practice of law when they
   provide mediation services. The Section recognizes that in
   some very extraordinary situations it might be possible for
   a mediator to inadvertently create an attorney-client
   relationship with a party in mediation. For example, if the
   parties were unrepresented, and the mediator did not clarify
   his/her role, it is possible that a party in mediation could
   mistakenly assume that the mediator's role was to advise
   and protect solely that party's interests. In mediations
   where the parties are represented by counsel or where the
   mediator properly explains (and preferably documents)
   his/her role, it would appear unlikely that either party in
   mediation could ever reasonably assume that the mediator
   was that person's attorney.

2.  *Ethical rules governing mediators*. There is a growing body
    of ethical principles and standards governing the practice of
    mediation. Accordingly, even if a mediator's conduct is not
    inconsistent with state UPL statutes or regulations, there
    may be other sources of authority governing the mediator's
    conduct. *See, e.g.*, Mass. Uniform Rules on Dispute
    Resolution 9(c)(iv) ("A neutral may use his or her knowledge
    to inform the parties' deliberations, but shall not provide
    legal advice, counseling, or other professional services in
    connection with the dispute resolution process.").

\* \* \*

5.  *Guidelines on legal advice*. The Virginia Guidelines on
    Mediation and the Unauthorized Practice of Law, drafted by
    the Department of Dispute Resolution Services of the
    Supreme Court of Virginia, and the North Carolina
    Guidelines for the Ethical Practice of Mediation and to
    Prevent the Unauthorized Practice of Law, adopted by the
    North Carolina Bar in 1999, articulate a UPL standard for
    mediators that differs from the standard articulated in this
    Resolution. According to those Guidelines, a mediator may
    provide the parties with legal information but may not give
    legal advice. The Guidelines define legal advice as applying
    the law to the facts of the case in such a way as to (a) predict
    the outcome of the case or an issue in the case, or (b)
    recommend a course of action based on the mediator's
    analysis. The Section believes that adoption of the Virginia
    and North Carolina standards in other jurisdictions would
    be harmful to the growth and development of mediation.

    It is important that mediators who are competent to engage
    in discussion about the strengths and weaknesses of a
    party's case be free to do so without running afoul of UPL
    statutes. Indeed, many parties, and their counsel, hire
    mediators precisely to obtain feedback about their case.
    Even though mediators who engage in these discussions do
    sometimes aid the parties by discussing possible outcomes
    of the dispute if a settlement is not reached and providing
    evaluative feedback about the parties' positions, this
    conduct is not the practice of law because the parties have
    no reasonable basis for believing that the mediator will

provide advice solely on behalf of any individual party. This is the important distinction between the mediator's role and the role of an attorney. Parties expect their attorney to represent solely their interests and to provide advice and counsel only for them. On the other hand, a mediator is a neutral, with no duty of loyalty to the individual parties. (Thus, for example, when a judge conducts a settlement conference, acting in a manner analogous to that of a mediator and providing evaluation to the parties about their case, no one suggests that the judge is practicing law.)

6.   *Discussion of legal issues*. This Resolution seeks to avoid the problem of a mediator determining, in the midst of a discussion of relevant legal issues, which particular phrasings would constitute legal advice and which would not. For example, during mediation of a medical malpractice case, if a mediator comments that "the video of the newborn (deceased shortly after birth) has considerable emotional impact and makes the newborn more real," is this legal advice or prediction or simply stating the obvious? In context, the mediator is implicitly or explicitly suggesting that it may affect a jury's damage award, and thus settlement value. S/he is raising, from the neutral's perspective, a point the parties (presumably the defendants) may have missed, which may distinguish this case from others (e.g., cases in which a baby died *in utero* or where there was no video of the newborn) in which lower settlement amounts were offered and accepted. Is the mediator absolved if s/he phrases the point as a "probing question"?

In their article, "A Well-Founded Fear of Prosecution: Mediation and the Unauthorized Practice of Law" (6 *Dispute Resolution Magazine* 20 (Winter 2000)), authors David A. Hoffman and Natasha A. Affolder illustrate this problem across a broader mediation context, setting out numerous alternative ways a mediator might phrase a point. They note that there would likely be very little professional consensus about which phrasings would constitute the practice of law and which would not. Even if mediators could agree as to where the line would be drawn among suggested phrasings, the intended meaning and impact of any particular statement might vary with the context and how the statement was delivered. Because mediation is almost always an informal and confidential process, it is virtually impossible—without an audio or video recording of a mediation—for regulators to police the nuances of the mediator's communications with the parties. Such recording would clearly be anathema to the mediation process.

7.   *Settlement agreements*. The Virginia and North Carolina Guidelines' approach to the drafting of settlement agreements by a mediator is similar to the approach outlined in this Resolution. See "Guidelines on Mediation and the Unauthorized Practice of Law," Department of Dispute Resolution Services of the Supreme Court of Virginia, at 27–28 ("Mediators who prepare written agreements for disputing parties should strive to use the parties' own words whenever possible and in all cases should write agreements in a manner that comports with the wishes of the disputants. . . . Unless required by law, a mediator should not add provisions to an agreement beyond those specified by the disputants.") Ethics opinions in some states have approved the drafting of formal settlement agreements by mediators who are lawyers, even where the mediator incorporates language that goes beyond the words specified by the parties, provided that the mediator has encouraged the parties to seek independent legal advice. *See, e.g.*, Massachusetts Bar Association Opinion 85–3 (attorney acting as mediator may draft a marital settlement agreement "but must advise the parties of the advantages of having independent legal counsel review any such agreement, and must obtain the informed consent of the parties to such joint representation"). * * *

# CHAPTER III

# WHEN DOES ASSISTING LAWYERS AMOUNT TO UPL?

■ ■ ■

## A.  PARALEGALS

### IN RE OPINION NO. 24 OF COMM. ON THE UNAUTHORIZED PRACTICE OF LAW

607 A.2d 962 (N.J. 1992)

The New Jersey Supreme Court Committee on the Unauthorized Practice of Law (the "Committee") concluded in Advisory Opinion No. 24, 126 *N.J.L.J.* 1306, 1338 (1990), that "paralegals functioning outside of the supervision of an attorney-employer are engaged in the unauthorized practice of law." Petitioners are several independent paralegals whom attorneys do not employ but retain on a temporary basis. They ask the Court to disapprove the Advisory Opinion.

Like paralegals employed by attorneys, independent paralegals retained by attorneys do not offer their services directly to the public. Nonetheless, the Committee determined that independent paralegals are engaged in the unauthorized practice of law because they are performing legal services without adequate attorney supervision. We agree with the Committee that the resolution of the issue turns on whether independent paralegals are adequately supervised by attorneys. We disagree with the Committee, however, that the evidence supports a categorical ban on all independent paralegals in New Jersey.

I

The Committee received inquiries from various sources regarding whether independent paralegals were engaged in the unauthorized practice of law. Pursuant to its advisory-opinion powers under *Rule* 1:22–2, the Committee solicited written comments and information from interested persons and organizations.

In response, the Committee received thirty-seven letters from a wide variety of sources. Additionally, the State Bar Association's Subcommittee on Legal Assistants ("Legal Assistant Subcommittee"), the National Association of Legal Assistants ("NALA"), and the National Federation of Paralegal Associates ("NFPA") provided the Committee with information on regulation, education, certification, and the ethical responsibilities of paralegals.

The Committee characterized the information that it received in two ways: first, the material expressed positive views on the value of the work performed by paralegals; second, all of the materials expressly or implicitly recognized that the work of paralegals must be performed under attorney supervision. None distinguished between paralegals employed by law firms and those functioning as independent contractors offering services to attorneys. Several recurring themes played throughout the submissions:

1.  One need not be a full- or part-time employee of a single attorney to be under the direct supervision of an attorney and independent paralegals in particular work under the direct supervision of attorneys.

2.  Independent paralegals provide necessary services for sole practitioners and small law firms who cannot afford to employ paralegals on a full-time basis.

3.  Independent paralegals confer an invaluable benefit on the public in the form of reduced legal fees.

4.  Independent paralegals maintain high standards of competence and professionalism.

5.  Rather than exacting a *per se* prohibition, the Committee should consider regulations or standards or other alternative forms of guidance, such as licensure and certification.

6. A blanket prohibition on independent paralegals would work a disservice to the paralegals and the general public.

After receiving those submissions, the Committee held a hearing at which four independent paralegals, three employed paralegals, and three attorneys testified. All the independent paralegals testifying before the Committee were well qualified. One independent paralegal noted that as an NALA member she is bound by both the *ABA Model Code of Professional Responsibility* and the ABA *Model Rules of Professional Conduct*. The independent paralegals stated that although they had worked with many attorneys during their careers, they had worked solely for those attorneys and only under their direct supervision.

The independent paralegals gave several reasons for being retained by attorneys. First, attorneys may be understaffed at any time and may need to devote additional resources to one case. Second, attorneys may need paralegal assistance but be unable to afford a full-time paralegal. Third, attorneys may hire independent paralegals who have expertise in a given field.

Client contact varied for each independent paralegal. Some see the attorney's client in the attorney's office, while others meet outside of the office. One paralegal testified that she carefully ensures that clients understand that she is not an attorney and that she cannot, as a paralegal, answer legal questions.

The independent paralegals correspond with clients on behalf of attorneys, using the attorney's or law firm's letterhead, which is usually kept in the paralegal's office. Although the paralegals noted that the attorneys generally receive copies of any correspondence, one paralegal testified that she did not provide copies of all correspondence to the attorneys. Another paralegal stated that some attorneys authorized her to send out letters without their prior review. All the paralegals pointed out that they use computer technology, which facilitates rapid transmission of letters and other written material to their supervising attorneys to review, correct, and return.

Three paralegals who were full-time employees of law firms also testified before the Committee. Each paralegal represented a paralegal organization, such as NFPA or NALA. They explained that many independent paralegals are members of those organizations and that both organizations have developed guidelines and standards for their paralegal members. In addition, NALA conducts a certification examination that takes over two days and requires extensive knowledge of a variety of legal matters.

All three employed paralegals expressed support for independent paralegals who work under the direct supervision of an attorney and who do not provide services directly to the public.

Two attorneys appeared before the Committee. One testified that as long as attorneys supervise independent paralegals, that those paralegals do not work full-time for one attorney or firm does not matter. The second attorney, a sole practitioner, testified that independent paralegals provide many benefits to both small firms and the general public alike. The Committee, he suggested, should focus on others, known as "legal technicians" or "forms practitioners," who offer their services directly to the public, rather than on independent paralegals who do not offer their services directly to the public but who are retained by attorneys.

## II

After the hearing, the Committee issued Advisory Opinion No. 24, 26 *N.J.L.J.* 1306 (1990), in which it compared the amount of supervision attorneys exercise over employed paralegals and retained paralegals. It concluded that attorneys do not adequately supervise retained paralegals. The Committee linked the absence of adequate attorney supervision to several different factors.

First, the Committee raised the concern that attorneys retaining independent paralegals do not carefully select those with sufficient training and experience because the short-term working relationship does not allow the attorney enough time to discover their levels of expertise. In contrast, the Committee presumed that employed paralegals undergo an interview process with an attorney, and the attorney's ongoing relationship with those paralegals allows him or her to determine whether they are qualified for the job.

Second, the Committee believed that attorneys are unable to undertake reasonable efforts to insure that the conduct of independent paralegals is compatible with the attorney's professional obligations pursuant to *Rule 5.3* of the *Model Rules of Professional Conduct* ("*RPC 5.3*"). The Committee reasoned that an attorney who hires an independent paralegal could not satisfy *RPC* 5.3(c)(3), which requires an attorney to make "reasonable investigations" into a paralegal's misconduct. That conclusion was based on the Committee's perception that the relationship between an attorney and an independent paralegal is more distant than the one between an attorney and a full-time employed paralegal.

Third, the Committee maintained that the relationship between attorneys and independent paralegals would cause significant conflicts of interest because the independent paralegal could work for numerous law firms and the attorney might not be able to monitor any conflict that might arise.

Fourth, the Committee concluded that attorneys not sufficiently skilled in a particular area of the law who charge a fee for the work done by the paralegal violate attorney-ethics considerations by assisting in the unauthorized practice of law. *[S]ee also RPC* 5.5(b) (a lawyer shall not assist a person who is not a member of the bar in the performance of activity that constitutes the unauthorized practice of law). The Committee observed that attorneys cannot supervise an independent paralegal who is working in a field that is unfamiliar to the attorney. It suggested as an alternative that sole practitioners could seek assistance in substantive legal matters from specialist attorneys or law firms rather than from independent paralegals.

Fifth, and finally, the Committee was troubled by correspondence and communication between attorneys and independent paralegals. The Committee was distressed to learn that paralegals had sent out letters on firm stationary without prior review by the attorney, creating potential for misunderstanding by the general public.

The Committee summarized its findings as follows:

> When the paralegal is employed by the attorney, the nature of the employment relationship makes it possible for the attorney to make the decisions as to which matters are appropriate for handling by the paralegal and which matters require direct hands-on work by the attorney. When the attorney and the paralegal are separated both by distance and the independent nature of the paralegal's relationship with the attorney, the opportunity for the exercise of that most important judgment by the attorney becomes increasingly difficult.
>
> This is not to say that there are not matters that could be handled by an independent paralegal with appropriate supervision by the attorney contracting with the paralegal. The problem is that the decisions as to what work may be done by the paralegal should be the attorney's to make but the distance between attorney and paralegal mandated by the independent relationship may result in the making of those decisions by the paralegal or by default.
>
> It is the view of the Committee, moreover, that the paralegal practicing in an independent paralegal organization, removed from the attorney both by distance and relationship, presents far too little opportunity for the direct supervision necessary to justify handling those legal issues that might be delegated. Without supervision, the work of the paralegal clearly constitutes the unauthorized practice of law. We found, from the testimony and materials presented to our Committee, that the opportunity for supervision of the independent paralegal diminishes to the point where much of the work of the independent paralegal, is, in fact, unsupervised. That being the case, the independent practice by the paralegal must involve the unauthorized practice of law. The fact that some of the work might actually be directly supervised cannot justify the allowance of a system which permits the independent paralegal to work free of attorney

supervision and control for such a large part of the time
and for such a large part of the work.

Based on those findings, the Committee concluded that
attorneys are currently unable to supervise adequately the
performance of independent paralegals, and that by performing
legal services without such adequate supervision those
paralegals are engaging in the unauthorized practice of law.
* * *

## III

No satisfactory, all-inclusive definition of what constitutes the
practice of law has ever been devised. None will be attempted
here. That has been left, and wisely so, to the courts when
parties present them with concrete factual situations.

Essentially, the Court decides what constitutes the practice of
law on a case-by-case basis. *See, e.g., New Jersey State Bar Ass'n
v. New Jersey Ass'n of Realtor Bds.,* 93 *N.J.* 470, 461 *A*.2d 1112
(1983) (permitting real-estate brokers to prepare certain
residential-sales and lease agreements, subject to right of
attorney review); *In re Education Law Center,* 86 *N.J.* 124, 429
*A*.2d 1051 (1981) (exempting non-profit corporations from
practice-of-law violations); *Auerbacher v. Wood,* 142 *N.J.Eq.* 484,
59 *A*.2d 863 (E. & A.1948) (holding that services of industrial-
relations consultant do not constitute practice of law).

The difficulties presented by our undefined conception of the
legal practice are reflected in this Court's review of decisions of
the Committee on the Unauthorized Practice of Law. For
example, in *In re Application of the New Jersey Society of
Certified Public Accountants,* 102 *N.J.* 231, 507 *A*.2d 711 (1986),
(hereinafter *Application of CPAs*), the Court stated:

> The practice of law is not subject to precise definition. It
> is not confined to litigation but often encompasses "legal
> activities in many non-litigious fields which entail
> specialized knowledge and ability." Therefore, the line
> between permissible business and professional
> activities and the unauthorized practice of law is often
> blurred.

The Court in *Application of CPAs* reviewed the Committee's Opinion No. 10, 95 *N.J.L.J.* 1209 (1972), which held that a nonlawyer's preparation of an inheritance-tax return for another person constituted the unauthorized practice of law. The Court disagreed, and emphasized that "in cases involving an overlap of professional discipline we must try to avoid arbitrary classifications and instead focus on the public's realistic need for protection and regulation." Applying that standard, the Court modified Opinion No. 10 to permit CPAs to prepare inheritance-tax returns subject to the condition that the accountant notify the client that an attorney's review of the return would be helpful because of the legal issues surrounding its preparation.

There is no question that paralegals' work constitutes the practice of law. *N.J.S.A.* 2A:170–78 and 79 deem unauthorized the practice of law by a nonlawyer and make such practice a disorderly-persons offense. However, *N.J.S.A.* 2A:170–81(f) excepts paralegals from being penalized for engaging in tasks that constitute legal practice if their supervising attorney assumes direct responsibility for the work that the paralegals perform. *N.J.S.A.* 2A:170–81(f) states:

> Any person or corporation furnishing to any person lawfully engaged in the practice of law such information or such clerical assistance in and about his professional work as, except for the provisions of this article, may be lawful, but the lawyer receiving such information or service shall at all times maintain full professional and direct responsibility to his client for the information and service so rendered.

Consequently, paralegals who are supervised by attorneys do not engage in the unauthorized practice of law.

## IV

Availability of legal services to the public at an affordable cost is a goal to which the Court is committed. The use of paralegals represents a means of achieving that goal while maintaining the quality of legal services. Paralegals enable attorneys to render legal services more economically and efficiently. During the last twenty years the employment of paralegals has greatly expanded, and within the last ten years the number of independent paralegals has increased.

Independent paralegals work either at a "paralegal firm" or freelance. Most are employed by sole practitioners or smaller firms who cannot afford the services of a full-time paralegal. Like large law firms, small firms find that using paralegals helps them provide effective and economical services to their clients. Requiring paralegals to be full-time employees of law firms would thus deny attorneys not associated with large law firms the very valuable services of paralegals.

The United States Supreme Court, in upholding an award of legal fees based on the market value of paralegal services, stated that the use of paralegal services whenever possible "encourages cost-effective legal services * * * by reducing the spiraling cost of * * * litigation." *Missouri v. Jenkins,* 491 *U.S.* 274, 288, 109 *S.Ct.* 2463, 2471, 105 *L.Ed.*2d 229, 243 (1989).

The Court further noted:

> It has frequently been recognized in the lower courts that paralegals are capable of carrying out many tasks, under the supervision of an attorney, that might otherwise be performed by a lawyer and billed at a higher rate. Such work might include locating and interviewing witnesses; assistance with depositions, interrogatories, and document production; compilation of statistical and financial data, checking legal citations, and drafting correspondence. Much such work lies in a gray area of tasks that might appropriately be performed either by an attorney or a paralegal. To the extent that fee applicants under § 1988 are not permitted to bill for the work of paralegals at market rates, it would not be surprising to see a greater amount of such work performed by attorneys themselves, thus increasing the overall cost of litigation.

New Jersey's Advisory Committee on Professional Ethics also has recognized the value of paralegals to the legal profession:

> It cannot be gainsaid that the utilization of paralegals has become, over the last 10 years, accepted, acceptable, important and indeed, necessary to the efficient

practice of law. Lawyers, law firms and, more importantly, clients benefit greatly by their work. Those people who perform paraprofessionally are educated to do so. They are trained and truly professional. They are diligent and carry on their functions in a dignified, proper, professional manner.

The New Jersey State Bar Association also specifically recognizes the important role of the paralegal. On September 15, 1989, its Board of Trustees voted to allow associate membership for paralegals and legal assistants.

We also note that the American Bar Association ("ABA") has long given latitude to attorneys to employ non-lawyers for a variety of tasks. For example, Ethical Consideration 3–6 of the ABA *Model Code of Professional Responsibility* provides as follows:

A lawyer often delegates tasks to clerks, secretaries, and other lay persons. Such delegation is proper if the lawyer maintains a direct relationship with his/her client, supervises the delegated work, and has complete professional responsibility for the work product. This delegation enables a lawyer to render legal services more economically and efficiently.

The ABA has further stated, in Formal Opinion 316, that "we do not limit the kind of assistance that a lawyer can acquire *in any way* to persons who are admitted to the Bar, so long as the non-lawyers do not do things that lawyers may not do or do the things that [only] lawyers[ ] may do." (emphasis added).

## V

No judicial, legislative, or other rule-making body excludes independent paralegals from its definition of a paralegal. For example, the ABA defines a paralegal as follows:

A person qualified through education, training or work experience; is employed or *retained* by a lawyer, law office, government agency, or other entity; works under the *ultimate* direction and supervision of an attorney; performs specifically delegated legal work, which, for the most part, requires a sufficient knowledge of legal concepts; and performs such duties that, absent such an assistant, the attorney would perform such tasks. (emphasis added).

The ABA definition expands the role of a legal assistant to include independent paralegals, recognizing that attorneys can and do retain the services of legal assistants who work outside the law office.

New Jersey's ethics Rules also recognize independent paralegals. This Court has adopted the ABA's *Model Rules of Professional Conduct* to govern the conduct of New Jersey State Bar members. *R.* 1:14 (adopting the ABA *Model Rules* "as amended and supplemented by the Supreme Court"). The central provision governing the attorney's use of lay employees is *RPC* 5.3:

With respect to a nonlawyer employed *or retained by* or associated with a lawyer:

(a) every lawyer or organization authorized by the Court rules to practice law in this jurisdiction shall adopt and maintain reasonable efforts to ensure that the conduct of nonlawyers *retained* or employed by the lawyer, law firm or organization is compatible with the professional obligations of the lawyer.

(b) a lawyer having direct supervisory authority over the nonlawyer shall make reasonable efforts to ensure that the person's conduct is compatible with the professional obligations of the lawyer; and

(c) a lawyer shall be responsible for conduct of such a person that would be a violation of the Rules of Professional Conduct if engaged in by a lawyer if:

(1) the lawyer orders or ratifies the conduct involved;

(2) the lawyer has direct supervisory authority over the person and knows of the conduct at a time when its consequences can be avoided or mitigated but fails to take reasonable remedial action; or

(3) the lawyer has failed to make reasonable investigation of circumstances that would disclose past instances of conduct by the nonlawyer incompatible with the professional obligations of a lawyer, which evidence a propensity for such conduct. (emphasis added).

The emphasized language indicates that *RPC* 5.3 applies to independent retained paralegals and not just to employed paralegals.

Moreover, the comment following *RPC* 5.3 does not distinguish between employees and independent contractors, stating as follows:

Lawyers generally employ assistants in their practice. * * * Such assistants, *whether employees or independent contractors,* act for the lawyer in rendition of the lawyer's professional services. (emphasis added).

Finally, *Rule* 4:42–9(b) implicitly recognizes that attorneys use paralegals by permitting awards of counsel fees to include costs of paraprofessional services. That Rule's definition of "legal assistant" is almost identical to that of the ABA's. The Rule, however, requires only that the paralegal operate under the direction and supervision of the attorney. It does not distinguish between an employed or retained paralegal.

VI

Under both federal law and New Jersey law, and under both the ABA and New Jersey ethics Rules, attorneys may delegate legal tasks to paralegals if they maintain direct relationships with their clients, supervise the paralegal's work and remain responsible for the work product.

Neither case law nor statutes distinguish paralegals employed by an attorney or law firm from independent paralegals retained by an attorney or a law firm. Nor do we. Rather, the important inquiry is whether the paralegal, whether employed or retained, is working directly for the attorney, under that attorney's supervision. Safeguards against the unauthorized practice of law exist through that supervision. Realistically, a paralegal can engage in the unauthorized practice of law whether he or she is an independent paralegal or employed in a law firm. Likewise, regardless of the paralegal's status, an attorney who does not properly supervise a paralegal is in violation of the ethical Rules. Although fulfilling the ethical requirements of *RPC* 5.3 is primarily the attorney's obligation and responsibility, a paralegal is not relieved from an independent obligation to refrain from illegal conduct and to work directly under the supervision of the attorney. A paralegal who recognizes that the attorney is not directly supervising his or her work or that such supervision is illusory because the attorney knows nothing about the field in which the paralegal is working must understand that he or she is engaged in the unauthorized practice of law. In such a situation an independent paralegal must withdraw from representation of the client. The key is supervision, and that supervision must occur regardless of whether the paralegal is employed by the attorney or retained by the attorney.

We were impressed by the professionalism of the paralegals who testified before the Committee. They all understood the need for direct attorney supervision and were sensitive to potential conflict-of-interest problems. Additionally, they all recognized that as the paralegal profession continues to grow, the need to define clearly the limits of the profession's responsibilities increases.

Those who testified voiced many of the same concerns expressed by the Committee. Indeed, Opinion No. 24 crystallized issues that both the legal profession and paralegals recognize should be addressed. The Committee enumerated five factors that are of vital importance to the profession and that confront every paralegal and every prospective employer:

(1) There have been no standards or guidelines set down by any body with regulatory authority to control and regulate the activities of independent paralegals.

(2) At least one New Jersey college provides an ABA-approved paralegal program and provides a certificate of completion to successful candidates. A bachelor of arts degree is a prerequisite to obtaining the certificate. Those requirements are applicable

only to matriculating students and it is clear that no law or regulation imposes the requirement of obtaining such a certificate on students who propose to practice.

(3) Neither the state of New Jersey, any bar association, nor any organization or affiliation of paralegals or legal assistants provides for a licensing procedure or any other procedure to regulate and control the identity, training and conduct of those who engage in the work.

(4) While the ABA definition states that a legal assistant should be "qualified through education, training or work experience" which serves as a guideline for its members in the use of paralegal assistance, that requirement is not imposed or binding upon a person who desires to engage in independent paralegal practice.

(5) There is no paralegal association or organization that imposes any uniform mechanism of standards of ethics, disciplinary proceedings, and rules and regulations to oversee the activities of paralegals. Those who function as paralegals, therefore, do so pursuant to standards and rules either of their own devising or of the devising of the variety of different groups or organizations, none of which have the power to impose adherence to standards or to control or discipline those who do not adhere to standards.

Following the introduction of *RPC* 5.3, the Practicing Law Institute correctly noted:

[M]any firms will not be prepared to shoulder [the responsibility of supervising paralegals] within their existing procedures. Accordingly, effective measures will have to be undertaken to ensure compliance. These will include not only procedures and controls, but also communication, training and education of staff employees in the responsibilities inherent in relevant Model Rules.

Although we agree that those concerns must be addressed, we emphasize that they apply equally to employed paralegals and to independent paralegals.

Although the ABA requires that paralegals be qualified through work, education, or training, the State currently requires neither certification nor licensure for paralegals. No regulatory body exists to prevent unqualified persons from working as paralegals. However, the same is true with regard to employed paralegals.

No rule requires that either employed paralegals or independent paralegals belong to any paraprofessional organization. Thus, only those paralegals who are members of such organizations are subject to regulation. Again, the problem is not with independent paralegals but with the absence of any binding regulations or guidelines.

The same holds true with regard to ethical issues. As with other laypersons, paralegals are not subject to any ethics rules governing the practice of law. The ethical prohibitions against paralegals, *RPC* 5.3, therefore focus on the attorney's conduct. However, the language of *RPC* 5.3 applies to attorneys who both employ and retain paralegals.

Underlying many of the Committee's concerns is its belief that the attorney will not be able to comply with *RPC* 5.3 due to the lack of physical proximity to the retained paralegal. That "physical distance" led the Committee to conclude that for an attorney to maintain direct supervisory authority over an independent paralegal who often will not work in the same office as the attorney is too difficult.

We recognize that distance between the independent paralegal and the attorney may create less opportunity for efficient, significant, rigorous supervision. Nonetheless, the site at which the paralegal performs services should not be the determinative factor. In large law firms that have satellite offices, an employed paralegal frequently has less face-to-face contact with the supervising attorney than would a retained paralegal.

Moreover, in this age of rapidly-expanding instant communications (including fax tele-transmissions, word processing, computer networks, cellular telephone service and other computer-modem communications), out-of-office paralegals can communicate frequently with their supervising attorneys. Indeed, as technology progresses, there will be more communication between employers and employees located at different sites, even different states. That arrangement will be helpful to both the paralegal and the attorney. Parents and disabled people, particularly, may prefer to work from their homes. Sole practitioners and small law firms will be able to obtain the services of paralegals otherwise available only to large firms.

Moreover, nothing in the record before the Committee suggested that attorneys have found it difficult to supervise independent paralegals. Indeed, the paralegals testified that the use of word processing made an attorney's quick review of their work possible. Most of the independent contractors who testified worked under the supervision of attorneys with whom they had regular communication.

Although a paralegal's unsupervised work does constitute the unauthorized practice of law, that issue is not unique to independent paralegals. Rather, we emphasize again, it is the lack of educational and regulatory standards to govern their practice that is at the heart of the problem.

Regulation may also solve another ethical problem-conflicts of interest. We agree with the Committee's observation that

> [t]he appearance of and potential for conflict will increase dramatically when independent paralegals offer their services to multiple law firms to assist them in litigated matters. Although the paralegal may be sensitive to avoid functioning for two adversary attorneys in the same case, the potential for conflict increases in the same magnitude as is represented by the number of different law firms represented by the one paralegal * * *. The problem is exacerbated to a point which may not be controllable when the relationships multiply by virtue of a single, independent paralegal representing multiple law firms.

However, the paralegals who testified were aware of potential conflict situations. An independent paralegal explained that she keeps accurate records on each attorney's clients:

> MS. SECOL: I have—I have all my files—they're all logged and noted. I have a list of all of the files for each attorney.

Moreover, in Opinion No. 647 the Advisory Committee on Professional Ethics recognized that paralegals are extremely aware of the potential ethical dilemmas of the legal profession:

> [Paralegals] understand ethical inhibitions and prohibitions. Lawyers assign them work expecting them to respect confidences which they obtain and to comport themselves in the best traditions of those who serve in the legal area * * *. It is too late in the day to view these paraprofessionals with suspicion of their morals or ethics.

Nonetheless, we recognize that because independent paralegals are retained by different firms and lawyers, a potential conflict exists. For example, the Advisory Committee on Professional Ethics has noted that "[h]iring a paralegal formerly employed by a firm with which the prospective employer presently is involved in adversarial matters would clearly be improper." In re Opinion No. 546 of the Advisory Committee on Ethics, 114 *N.J.L.J.* 496 (1984). Opinion No. 546 is extremely brief, however, and does not detail the circumstances under which such employment would be improper.

The ABA, however, has also considered whether an employing firm can be disqualified by a change in employment of a nonlawyer employee, specifically a paralegal, in Informal Ethics Opinion 88–1526 (June 22, 1988). The ABA determined that such firms can be disqualified unless they thoroughly screen the paralegal and ensure that the paralegal reveals no information relating to the representation of the client at the former firm to any person in the employing firm. The ABA also noted its concern that paralegals could potentially lose the ability to earn a livelihood if they were prevented from working for different law firms:

It is important that nonlawyer employees have as much mobility in employment opportunities as possible consistent with the protection of clients' interests. To so limit employment opportunities that some nonlawyers trained to work with law firms might be required to leave the careers for which they are trained would disserve clients as well as the legal profession. Accordingly, any restrictions on the nonlawyer's employment should be held to the minimum necessary to protect the confidentiality of client information.

We again conclude that regulations and guidelines can be drafted to address adequately the conflict-of-interest problem. For example, as urged by paralegal associations, there could be a requirement that paralegals must keep records of each case, listing the names of the parties and all counsel. Before undertaking new employment, paralegals would check the list. Likewise, attorneys should require the paralegals to furnish them with such a list. The attorney could thus examine whether such matters would conflict with the attorney's representation of a client before retaining that paralegal. Regulation can also remedy any problems resulting from the attendant problem of paralegals sending correspondence directly to clients without the attorney's review and approval.

Although we have not incorporated use of paralegals into New Jersey Court Rules, the Advisory Committee on Professional Ethics has considered the practice of paralegals on four prior occasions, most recently in Opinion No. 647, 126 *N.J.L.J.* 1525 (1990). In that opinion the Advisory Committee on Professional Ethics held that paralegals working under the direct supervision of an attorney may carry business cards so long as the name of the attorney or firm appears on the card and the card is authorized by the attorney or law firm.

Giving to them the ability of clearly identifying themselves and for whom they work can only better serve their employers and clients. The business card, as is true in every area where business cards are used, serves to define the status of the person presenting that card and has the desired effect of eliminating confusion.

Other states, bar associations, and paralegal organizations have also begun to regulate paralegals and attorneys' use of them. A significant number of state courts have incorporated into their court rules or ethics opinions rules for the use of legal assistants. Kentucky has promulgated a Paralegal Code of Ethics, which sets forth certain exclusions to the unauthorized practice of law:

> For purposes of this rule, the unauthorized practice of law shall not include any service rendered involving legal knowledge or advice, whether representation, counsel or advocacy, in or out of court, rendered in respect to the acts, duties, obligations, liabilities or business relations of the one requiring services where:
>
> A.  The client understands that the paralegal is not a lawyer;
>
> B.  The lawyer supervises the paralegal in the performance of his duties; and
>
> C.  The lawyer remains fully responsible for such representation, including all actions taken or not taken in connection therewith by the paralegal to the same extent as if such representation had been furnished entirely by the lawyer and all such actions had been taken or not taken directly by the attorney. Paralegal Code, Ky.S.Ct.R. 3.700, Sub-Rule 2.

Several states' bar associations have also promulgated guidelines to regulate the paralegal profession. For example, the Colorado Bar Association has issued a set of guidelines under which a lawyer may permit a paralegal to assist in all aspects of the lawyer's representation of a client, provided that:

1.  the status of the [paralegal] is disclosed at the outset of any professional relationship with a client, other attorneys, courts or administrative agencies or members of the general public;

2.  the lawyer establishes the attorney-client relationship, is available to the client and maintains control of all client matters;

3.   the lawyer reviews the [paralegal's] work product and supervises the performance of duties assigned to the [paralegal];

4.   the lawyer remains responsible for the services performed by the [paralegal] to the same extent as if such services had been furnished entirely by the lawyer and such actions were those of the lawyer;

5.   the services performed by the [paralegal] supplement, merge with and become part of the attorney's work product;

6.   the services performed by the [paralegal] do not require the exercise of unsupervised legal judgment; and

7.   the lawyer instructs the [paralegal] concerning standards of client confidentiality.

The guidelines also provide:

1.   A [paralegal] may author and sign correspondence on the lawyer's letterhead, provided the [paralegal] status is indicated and the correspondence does not contain legal opinions or give legal advice.

2.   A [paralegal] may have a business card with the firm name appearing on it so long as the status of the legal assistant is disclosed. However, the name of the [paralegal] may not appear on the letterhead of the firm.

3.   A [paralegal] may conduct client interviews and maintain general contact with the client once the attorney-client relationship has been established, so long as the client is aware of the status and duties of the [paralegal], and the client contact is authorized by the attorney.

The Colorado Bar Association has also promulgated a set of ethical requirements for the attorney who hires paralegals:

1.   A lawyer shall ascertain the paralegal's abilities, limitations and training, and must limit the paralegal's duties and responsibilities to those that

can be competently performed in view of those abilities, limitations and training.

2. A lawyer shall educate and train [paralegals] with respect to the ethical standards which apply to the lawyer.

3. A lawyer is responsible for monitoring and supervising the conduct of [paralegals] to prevent the violation of the ethical standards which apply to the lawyer, and the lawyer is responsible for assuring that [paralegals] do not do anything which the lawyer could not do.

4. A lawyer shall continuously monitor and supervise the work of [paralegals] in order to assure that the services rendered by the [paralegals] are performed competently and in a professional manner.

5. A lawyer is responsible for assuring that the [paralegal] does not engage in the unauthorized practice of law.

6. A lawyer shall assume responsibility for the improper conduct of [paralegals] and must take appropriate action to prevent recurrence of improper behavior or activities.

7. [Paralegals] who deal directly with lawyers' clients must be identified to those clients as non-lawyers, and the lawyer is responsible for obtaining the understanding of the clients with respect to the role of and the limitations which apply to those assistants.

The Michigan, Missouri, and New York Bar Associations have adopted similar requirements.

Additionally, two of the largest paralegal associations have proposed standards for paralegals. NALA has developed an examination procedure for certifying paralegals and has developed ethics guidelines for their work, and NFPA has developed a detailed list of "Paralegal Responsibilities" and maintains a repository of the latest state-by-state statutory and case developments regulating the use of paralegals.

### VII

Regulation and guidelines represent the proper course of action to address the problems that the work practices of all paralegals may create. Although the paralegal is directly accountable for engaging in the unauthorized practice of law and also has an obligation to avoid conduct that otherwise violates the Rules of Professional Conduct, the attorney is ultimately accountable. Therefore, with great care, the attorney should ensure that the legal assistant is informed of and abides by the provisions of the Rules of Professional Conduct.

Although an attorney must directly supervise a paralegal, no rational basis exists for the disparate way in which the Committee's opinion treats employed and independent paralegals. The testimony overwhelmingly indicates that the independent paralegals were subject to direct supervision by attorneys and were sensitive to potential conflicts of interest. We conclude that given the appropriate instructions and supervision, paralegals, whether as employees or independent contractors, are valuable and necessary members of an attorney's team in the effective and efficient practice of law.

Subsequent to the issuance of the Committee's decision, the State Bar Association forwarded a resolution to this Court requesting the establishment of a standing committee on paralegal education and regulation. We agree that such a committee is necessary, and will shortly establish it to study the practice of paralegals and make recommendations. The committee may consider guidelines from other states, bar associations, and paralegal associations in formulating regulations for New Jersey paralegals. Any such regulations or guidelines should encourage the use of paralegals while providing both attorneys and paralegals with a set of principles that together with the Rules of Professional Conduct can guide their practices. The guidelines drafted will not be static but subject to modification as new issues arise.

We modify Opinion No. 24 in accordance with this opinion.

## GUIDELINES FOR THE UTILIZATION OF PARALEGAL SERVICES

\* \* \*

GUIDELINE 2: PROVIDED THE LAWYER MAINTAINS RESPONSIBILITY FOR THE WORK PRODUCT, A LAWYER MAY DELEGATE TO A PARALEGAL ANY TASK NORMALLY PERFORMED BY THE LAWYER EXCEPT THOSE TASKS PROSCRIBED TO A NONLAWYER BY STATUTE, COURT RULE, ADMINISTRATIVE RULE OR REGULATION, CONTROLLING AUTHORITY, THE APPLICABLE RULE OF PROFESSIONAL CONDUCT OF THE JURISDICTION IN WHICH THE LAWYER PRACTICES, OR THESE GUIDELINES.

### Comment to Guideline 2

The essence of the definition of the term "legal assistant" first adopted by the ABA in 1986 and subsequently amended in 1997 is that, so long as appropriate supervision is maintained, many tasks normally performed by lawyers may be delegated to paralegals. EC 3–6 under the Model Code mentioned three specific kinds of tasks that paralegals may perform under appropriate lawyer supervision: factual investigation and research, legal research, and the preparation of legal documents. Various states delineate more specific tasks in their guidelines including attending client conferences, corresponding with and obtaining information from clients, witnessing the execution of documents, preparing transmittal letters, and maintaining estate/guardianship trust accounts. *See, e.g.,* Colorado Bar Association Guidelines for the Use of Paralegals (the Colorado Bar Association adopted guidelines in 1986 for the use of paralegals in 21 specialty practice areas including, bankruptcy, civil litigation, corporate law and estate planning. The Colorado Bar Association Guidelines were revised in 2008); NALA Guideline 5.

While appropriate delegation of tasks is encouraged and a broad array of tasks is properly delegable to paralegals, improper delegation of tasks will often run afoul of a lawyer's obligations under applicable rules of professional conduct. A common consequence of the improper delegation of tasks is that the lawyer will have assisted the paralegal in the unauthorized "practice of law" in violation of Rule 5.5 of the Model Rules, Model Code DR 3–101, and the professional rules of most states. Neither the Model Rules nor the Model Code defines the "practice of law." EC 3–5 under the Model Code gave some guidance by equating the practice of law to the application of the professional judgment of the lawyer in solving clients' legal problems. This approach is consistent with that taken in ABA Opinion 316 (1967) which states: "A lawyer . . . may employ nonlawyers to do any task for him except counsel clients about law matters, engage directly in the practice of law, appear in court or appear in formal proceedings as part of the judicial process, so long as it is he who takes the work and vouches for it to the client and becomes responsible for it to the client."

As a general matter, most state guidelines specify that paralegals may not appear before courts, administrative tribunals, or other adjudicatory bodies unless the procedural rules of the adjudicatory body authorize such appearances. *See, e.g., State Bar of Arizona, Committee on the Rules of Prof'l Conduct, Opinion No. 99–13 (December 1999)* (http://www.azbar. org/Ethics/EthicsOpinions/ViewEthicsOpinion?id=507) (attorney did not assist in unauthorized practice of law by supervising paralegal in tribal court where tribal court rules permit non-attorneys to be licensed tribal advocates). Additionally, no state permits paralegals to conduct depositions or give legal advice to clients. *E.g.,* Guideline 2, Connecticut Bar Association Guidelines for Lawyers Who Employ or Retain Legal Assistants (the "Connecticut Guidelines"); Guideline 2, State Bar of Michigan Guidelines for Utilization of Legal Assistants (www. michbar.org/opinions/ethics/utilization.cfm); State Bar of Georgia, State Disciplinary Board Advisory Opinion No. 21 (September 16, 1977) (https://www.gabar.org/Handbook/index. cfm#handbook/rule469); Doe v. Condon, 532 S.E.2d 879 (S.C. 2000) (it is the unauthorized practice of law for a paralegal to conduct educational seminars and answer estate planning questions because the paralegal will be implicitly advising participants that they require estate planning services). *See also* NALA Guidelines II, III, and V.

Ultimately, apart from the obvious tasks that virtually all states argue are proscribed to paralegals, what constitutes the "practice of law" is governed by state law and is a fact specific question. *See, e.g.*, Louisiana Rules of Prof'l Conduct Rule 5.5 (www.lasc.org/rules/orders/2005/ROPC5.5_8.5.pdf) which sets out specific tasks considered to be the "practice of law" by the Supreme Court of Louisiana. Thus, some tasks that have been specifically prohibited in some states are expressly delegable in others. *Compare*, Guideline 2, Connecticut Guidelines (permitting paralegal to attend real estate closings even though no supervising lawyer is present provided that the paralegal does not render opinion or judgment about execution of documents, changes in adjustments or price or other matters involving documents or funds) *and* The Florida Bar, Opinion 89–5 (November 1989) (https://www.floridabar.org/etopinions/et opinion-89-5/) (permitting paralegal to handle real estate closing at which no supervising lawyer is present provided, among other things, that the paralegal will not give legal advice or make impromptu decisions that should be made by a lawyer) *with* Supreme Court of Georgia, Formal Advisory Opinion No. 86–5 (May 1989) (www.gabar.org/barrules/handbookdetail.cfm?what =rule&id=505) (closing of real estate transactions constitutes the practice of law and it is ethically improper for a lawyer to permit a paralegal to close the transaction). It is thus incumbent on the lawyer to determine whether a particular task is properly delegable in the jurisdiction at issue.

Once the lawyer has determined that a particular task is delegable consistent with the professional rules, utilization guidelines, and case law of the relevant jurisdiction, the key to Guideline 2 is proper supervision. A lawyer should start the supervision process by ensuring that the paralegal has sufficient education, background and experience to handle the task being assigned. The lawyer should provide adequate instruction when assigning projects and should also monitor the progress of the project. Finally, it is the lawyer's obligation to review the completed project to ensure that the work product is appropriate for the assigned task. *See* Guideline 1, Connecticut Guidelines; *See also, e.g., Spencer v. Steinman,* 179 F.R.D. 484 (E.D. Penn. 1998) (lawyer sanctioned under Rule 11 for paralegal's failure to serve subpoena duces tecum on parties to the litigation because the lawyer "did not assure himself that [the paralegal] had adequate training nor did he adequately supervise her once he assigned her the task of issuing subpoenas").

Serious consequences can result from a lawyer's failure to properly delegate tasks to or to supervise a paralegal properly. For example, the Supreme Court of Virginia upheld a malpractice verdict against a lawyer based in part on negligent actions of a paralegal in performing tasks that evidently were properly delegable. *Musselman v. Willoughby Corp.,* 230 Va. 337, 337 S.E. 2d 724 (1985). *See also* C. Wolfram, Modern Legal Ethics 236, 896 (1986). Disbarment and suspension from the practice of law have resulted from a lawyer's failure to properly supervise the work performed by paralegals. *See Matter of Disciplinary Action Against Nassif,* 547 N.W.2d 541 (N.D. 1996) (disbarment for failure to supervise which resulted in the unauthorized practice of law by office paralegals); *Attorney Grievance Comm'n of Maryland v. Hallmon,* 681 A.2d 510 (Md. 1996) (90-day suspension for, among other things, abdicating responsibility for a case to paralegal without supervising or reviewing the paralegal's work). Lawyers have also been subject to monetary and other sanctions in federal and state courts for failing to properly utilize and supervise paralegals. *See In re Hessinger & Associates,* 192 B.R. 211 (N.D. Cal. 1996) (bankruptcy court directed to reevaluate its $100,000 sanction but district court finds that law firm violated Rule 3–110(A) of the California Rules of Professional Conduct by permitting bankruptcy paralegals to undertake initial interviews, fill out forms and complete schedules without attorney supervision).

Finally, it is important to note that although the attorney has the primary obligation to not permit a nonlawyer to engage in the unauthorized practice of law, some states have concluded that a paralegal is not relieved from an independent obligation to refrain from illegal conduct and to work directly under an attorney's supervision. *See In re Opinion No. 24 of the Committee on the Unauthorized Practice of Law,* 607 A.2d 962, 969 (N.J. 1992) (a "paralegal who recognizes that the attorney is not directly supervising his or her work or that such supervision is illusory because the attorney knows nothing about the field in which the paralegal is working must understand that he or she is engaged in the unauthorized practice of law"); Kentucky Supreme Court Rule (SCR) 3.700 (stating that "the paralegal does have an independent obligation to refrain from illegal conduct"). Additionally, paralegals must also familiarize themselves with the specific statutes governing the particular area of law with which they might come into contact while providing paralegal services. *See, e.g.,* 11 U.S.C. § 110 (provisions governing nonlawyer preparers of bankruptcy petitions); *In Re Moffett,* 263 B.R. 805 (W.D. Ky. 2001) (nonlawyer bankruptcy petition preparer fined for advertising herself as "paralegal" because that is prohibited by 11 U.S.C. § 110(f)). Again, the lawyer must remember that any independent obligation a paralegal might have under state law to refrain from the unauthorized practice of law does not in any way diminish or vitiate the lawyer's obligation to properly delegate tasks and supervise the paralegal working for the lawyer.

GUIDELINE 3: A LAWYER MAY NOT DELEGATE TO A PARALEGAL:

    (A) RESPONSIBILITY FOR ESTABLISHING AN ATTORNEY-CLIENT RELATIONSHIP.

    (B) RESPONSIBILITY FOR ESTABLISHING THE AMOUNT OF A FEE TO BE CHARGED FOR A LEGAL SERVICE.

    (C) RESPONSIBILITY FOR A LEGAL OPINION RENDERED TO A CLIENT.

**Comment to Guideline 3**

Model Rule 1.4 and most state codes require lawyers to communicate directly with their clients and to provide their clients information reasonably necessary to make informed decisions and to effectively participate in the representation. While delegation of legal tasks to nonlawyers may benefit clients by enabling their lawyers to render legal services more economically and efficiently, Model Rule 1.4 and EC 3–6 under the Model Code emphasize that delegation is proper only if the lawyer "maintains a direct relationship with his client, supervises the delegated work and has complete professional responsibility for the work product." NALA Ethics Canon 2, echoes the Model Rule when it states: "A legal assistant may perform any task which is properly delegated and supervised by an attorney as long as the attorney is ultimately responsible to the client, maintains a direct relationship with the client, and assumes professional responsibility for the work product." Most state guidelines also stress the paramount importance of a direct attorney-client relationship. *See* Ohio EC 3–6 and New Mexico Rule 20–106. The direct personal relationship between client and lawyer is critical to the exercise of the lawyer's trained professional judgment.

Fundamental to the lawyer-client relationship is the lawyer's agreement to undertake representation and the related fee arrangement. The Model Rules and most states require lawyers to make fee arrangements with their clients and to clearly communicate with their clients concerning the scope of the representation and the basis for the fees for which the client will be responsible. Model Rule 1.5 and Comments. Many state guidelines prohibit paralegals from "setting fees" or "accepting cases." *See, e.g.*, Pennsylvania Eth. Op. 98–75, 1994 Utah Eth. Op. 139. NALA Ethics Canon 3 states that a paralegal must not establish attorney-client relationships or set fees.

Model Code EC 3–5 states: "[T]he essence of the professional judgment of the lawyer is his educated ability to relate the general body and philosophy of law to a specific legal problem of a client; and thus, the public interest will be better served if only lawyers are permitted to act in matters involving professional judgment." Clients are entitled to their lawyers' professional judgment and opinion. Paralegals may, however, be authorized to communicate a lawyer's legal advice to a client so long as they do not interpret or expand on that advice. Typically, state guidelines phrase this prohibition in terms of paralegals being forbidden from "giving legal advice" or "counseling clients about legal matters." *See, e.g.*, New Hampshire Rule 35, Sub-Rule 1, Kentucky SCR 3.700, Sub-Rule 2. NALA Ethics Canon 3 states that a paralegal must not give legal opinions or advice. Some states have more expansive wording that prohibits paralegals from engaging in any activity that would require the exercise of independent legal judgment. *See, e.g.*, New Mexico Rule 20–103. Nevertheless, it is clear that all states and the Model Rules

encourage direct communication between clients and a paralegal insofar as the paralegal is performing a task properly delegated by a lawyer. It should be noted that a lawyer who permits a paralegal to assist in establishing the attorney-client relationship, in communicating the lawyer's fee, or in preparing the lawyer's legal opinion is not delegating responsibility for those matters and, therefore, is not in violation of this guideline.
\* \* \*

## MODEL STANDARDS AND GUIDELINES
## FOR UTILIZATION OF PARALEGALS
NALA—The Association of Paralegals

\* \* \*

## Guideline 3

Paralegals may perform services for an attorney in the representation of a client, provided:

- The services performed by the paralegal do not require the exercise of independent professional legal judgment;

- The attorney maintains a direct relationship with the client and maintains control of all client matters;

- The attorney supervises the paralegal;

- The attorney remains professionally responsible for all work on behalf of the client, including any actions taken or not taken by the paralegal in connection therewith; and

- The services performed supplement, merge with and become the attorney's work product.

## Comment

Paralegals, whether employees or independent contractors, perform services for the attorney in the representation of a client. Attorneys should delegate work to paralegals commensurate with their knowledge and experience and provide appropriate instruction and supervision concerning the delegated work, as well as ethical acts of their employment. Ultimate responsibility for the work product of a paralegal rests with the attorney. However, a paralegal must use discretion and professional judgment and must not render independent legal judgment in place of an attorney.

The work product of a paralegal is subject to civil rules governing discovery of materials prepared in anticipation of litigation, whether the paralegal is viewed as an extension of the attorney or as another representative of the party itself. Fed.R.Civ.P. 26(b)(3) and (5). * * *

## B. OTHER SERVICES

### TENN. CODE ANN. § 23–3–103.
#### UNLAWFUL PRACTICE PROHIBITED—PENALTY

(a) No person shall engage in the practice of law or do law business, or both, as defined in § 23–3–101, unless the person has been duly licensed and while the person's license is in full force and effect, nor shall any association or corporation engage in the practice of the law or do law business, or both. * * *

### TENN. CODE ANN. § 23–3–101.
#### CHAPTER DEFINITIONS

As used in this chapter, unless the context otherwise requires:

(1) "Law business" means the advising or counseling for valuable consideration of any person as to any secular law, the drawing or the procuring of or assisting in the drawing for valuable consideration of any paper, document or instrument affecting or relating to secular rights, the doing of any act for valuable consideration in a representative capacity, obtaining or tending to secure for any person any property or property rights whatsoever, or the soliciting of clients directly or indirectly to provide such services; * * *

(3) "Practice of law" means the appearance as an advocate in a representative capacity or the drawing of papers, pleadings or documents or the performance of any act in such capacity in connection with proceedings pending or prospective before any court, commissioner, referee or any body, board, committee or commission constituted by law or having authority to settle controversies, or the soliciting of clients directly or indirectly to provide such services.

## D.C. CT. APP. RULE 49.
### UNAUTHORIZED PRACTICE OF LAW

**(a) General Rule.** No person shall engage in the practice of law in the District of Columbia or in any manner hold out as authorized or competent to practice law in the District of Columbia unless enrolled as an active member of the District of Columbia Bar, except as otherwise permitted by these Rules.

**(b) Definitions.** * * *

(2) **"Practice of Law"** means the provision of professional legal advice or services where there is a client relationship of trust or reliance. One is presumed to be practicing law when engaging in any of the following conduct on behalf of another:

(A) Preparing any legal document, including any deeds, mortgages, assignments, discharges, leases, trust instruments or any other instruments intended to affect interests in real or personal property, will, codicils, instruments intended to affect the disposition of property of decedents' estates, other instruments intended to affect or secure legal rights, and contracts except routine agreements incidental to a regular course of business;

(B) Preparing or expressing legal opinions;

(C) Appearing or acting as an attorney in any tribunal;

(D) Preparing any claims, demands or pleadings of any kind, or any written documents containing legal argument or interpretation of law, for filing in any court, administrative agency or other tribunal;

(E) Providing advice or counsel as to how any of the activities described in subparagraph (A) through (D) might be done, or whether they were done, in accordance with applicable law;

(F) Furnishing an attorney or attorneys, or other persons, to render the services described in subparagraphs (a) through (e) above. * * *

**(4)** **"Hold out as authorized or competent to practice law in the District of Columbia"** means to indicate in any manner to any other person that one is competent, authorized, or available to practice law from an office or location in the District of Columbia. Among the characterizations which give such an indication are "Esq.," "lawyer," "attorney at law," "counselor at law," "contract lawyer," "trial or legal advocate," "legal representative," "legal advocate," and "judge." \* \* \*

### DISTRICT OF COLUMBIA COMMITTEE ON UNAUTHORIZED PRACTICE OF LAW: OPINION 21–12. APPLICABILITY OF RULE 49 TO DISCOVERY SERVICES COMPANIES
Issued January 12, 2012

Pursuant to District of Columbia Court of Appeals Rule 49, and specifically its section 49(d)(3)(G), the District of Columbia Court of Appeals Committee on the Unauthorized Practice of Law, by a majority vote of a quorum of its members then present, approved the following opinion at its meeting on January 12, 2012:

The D.C. Court of Appeals Committee on Unauthorized Practice of Law has recently received a number of inquiries regarding the applicability of D.C. Court of Appeals Rule 49 to "discovery services companies"—companies that state they offer comprehensive discovery services, including assistance with large scale document review, to legal services organizations. The Committee has previously issued two opinions that bear on this question, both of which also relate to document review: The Committee's Opinion 6–99 discusses Rule 49's application to legal staffing services, and Opinion 16–05 provides guidance on the applicability of Rule 49 to the work of "contract attorneys."

Having investigated the matter, it is the Committee's opinion that the business practices of discovery services companies have advanced sufficiently beyond the discussion in the Committee's prior opinions that it would be useful to provide guidance to assist these companies and the legal services organizations that employ them in complying with Rule 49.

A.   Prior Opinions of the Committee on Unauthorized Practice of Law.

In 1999, the Committee issued Opinion 6–99 to address the applicability of D.C. Court of Appeals Rule 49 to the conduct of legal staffing services—companies that place attorneys on a temporary basis with legal services organizations. That opinion was prompted by the increasing practice of law firms and other legal services organizations seeking to retain attorneys on a temporary basis for particular projects, and the consequent emergence of companies offering to identify attorneys for such temporary placements. More often than not, the projects for which legal services organizations seek the assistance of temporary attorneys involve "document review"—the process of reviewing very large numbers of documents for large scale litigation or investigation matters.

Rule 49 of the District of Columbia Court of Appeals provides, "No person shall engage in the practice of law in the District of Columbia . . . unless enrolled as an active member of the District of Columbia Bar, except as otherwise permitted by these Rules." Subsection (b)(2)(F) of Rule 49 states that the practice of law includes "[f]urnishing an attorney or attorneys, or other persons" to provide legal services.

In Opinion 6–99 the Committee noted that "furnishing," within the meaning of the rule "involves more than simply recommending a particular attorney." Rather, "section (b)(2)(F) is generally addressed to the business of providing attorneys in response to a request from a non-lawyer member of the public for representation in a specific, pending legal matter." * * * "This activity is included in the definition of the 'practice of law,' because, properly made, such referrals generally involve the exercise of the trained judgment of a lawyer."

The Committee concluded that legal staffing companies do not engage in the practice of law by providing attorneys to legal services organizations so long as: (1) an attorney with an attorney-client relationship with the prospective client selects the temporary attorney; (2) the temporary attorney is directed or supervised by a lawyer representing the client; and (3) the staffing company does not otherwise engage in the practice of law within the meaning of Rule 49 or attempt to supervise the practice of law by the attorneys it places.

Six years later, the Committee issued Opinion 16–05 to address another issue related to document review—the applicability of Rule 49 to "contract attorneys," that is, the attorneys placed by legal staffing companies on temporary assignments or hired temporarily by legal services organizations. The Committee noted that contract attorneys are typically hired to fill temporary staffing needs resulting "from large, document-intensive litigations or investigations."

The Committee concluded that "practicing law in the District of Columbia as a contract lawyer is no different than practicing law as a non-contract partner, associate or other employee." Accordingly, attorneys regularly practicing in the District of Columbia, even as contract attorneys, must be members of the D.C. Bar. Nevertheless, the Committee acknowledged that certain document review tasks "seem[ ] to call for little or no application of legal knowledge, training, or judgment."

The Committee cited as one common example "review of documents for potential relevance or potential privilege, where the ultimate decision to assert the privilege and produce or not produce the document will be made by someone else." The Committee explained that persons performing this work, which is "the same basic function as a paralegal," must be members of the D.C. Bar if "the person is being held out, and billed out, as a lawyer." Whereas Rule 49 does not apply to persons hired as and performing the work of a paralegal, "[w]hen a person is hired and billed as a lawyer, . . . the person is generally engaged in the practice of law, and is certainly being held out as authorized or competent to practice law."

B.   Applicability of Rule 49 to Discovery Services Companies.

In recent years, companies seeking to assist legal services organizations with document review have dramatically expanded the scope of their services. For example, some companies offer not only attorneys to staff document review projects, but also offer the physical space where the document review will take place, computers for conducting the review, and servers for hosting the documents to be reviewed. These companies also offer a host of related services, from e-discovery consulting to database management to the eventual production of documents in litigation.

At the same time, discovery services companies have begun to describe their services in increasingly broad language. They use terms like "one-stop shopping," "comprehensive review and project management," and "fully managed document review." Other statements these companies have made in their promotional materials include the following:

- "We design, develop, and manage the entire review process instead of just providing contract attorneys and software and leaving the rest to the client."

- "Simply put, our experience in running your project . . . managing a soup-to-nuts document project from process to production—is unparalleled."

- "[We have] the ability to run every aspect of discovery management and document review with as much or as little involvement as you require."

- "Our consultants develop and implement methods and manage the overall discovery process to yield efficiency and cost savings."

- "Our managed services are tailored to specific project needs and include comprehensive project planning, on-site review team supervision, privilege log preparation, e-vender selection, and more."

In addition, some companies have sought to distinguish their services by promoting the legal expertise or qualifications of their staff. These statements do not appear to refer to the expertise of attorneys that the company seeks to place for document review projects.

Instead, these companies tout the expertise of persons who work for the discovery services company itself. Some companies have described these individuals as "seasoned litigators," and have promoted particular "practice areas" such as intellectual property, patent litigation, class action lawsuits, and mergers and acquisitions. Statements about discovery services companies' legal expertise include the following:

- "With significant in-house corporate legal experience, our experts have a deep knowledge of the issues clients face and bring strategies that help clients optimize their review."

- "[Our] team of attorneys is highly skilled and experienced in handling the complexities associated with litigation. We can readily assist you with any pre-litigation discovery issues, as well as draft discovery requests and responses. [We] can prepare all types of standard litigation related documents including: Preparation of Summons & Complaints, Discovery Requests and Responses."

- "[O]ur teams are built around the notion that seasoned attorneys provide the best service to our clients because they've experienced the issues you face today."

- "Led by seasoned attorneys, [our] competitive advantage is [our] subject matter expertise and proven ability to manage all aspects of document review, e-discovery and contract attorney placement services."

Many of these companies have offices in the District of Columbia or state that they serve the Washington, D.C. market.

The expanded scope of services offered by discovery services companies and the way that they are promoted raise questions as to whether their activities constitute the practice of law under Rule 49, and whether the companies' promotional statements constitute holding out as authorized to practice law in the District of Columbia under Rule 49(a). For example, a statement that a given company "design[s], develop[s], and manage[s] the entire review process" could mean that the company is selecting attorneys to work on a project and supervising the exercise of their legal judgment. If the company does so in the District of Columbia, it would be engaging in the practice of law under Rule 49, as discussed in the Committee's Opinion 6–99.

To the extent the statement is ambiguous as to the scope of services offered, it could also be construed as holding the company out as authorized to practice law in the District of Columbia. Similarly, statements regarding the legal expertise of discovery services companies could be read to indicate that these companies are offering their staff members to provide legal judgment to members of the public. To the extent these companies are located in the District of Columbia, such statements could imply that the companies are authorized to practice law in the District.

On the other hand, the broad marketing statements made by these companies could also be consistent with services that do not cross the line into legal practice. A company's statement that it "design[s], develop[s], and manage[s] the entire review process" could also mean that the company takes care of all of the administrative and technical tasks associated with document review but none of the legal tasks. This could include locating and interviewing document reviewers, obtaining the physical space where they will work, obtaining computers, servers, and software sufficient to handle the review, handling payroll and taxes, making sure the document reviewers show up to work and work at an appropriate pace, and similar administrative tasks. The discovery services company could leave all of the tasks involving the exercise of legal judgment, such as the final selection of attorneys to work on the project and overseeing project attorneys' legal work, to a lawyer with a client relationship. Indeed, in response to the Committee's inquiries, discovery services companies uniformly stated that, in spite of their promotional materials, this is precisely the scope of services that they provide.

Similarly, the expertise of discovery services companies' staff as litigators or in-house counsel and in particular areas of the law is likely to be useful in managing even the non-legal aspects of document review projects. Cases involving a particular area of the law may share common technical or other administrative requirements that do not involve the exercise of legal judgment. Discovery services companies' promotional statements regarding their staff's legal expertise could therefore be read not as holding out, but rather as attempting to demonstrate how particular expertise assists with the permissible non-legal services that the company provides. Again, the discovery services companies contacted by the Committee stated that this is the intent of the cited statements.

In order to provide guidance to discovery services companies regarding the permissible scope of services that may be performed without engaging in the practice of law and the extent to which the companies may promote their services without holding out as authorized to practice law in the District of Columbia, the Committee offers the following principles:

First, the Committee notes that some of the largest discovery services companies are not based in the District of Columbia but state that they serve the Washington, D.C. legal market. Rule 49's prohibition on unauthorized practice applies to "the practice of law in the District of Columbia." The rule thus applies specifically to companies that are located in the District of Columbia or that conduct document reviews that take place in the District of Columbia. To the extent discovery services companies located elsewhere conduct document review projects outside of the District, those projects are not governed by Rule 49.

However, Rule 49's prohibition on holding out is not likewise geographically restricted. Rather, the Rule prohibits holding out "in any manner," as authorized to practice law in the District, even if the person or entity is not physically within the District of Columbia. D.C. Ct. App. R. 49(a). Thus, to the extent that discovery services use a District of Columbia address, or advertise themselves as available to assist with discovery projects in the District, Rule 49's holding out prohibition does apply.

Second, to comply with Rule 49's unauthorized practice restrictions, companies that provide lawyers for document review in the District of Columbia must abide by Rule 49 and the Committee's Opinion 6–99. Thus, the final selection of attorneys to staff a document review project must be made by a member of the D.C. Bar with an attorney-client relationship with the client, the attorney's legal work must be directed or supervised by a D.C. Bar member who represents the client, and the discovery services company may not otherwise violate Rule 49 or attempt to supervise the document review attorney.

As Opinion 6–99 made clear, however, the touchstone of Rule 49(b)(2)(F) is the exercise of professional legal judgment. Accordingly, discovery services companies do not run afoul of Rule 49 by handling the administrative aspects of hiring and supervising a document review attorney. This could include interviewing individuals to create a roster of attorneys available to assist with document review projects, providing the lawyer's working space and equipment, ensuring that he or she works a regular day and works at an acceptable pace, providing salary and benefits, and similar supervisory activities that do not require the application of professional legal judgment. Moreover, as the Committee acknowledged in Opinion 16–05, "Rule 49 does not regulate the hiring of a person as a paralegal or a law clerk, even though the person may be admitted to the practice of law in another jurisdiction." Accordingly, discovery services companies do not violate Rule 49 when hiring persons to perform work that does not involve the application of legal knowledge, training, or judgment, and the person is not held out or billed as a lawyer.

Third, discovery services companies that are not otherwise authorized to practice law in the District of Columbia may not provide legal advice to their clients, nor may they hold out themselves or any attorneys on their staff as authorized to practice law in the District of Columbia. The commentary to Rule 49 provides that the holding out provision "prohibits both the implicit representation of authority or competency by engaging in the practice of law, and the express holding out of oneself as authorized or qualified to practice law in the District of Columbia." To avoid running afoul of the holding out prohibition, discovery services companies must avoid making statements in their promotional materials that are ambiguous or misleading regarding their capabilities.

For example, terms like "document review" and "the discovery process" encompass numerous discrete tasks, some of which involve the application of legal judgment and some of which do not. Broad statements that a company can manage the entire document review or discovery process—by providing "soup-to-nuts" or "end-to-end" solutions, e.g.—have a serious potential to mislead. Accordingly, discovery services companies should avoid making such broad statements or at a minimum must include a prominent disclaimer stating that the company is not authorized to practice law or provide legal services in the District of Columbia, and that the services offered by the company are limited to the non-legal, administrative aspects of document review and discovery projects. In order to be effective, such a disclaimer must appear on the same page as the potentially misleading claim, must be in the same font size and in close proximity to the claim.

In addition, while marketing statements promoting the legal expertise of discovery services companies' staff may be intended only to demonstrate that those staff members have backgrounds that enable them to effectively manage the non-legal aspects of document review projects, standing alone such statements can be misconstrued as implying that those persons will apply their legal judgment or expertise in a given project. Accordingly, in order to avoid creating the impression that the company or its staff is authorized to practice law in the District of Columbia, statements regarding the legal experience of the companies' staff must be accompanied by a prominent disclaimer that the company is not authorized to practice law or provide legal services in the District of Columbia, and that the company's staff members cannot represent outside clients or provide legal advice.

To be clear, the requirement that discovery services companies avoid misleading statements regarding their staff members' authorization to practice law is directed to statements regarding the discovery services company's own staff members, not to attorneys that it places for discovery projects. The requirement applies even if the company's staff members are members of the D.C. Bar. While a D.C. Bar member may individually be authorized to practice law in the District, a company providing such an attorney's legal services would necessarily run afoul of the restrictions placed on attorney referral articulated in the Committee's Opinion 6–99. The requirement does not apply to a company's description of its roster of attorneys available to be placed on document review projects, so long as the referral of such attorneys complies with Rule 49 and Opinion 6–99.

Consistent with prior opinions of the Committee, this Opinion addresses only the application of Rule 49 to the discovery-related services described above. It does not address the activities of professional search companies that provide different services, nor to the non-discovery services offered by discovery services companies or their affiliated entities. * * *

CHAPTER IV

# WHEN DOES PROVIDING FORMS OR TECHNOLOGY AMOUNT TO UPL?

■ ■ ■

Typically, a person who completes a legal form drafted and supplied by her lawyer is not engaged in the unauthorized practice of law. Neither of them is.

A trickier situation involves a stranger who prepares legal "forms" that are sold to and used by the public when doing deals, planning an estate, or engaging in other activities that require compliance with the law. The "forms" may be old-fashioned, hard-copy paper completed with a pen or pencil; or they may be digitized, powered by learning algorithms, driven by a lay-person friendly user interface, and designed for completion anywhere and anytime, without a lawyer's advice.

In any case, the form or technology essentially identifies and translates the requirements of applicable law and provides for and allows the user to satisfy these requirements in specific situations by supplying facts and information, very little judgment, and no legal knowledge beyond that embedded in the form or technology.

In every case, the core issue is whether providing the forms or technology is the unauthorized practice of law.

### NEW YORK COUNTY LAWYERS' ASS'N V. DACEY
234 N.E.2d 459 (1967)

Proceeding was brought by New York County Lawyers' Association against author of book entitled 'How to Avoid Probate!', and the publishers, distributors, and sellers of the book pursuant to the Judiciary Law, Consol. Laws, c. 30, § 750, subd. B, to punish them for contempt and for an injunction for the unlawful practice of law.

131

The Supreme Court, Special Term, New York County, 54 Misc.2d 564, 282 N.Y.S.2d 985, entered a judgment adjudging the author guilty of criminal contempt because of the allegedly unlawful practice of law, fining him, and granting an injunction against him and the publishers, distributors, and sellers of the book.

The Appellate Division, 28 A.D.2d 161, 283 N.Y.S.2d 984, by a divided court, entered an order . . . which affirmed the judgment as to the author and modified the judgment, on the law, as to the publishers, distributors, and sellers by limiting injunction granted against the publishers, distributors and sellers so as to restrain from the publication, distribution and sale in New York, and from advertising or soliciting purchases of the book in New York. Stevens, J., dissented, on ground that it could not be claimed that the publication of a legal text which purported to say what the law is amounts to legal practice, and that the mere fact that the principles or rules stated in the text may be accepted by a particular reader as a solution to his problem, does not affect the matter, and that the publication of a multitude of forms for all manner of legal situations is a commonplace activity and their use by the Bar and public is general, and that the conjoining of the text and the forms with advice as to how the forms should be filled out does not constitute the unlawful practice of law, and that the order appealed from should be vacated on the law and the petition should be dismissed.

The author, publishers, distributors and sellers appealed to the Court of Appeals.

Order reversed and the petition dismissed with costs on the dissenting opinion at the Appellate Division.

### THE FLA. BAR V. BRUMBAUGH
355 So.2d 1186 (Fla. 1978)

Respondent, Marilyn Brumbaugh, is not and has never been a member of the Florida Bar, and is, therefore, not licensed to practice law within this state. She has advertised in various local newspapers as "Marilyn's Secretarial Service" offering to perform typing services for "Do-It-Yourself" divorces, wills, resumes, and bankruptcies. The Florida Bar charges that she performed unauthorized legal services by preparing for her customers those legal documents necessary in an uncontested dissolution of marriage proceeding and by advising her customers as to the costs involved and the procedures which should be followed in order to obtain a dissolution of marriage. For this service, Ms. Brumbaugh charges a fee of $50. * * *

The Florida Bar argues that the above activities of respondent violate the rulings of this Court in The Florida Bar v. American Legal and Business Forms, Inc., 274 So.2d 225 (Fla.1973), and The Florida Bar v. Stupica, 300 So.2d 683 (Fla.1974). In those decisions we held that it is lawful to sell to the public printed legal forms, provided they do not carry with them what purports to be instructions on how to fill out such forms or how to use them. We stated that legal advice is inextricably involved in the filling out and advice as to how to use such legal forms, and therein lies the danger of injury or damage to the public if not properly performed in accordance with law.

In *Stupica*, supra, this Court rejected the rationale of the New York courts in New York County Lawyer's Association v. Dacey, 28 A.D.2d 161, 283 N.Y.S.2d 984, reversed and dissenting opinion adopted 21 N.Y.2d 694, 287 N.Y.S.2d 422, 234 N.E.2d 459 (N.Y.1967), which held that the publication of forms and instructions on their use does not constitute the unauthorized practice of law if these instructions are addressed to the public in general rather than to a specific individual legal problem. The Court in *Dacey* stated that the possibility that the principles or rules set forth in the text may be accepted by a particular reader as solution to his problem, does not mean that the publisher is practicing law. Other states have adopted the principle of law set forth in Dacey, holding that the sale of legal forms with instructions for their use does not constitute unauthorized practice of law. See State Bar of Michigan v. Cramer, 399 Mich. 116, 249 N.W.2d 1 (1976); Oregon State Bar v. Gilchrist, 272 Or. 552, 538 P.2d 913 (1975). However, these courts have prohibited all personal contact between the service providing such forms and the customer, in the nature of consultation, explanation, recommendation, advice, or other assistance in selecting particular forms, in filling out any part of the forms, suggesting or advising how the forms should be used in solving the particular problems.

Although persons not licensed as attorneys are prohibited from practicing law within this state, it is somewhat difficult to define exactly what constitutes the practice of law in all instances. This Court has previously stated that:

> . . . if the giving of such advice and performance of such services affect important rights of a person under the law, and if the reasonable protection of the rights and property of those advised and served requires that the persons giving such advice possess legal skill and a knowledge of the law greater than that possessed by the average citizen, then the giving of such advice and the performance of such services by one for another as a course of conduct constitute the practice of law.

This definition is broad and is given content by this Court only as it applies to specific circumstances of each case. We agree that "any attempt to formulate a lasting, all encompassing definition of 'practice of law' is doomed to failure 'for the reason that under our system of jurisprudence such practice must necessarily change with the everchanging business and social order.' "

In determining whether a particular act constitutes the practice of law, our primary goal is the protection of the public. However, any limitations on the free practice of law by all persons necessarily affects important constitutional rights. Our decision here certainly affects the constitutional rights of Marilyn Brumbaugh to pursue a lawful occupation or business. Our decision also affects respondent's First Amendment rights to speak and print what she chooses. In addition, her customers and potential customers have the constitutional right of self representation, and the right of privacy inherent in the marriage relationship. All citizens in our state are also guaranteed access to our courts by Article I, Section 21, Florida Constitution (1968).

Although it is not necessary for us to provide affirmative assistance in order to ensure meaningful access to the courts to our citizens, as it is necessary for us to do for those incarcerated in our state prison system, we should not place any unnecessary restrictions upon that right. We should not deny persons who wish to represent themselves access to any source of information which might be relevant in the preparation of their cases. There are numerous texts in our state law libraries which describe our substantive and procedural law, purport to give legal advice to the reader as to choices that should be made in various situations, and which also contain sample legal forms which a reader may use as an example. We generally do not restrict the access of the public to these law libraries, although many of the legal texts are not authored by attorneys licensed to practice in this state. These texts do not carry with them any guarantees of accuracy, and only some of them purport to update statements which have been modified by subsequently enacted statutes and recent case law.

The policy of this Court should continue to be one of encouraging persons who are unsure of their legal rights and remedies to seek legal assistance from persons licensed by us to practice law in this state. However, in order to make an intelligent decision as whether or not to engage the assistance of an attorney, a citizen must be allowed access to information which will help determine the complexity of the legal problem. Once a person has made the decision to represent himself, we should not enforce any unnecessary regulation which might tend to hinder the exercise of this constitutionally protected right. However, any restriction of constitutional rights must be "narrowly drawn to express only the legitimate state interests at stake." NAACP v. Button, 371 U.S. 415, 438, 83 S.Ct. 328, 340, 9 L.Ed.2d 405 (1963). "And if there are other reasonable ways to achieve those goals with a lesser burden on constitutionally protected activity, a state may not choose the way of greater interference. If it acts at all, it must choose less drastic means. Shelton v. Tucker, 364 U.S. 479, 488, 81 S.Ct. 247, 252, 5 L.Ed.2d 231 (1960). * * *

Families usually undergo tremendous financial hardship when they decide to dissolve their marital relationships. The Legislature simplified procedures so that parties would not need to bear the additional burden of expensive legal fees where they have agreed to the settlement of their property and the custody of their children. This Court should not place unreasonable burdens upon the obtaining of such divorces, especially where both parties consent to the dissolution.

Present dissolution procedures in uncontested situations involve a very simplified method of asserting certain facts required by statute, notice to the other parties affected, and a simple hearing where the trial court may hear proof and make inquiries as to the facts asserted in those pleadings.

The legal forms necessary to obtain such an uncontested dissolution of marriage are susceptible of standardization. This Court has allowed the sale of legal forms on this and other subjects, provided that they do not carry with them what purports to be instructions on how to fill out such forms or how they are to be used. These decisions should be reevaluated in light of those recent decisions in other states which have held that the sale of forms necessary to obtain a divorce, together with any related textual instructions directed towards the general public, does not constitute the practice of law. The reasons for allowing the sale of such legal publications which contain sample forms to be used by individuals who wish to represent themselves are persuasive. *State Bar of Michigan v. Cramer*, supra, reasoned that such instructional material should be no more objectionable than any other publication placed into the stream of commerce which purports to offer general advice on common problems and does not purport to give a person advice on a specific problem particular to a designated or readily identified person.

In Bates v. State Bar of Arizona, 433 U.S. 350, 97 S.Ct. 2691, 2699, 53 L.Ed.2d 810 (1977) the Supreme Court discussed at length the substantial interests in the free flow of commercial speech. The Court said that the choice between the dangers of suppressing information and the dangers arising from its free flow is precisely the choice "that the First Amendment makes for us." There the Court, in approving legal advertising, reasoned that the state cannot assume a paternalistic approach which rests in large part on its citizens being kept in ignorance. The Court stated that we must assume that this information is not in itself harmful, and "that people will perceive their own best interests if only they are well enough informed, and that the best means to that end is to open the channels of communication rather than to close them."

Although there is a danger that some published material might give false or misleading information, that is not a sufficient reason to justify its total ban. We must assume that our citizens will generally use such publications for what they are worth in the preparation of their cases, and further assume that most persons will not rely on these materials in the same way they would rely on the advice of an attorney or other persons holding themselves out as having expertise in the area. The tendency of persons seeking legal assistance to place their trust in the individual purporting to have expertise in the area necessitates this Court's regulation of such attorney-client relationships, so as to require that persons giving such advice have at least a minimal amount of legal training and experience.

Although Marilyn Brumbaugh never held herself out as an attorney, it is clear that her clients placed some reliance upon her to properly prepare the necessary legal forms for their dissolution proceedings. To this extent we believe that Ms. Brumbaugh overstepped proper bounds and engaged in the unauthorized practice of law. We hold that Ms. Brumbaugh, and others in similar situations, may sell printed material purporting to explain legal practice and procedure to the public in general and she may sell sample legal forms. To this extent we limit our prior holdings in *Stupica* and *American Legal and Business Forms, Inc.* Further, we hold that it is not improper for Marilyn Brumbaugh to engage in a secretarial service, typing such forms for her clients, provided that she only copy the information given to her in writing by her clients. In addition, Ms. Brumbaugh may advertise her business activities of providing secretarial and notary services and selling legal forms and general printed information.

However, Marilyn Brumbaugh must not, in conjunction with her business, engage in advising clients as to the various remedies available to them, or otherwise assist them in preparing those forms necessary for a dissolution proceeding. More specifically, Marilyn Brumbaugh may not make inquiries nor answer questions from her clients as to the particular forms which might be necessary, how best to fill out such forms, where to properly file such forms, and how to present necessary evidence at the court hearings. Our specific holding with regard to the dissolution of marriage also applies to other unauthorized legal assistance such as the preparation of wills or real estate transaction documents. While Marilyn Brumbaugh may legally sell forms in these areas, and type up instruments which have been completed by clients, she must not engage in personal legal assistance in conjunction with her business activities, including the correction of errors and omissions.

Accordingly, having defined the limits within which Ms. Brumbaugh and those engaged in similar activities may conduct their business without engaging in the unauthorized practice of law, the rule to show cause is dissolved. It is so ordered.

### JOHN O. MCGINNIS & RUSSELL G. PEARCE, THE GREAT DISRUPTION: HOW MACHINE INTELLIGENCE WILL TRANSFORM THE ROLE OF LAWYERS IN THE DELIVERY OF LEGAL SERVICES
82 Fordham L. Rev. 3041, 3041–42 (2014)

Law is an information technology—a code that regulates social life. In our age, the machinery of information technology is growing exponentially in power, not only in hardware, but also in the software capacity of the programs that run on computers. As a result, the legal profession faces a great disruption. * * *

The disruption has already begun. In discovery, for instance, computationally based services are already replacing the task of document review that lawyers have performed in the past. But computational services are on the cusp of substituting for other legal tasks—from the generation of legal documents to predicting outcomes in litigation. And when machine intelligence becomes as good as lawyers in developing some service or some factor of production that contributes to a service, it does not stop improving. Intelligent machines will become better and better, both in terms of performance and cost. And unlike humans, they can work ceaselessly around the clock, without sleep or caffeine. Such continuous technological acceleration in computational power is the difference between previous technological improvements in legal services and those driven by machine intelligence. This difference makes it the single most important phenomenon with which the legal profession will need to grapple in the coming decades.

### JANSON V. LEGALZOOM.COM, INC.
802 F.Supp.2d 1053 (W.D. Mo. 2011)

LegalZoom is a privately held corporation with its principal place of business in California. LegalZoom maintains a website—www.legalzoom.com—which offers online legal document forms and services.

First, LegalZoom's website offers blank legal forms that customers may download, print, and fill in themselves. Among the blank legal forms customers may download from the LegalZoom website are affidavits, bills of sale, letters, releases, promissory notes, and various types of agreements. Plaintiffs make no claim with respect to these blank legal forms that customers may download, print, and fill-in themselves.

In addition to such blank forms, LegalZoom's website also offers an internet portal, which is the subject of this dispute. With respect to the services offered through the internet portal, LegalZoom has aired a television advertisement stating:

> Over a million people have discovered how easy it is to use LegalZoom for important legal documents, and LegalZoom will help you incorporate your business, file a patent, make a will and more. You can complete our online questions in minutes. Then we'll prepare your legal documents and deliver them directly to you.

Another LegalZoom advertisement states:

> Log on to LegalZoom.com and check out filing incorporation papers for a new business. Click the tab marked "Incorporations, LLCs and DBAs." Then click the "get started" button, and you're in. Just answer a few simple online questions and LegalZoom takes over. You get a quality legal document filed for you by real helpful people.

These advertisements also contain LegalZoom's disclaimer: "LegalZoom isn't a law firm. They provide self-help services at your specific direction."

Among the legal documents available through LegalZoom's internet portal are business formation documents, estate planning documents, pet protection agreements, and copyright, trademark, and patent applications. After making an initial selection, the customer enters answers to questions via a "branching intake mechanism" (or decision tree), referred to on the website as an "online questionnaire." Customers type in answers to the questions contained in the online questionnaire. In some cases, customers select an alternative from a list of choices or checkboxes provided by LegalZoom. The branching mechanism skips questions for sections of the questionnaire that are inapplicable based on the customer's prior answers. For example, the questionnaire for a last will and testament asks if the customer has children; if the customer's answer is "no," questions about the customer's children are skipped and the customer is taken to a different next question than if the customer's answer had been "yes."

The online questionnaire process is fully automated. No LegalZoom employee offers or gives personal guidance on answering the questions, although information relevant to the customer's choice sometimes appears on the screen. For example, when completing the questionnaire to purchase a last will and testament, a question appears: "Would you like to protect your personal representative from liability?" After the question, there appears on the screen: "How did most people answer this question?" followed by "yes."

When the customer has completed the online questionnaire, LegalZoom's software creates a completed data file containing the customer's responses. A LegalZoom employee then reviews that data file for completeness, spelling and grammatical errors, and consistency of names, addresses, and other factual information. If the employee spots a factual error or inconsistency, the customer is contacted and may choose to correct or clarify the answer.

After the review of the data file, LegalZoom's software automatically enters the information provided by the customer via the online questionnaire into the LegalZoom template that corresponds with the type of document sought by the customer. LegalZoom's templates include standardized language created by attorneys (licensed outside the state of Missouri) to apply to common consumer and business situations. The software also removes sections of the template that are inapplicable based on the customer's answers to the questionnaire. For instance, if a customer has answered that she has no children in responding to the online questionnaire for a last will, no provisions for bequests to children are included in the final document. All information entered by a customer (other than payment and shipping) is used by the software to fill in LegalZoom's template. In other words, the software does not edit or select from the information entered by the customer.

After the customer's data has been input into the template, a LegalZoom employee reviews the final document for quality in formatting—e.g., correcting word processing "widows," "orphans," page breaks, and the like. The employee then prints and ships the final, unsigned document to the customer. In rare cases, upon request, the document is emailed to the customer. A customer does not see the purchased document until it is delivered. All Missouri customers who select a given document and provide the same information will receive an identical final product.

After receiving the document, the customer may review, sign, execute, and use the final document at his convenience. The customer may take the unexecuted document to an attorney for review and choose not to use the document at all. Under LegalZoom's refund policy, customers can obtain a full refund (less charges paid to third parties for filing fees or other costs) for 60 days after their transaction if they are not satisfied.

With respect to some of the intellectual property documents, LegalZoom files the government document for the customer based on the customer's answers to the questionnaire. For example, a copyright application is completed using the information gathered through the customer's answers to the questionnaire and then uploaded directly from LegalZoom to the appropriate government office. In the copyright example, the customer will also, at the time of the application or later, send LegalZoom the work for which copyright protection is sought, and LegalZoom will also provide that material to the appropriate government office for the customer. At the time the copyright application is submitted to the appropriate government office by LegalZoom for the customer, LegalZoom reviews the entire submission to make sure it complies with what the customer wished to copyright as set forth in the answers provided to the questionnaire. Similarly, there are two different methods by which a person may create a trademark. LegalZoom determines the trademark-registration method after the customer that selected a trademark document answers questions in the branching questionnaire developed by LegalZoom for the trademark process. Like a copyright application, the customer never sees the trademark application before it is uploaded to the government office by LegalZoom. For documents in the business-services division, LegalZoom also determines what particular government document to use based on the consumer's answers to the questionnaires.

Limited customer service is available to LegalZoom customers by email and telephone. LegalZoom customer-service representatives receive training concerning the company's policy against providing legal advice and are regularly instructed not to recommend forms or documents or give any legal advice. LegalZoom customer-service representatives are repeatedly informed that giving legal advice to a customer will result in dismissal, and that even approaching giving legal advice to a customer will result in discipline up to and including dismissal.

The named Plaintiffs had no personal interaction with any LegalZoom employee while using the LegalZoom website or afterward. The named Plaintiffs never believed that they were receiving legal advice while using the LegalZoom website. Plaintiff Todd Janson paid LegalZoom $121.95 for his will, while Plaintiffs Gerald Ardrey and Chad Ferrell paid LegalZoom $249 for the articles of organization of Plaintiff C & J Remodeling. * * *

This action was removed to federal court. . . . Plaintiffs' Amended Petition contains four counts. Count I asserts a claim for unlawful practice of law pursuant to Mo.Rev.Stat. § 484.020. * * *

## B. Missouri's Unauthorized Practice of Law Statute

As Plaintiffs have stated, the overarching issue in this case is whether Defendant LegalZoom has violated Missouri law by engaging in the unauthorized practice of law. Section 484.020 provides:

> 1. No person shall engage in the practice of law or do law business, as defined in section 484.010, unless he shall have been duly licensed therefor. . . .

2. Any person, association, partnership, limited liability company or corporation who shall violate the foregoing prohibition of this section shall be guilty of a misdemeanor and upon conviction therefor shall be punished by a fine not exceeding one hundred dollars and costs of prosecution and shall be subject to be sued for treble the amount which shall have been paid him or it for any service rendered in violation hereof by the person, firm, association, partnership, limited liability company or corporation paying the same within two years from the date the same shall have been paid and if within said time such person, firm, association, partnership, limited liability company or corporation shall neglect and fail to sue for or recover such treble amount, then the state of Missouri shall have the right to and shall sue for such treble amount and recover the same and upon the recovery thereof such treble amount shall be paid into the treasury of the state of Missouri.

Section 484.010 provides:

1. The "practice of the law" is hereby defined to be and is the appearance as an advocate in a representative capacity or the drawing of papers, pleadings or documents or the performance of any act in such capacity in connection with proceedings pending or prospective before any court of record, commissioner, referee or any body, board, committee or commission constituted by law or having authority to settle controversies.

2. The "law business" is hereby defined to be and is the advising or counseling for a valuable consideration of any person, firm, association, or corporation as to any secular law or the drawing or the procuring of or assisting in the drawing for a valuable consideration of any paper, document or instrument affecting or relating to secular rights or the doing of any act for a valuable consideration in a representative capacity, obtaining or tending to

> obtain or securing or tending to secure for any
> person, firm, association or corporation any
> property or property rights whatsoever.

This Court is bound to apply the decisions of the Missouri
Supreme Court regarding substantive issues in a diversity case
controlled by Missouri law. Here, the Court must interpret
Missouri's unauthorized practice of law statute as would the
Missouri Supreme Court.

## C. The Missouri Supreme Court's Interpretation of the Unauthorized Practice of Law

The Missouri Supreme Court has repeatedly emphasized that
the "judicial branch of government has the power to regulate the
practice of law." When applying Missouri's unauthorized
practice of law statute, the Missouri Supreme Court has written:

> This [statutory] definition of "law business" .... is
> adequate for the issue before us, [but] it should also be
> noted that it is impossible to lay down an exhaustive
> definition of "the practice of law." ... In any event, the
> General Assembly may only *assist* the judiciary by
> providing penalties for the unauthorized practice of law,
> the ultimate definition of which is always within the
> province of this Court.

In re First Escrow, Inc., 840 S.W.2d 839, 843 n. 6, 7 (Mo.1992).
Thus, to apply Missouri's unauthorized practice of law statute,
this Court must decide whether LegalZoom's conduct fits within
the Missouri Supreme Court's definition of the unauthorized
practice of law.

### 1.   *Hulse* and *Thompson*

Two foundational cases are cited throughout the Missouri
Supreme Court's jurisprudence on the unauthorized practice of
law. Plaintiffs urge the Court to follow the cases that apply
Hulse v. Criger, 363 Mo. 26, 247 S.W.2d 855 (1952) (en banc),
which generally involve businesses providing a legal document
preparation service for their customers. Meanwhile, Defendant
LegalZoom argues that its website providing access to online
document assembly software is the functional equivalent of the

"do-it-yourself" divorce kit approved for sale by the Missouri Supreme Court in In re Thompson, 574 S.W.2d 365 (Mo. 1978).

In 1952, the Missouri Supreme Court decided *Hulse,* explaining that its regulation of the unauthorized practice of law "is not to protect the Bar from competition but to protect the public from being advised or represented in legal matters by incompetent or unreliable persons." In *Hulse:*

> Respondent admit[ted] that in numerous transactions in the general and ordinary course of his business as a licensed real estate broker and incidental thereto, respondent . . . has prepared for persons other than himself, many instruments relating to and affecting real estate and the title to real estate, including deeds conveying real estate, deeds of trust and mortgages encumbering real estate, promissory notes secured by such deeds of trust or mortgages; leases of real estate, options for purchase, contracts of sale and agreements. . . .

> Respondent also admit[ted] that [he] . . . customarily in each instance conferred with one or more of the parties to the transaction . . . elicit[ing] in such conference what were considered to be the pertinent facts. . . .

In other words, customers provided the defendant with information that would allow him to prepare their legal documents, which were ancillary to his real estate business. Indeed, the defendant in *Hulse* had argued that "preparing and completing instruments necessary to the closing of real estate transactions is one of the most important services performed by realtors. . . ." *Hulse* concluded that realtors could perform such a legal document preparation service for customers, but only when ancillary to their main business, and only if they did not charge a separate fee for that service.

*Thompson,* in contrast, concerned an Oregon resident sending "do-it-yourself" divorce kits to franchisees in Missouri:

> The "Divorce Kits" offered for sale in this state consist of a packet approximately one-fourth inch in thickness. Much of the kit consists of various forms pertaining to an action for an uncontested dissolution of marriage.

> Blank spaces, with instructions on practice forms, are provided for the insertion of specific items applicable to the parties involved in the dissolution. These forms include two forms for a petition for dissolution of marriage, one a "joint" petition, and one an individual petition, as well as other forms including affidavits of nonmilitary service, waivers of notice of hearing, affidavits needed to obtain service by publication, financial statements, and a decree form. These forms are accompanied by two kinds of instructions, a set of general procedural instructions designed to instruct as to what forms to file, in what order and where, and instructions on how to prepare the forms.

\* \* \*

*Thompson* relied most heavily on the Florida Supreme Court's reasoning in Florida Bar v. Brumbaugh, 355 So.2d 1186 (Fla.1978). *Thompson* quoted *Brumbaugh's* holding as follows:

> We hold that Ms. Brumbaugh, and others in similar situations, may sell printed material purporting to explain legal practice and procedure to the public in general and she may sell sample legal forms. . . . In addition, Ms. Brumbaugh may advertise her business activities of providing secretarial and notary services and selling legal forms and general printed information. However, Marilyn Brumbaugh must not, in conjunction with her business, engage in advising clients as to the various remedies available to them, or otherwise assist them in preparing those forms necessary for a dissolution proceeding.

\* \* \*

While *Thompson* did not involve notary services of any kind, it reached a similar conclusion as *Brumbaugh* with respect to the sale of legal self-help goods: "[T]he advertisement and sale by the respondents of the divorce kits does not constitute the unauthorized practice of law so long as the respondents and other[s] similarly situated refrain from giving personal advice as to legal remedies or the consequences flowing therefrom." Thus, it became the law in Missouri, as it is in other jurisdictions, that

the practice of law does not include the sale of "do-it-yourself"
kits, which include blank legal forms and general instructions.

## 2. Subsequent Cases

In 1992, the Missouri Supreme Court decided *First Escrow,*
which involved two escrow companies that provided "real estate
closing or settlement services":

> [Defendant escrow companies] complete pre-printed
> forms of documents, including but not limited to general
> warranty deeds, corporation warranty deeds, quit claim
> deeds, promissory notes, deeds of trust, affidavits of
> possession and title, HUD settlement statements and
> receipts, IRS Forms 1099, and property inspection
> certificates. [Defendants] discern the information
> needed to complete these forms from the written real
> estate contract and from communications with the
> parties and any attorneys, title insurers, or lenders
> involved in the transaction.

*First Escrow* applied the principles laid out in *Hulse:*

> [T]he *Hulse* Court rested its decision upon two grounds.
> First, that the transactions involved were "simple
> enough so that such a [standardized] form will suffice,"
> and second, that the broker had sufficient identity of
> interest with the seller he represented to safeguard the
> proper completion of the transaction.

> The situation presented here regarding escrow
> companies, however, does not fall within the *Hulse*
> exception. While the relatively simple nature of the task
> of filling in form documents remains unchanged, and
> while the completion of these documents may be
> "incidental" to the closing process, the escrow company
> does not have the requisite personal financial interest
> to safeguard the transaction.

However, the finding that the person filling in the document for
the customer could have adverse interests was not the end of the
analysis:

> Nonetheless, we are reluctant to automatically brand
> respondents' activities as the unauthorized doing of law

business. *Hulse* established our duty to strike a workable balance between the public's protection and the public's convenience. . . .

In short, we are willing to allow the *Hulse* test to be expanded to permit escrow companies to fill in the blanks of certain standardized form documents required to close real estate transactions only if they do so under the supervision of, and as agents for, a real estate broker, a mortgage lender, or a title insurer who has a direct financial interest in the transaction.

Still, the Missouri Supreme Court held that escrow companies "may not prepare or complete nonstandard or specialized documents" and "may not charge a separate fee for document preparation. . . ."

In 1996, the Missouri Supreme Court decided In re Mid-America Living Trust Associates, Inc., 927 S.W.2d 855 (Mo.1996) (en banc). The Court first reaffirmed the rules in *Hulse* and *Thompson*:

We allow non-attorneys to perform routine services, ancillary to other valid activities and without compensation, such as the filling in of blanks in approved form real estate documents. Also, non-attorneys may sell *generalized* legal publications and "kits", so long as no "personal advice as to the legal remedies or consequences flowing therefrom" is given.

Under *Mid-America's* facts, the Missouri Supreme Court found that the defendant's "trust associates" had engaged in the unauthorized practice of law:

This is not a situation such as in *In re Thompson* where a generalized "kit" was sold. Instead, specific individuals were solicited and Mid-America's trusts were recommended and sold to them for valuable consideration as estate planning devices. . . .

The trust associates were not merely collecting information to fill in standardized forms as otherwise might have been approved by *Hulse* and *In re First Escrow*. Instead, they also were giving legal advice to the clients about choices to be made and the legal effects of those choices. . . .

In *Hulse* and *In re First Escrow,* we held that non-attorneys could properly fill in blanks in standard real estate forms when they performed such a service *without compensation* and ancillary to other valid duties. Mid—America does not fall within this exception. The documents sold are not standardized forms accepted generally within a particular business or industry, but propriety documents unique to Mid—America. Mid—America markets, drafts, and executes customized legal documents *for compensation*. This service is not ancillary to any other valid business, but is the end business itself.

Most recently, in 2007, the Missouri Supreme Court decided Eisel v. Midwest BankCentre, 230 S.W.3d 335 (Mo. 2007). There, the defendant bank had charged a separate fee for preparing legal documents for its customers, in violation of the rules laid out in *Hulse* and reaffirmed in *Mid-America*. The Missouri Supreme Court wasted little time in affirming the judgment against the bank under Missouri's unauthorized practice of law statute:

This Court has prohibited a company and its non-lawyer agents, servants, employees, and trust associates from drawing, preparing, or assisting in the preparation of trust workbooks, trusts, wills, and powers of attorney, for valuable consideration, for Missouri residents without the direct supervision of an independent licensed attorney selected by and representing those individuals. Escrow companies may not charge a separate fee for document preparation or vary their customary charges for closing services based upon whether documents are to be prepared in the transaction. Similarly, this Court noted that the charging of a separate additional charge tends to place emphasis on conveyancing and legal drafting as a business rather than on the business of being a real estate broker. With respect to [defendant], no conflict exists between section 484.020 and this Court's regulation of the practice of law.

### 3. Application of Missouri Law to LegalZoom's Conduct

In its Motion for Summary Judgment, Defendant LegalZoom argues that, as a matter of law, it did not engage in the unauthorized practice of law in Missouri. Thus, the Court must decide whether a reasonable juror could conclude that LegalZoom did engage in the unauthorized practice of law, as it has been defined by the Missouri Supreme Court.

Plaintiffs argue that the Missouri Supreme Court has declared on multiple occasions that a non-lawyer may not charge a fee for their legal document preparation service. Defendant responds that its customers—rather than LegalZoom itself—complete the standardized legal documents by entering their information via the online questionnaire to fill the document's blanks, which it concedes that customers never see. While the parties dispute the proper characterization of the underlying facts, there is no dispute regarding how LegalZoom's legal document service functions.

It is uncontroverted that Defendant LegalZoom's website performs two distinct functions. First, the website offers blank legal forms that customers may download, print, and fill in themselves. Plaintiffs make no claim regarding these blank forms. Indeed, this function is analogous to the "do-it-yourself" kit in *Thompson* containing blank forms and general instructions regarding how those forms should be completed by the customer. Such a "do-it-yourself" kit puts the legal forms into the hands of the customers, facilitating the right to pro se representation.

It is the second function of LegalZoom's website that goes beyond mere general instruction. LegalZoom's internet portal is not like the "do-it-yourself" divorce kit in *Thompson*. Rather, LegalZoom's internet portal service is based on the opposite notion: we'll do it for you. Although the named Plaintiffs never believed that they were receiving legal advice while using the LegalZoom website, LegalZoom's advertisements shed some light on the manner in which LegalZoom takes legal problems out of its customers' hands. While stating that it is not a "law firm" (yet "provide[s] self-help services"), LegalZoom reassures consumers that "we'll prepare your legal documents," and that "LegalZoom takes over" once customers "answer a few simple online questions."

None of the Missouri Supreme Court cases cited by the parties are directly on point, due to the novelty of the technology at issue here. However, the weight of the authority that does exist indicates that businesses may not charge fees for a legal document preparation service, although they may sell goods— including blank forms and general instructions—to facilitate the consumer's own preparation of legal documents. The "do-it-yourself" divorce kit in *Thompson,* upon which Defendant relies so heavily, was not a service but purely a product. *Thompson* did not even address the question of document preparation in *Thompson* because the issue was not before it—the purchaser of the kit prepared the document, not the company that sold the kit.

*Thompson* relied heavily on *Brumbaugh,* where the Florida Supreme Court allowed not only the sale of self-help legal goods, but also allowed for parallel notary services. Nonetheless, *Brumbaugh* held that the notary could only "type up instruments which have been completed by clients," and could not "assist them in preparing those forms" or otherwise "engage in personal legal assistance in conjunction with her business activities, including the correction of errors and omissions." LegalZoom also cites Colorado Bar Association v. Miles, 192 Colo. 294, 557 P.2d 1202 (1976) (en banc), as an example of the permissibility of a scrivener service related to legal documents. But that case affirmed the prohibition of "[p]reparing for other persons pleadings or other written instruments relating to dissolution of marriage other than in the manner performed by a scrivener or public stenographer." In other words, the scrivener or notary service is a limited exception to the rule that the practice of law does include legal services such as "assisting [customers] in preparing forms" and "the correction of errors or omissions."

Here, LegalZoom's internet portal offers consumers not a piece of self-help merchandise, but a legal document service which goes well beyond the role of a notary or public stenographer. The kit in *Thompson* offered page upon page of detailed instructions but left it to the purchaser to select the provisions applicable to their situation. The purchaser understood that it was their responsibility to get it right. In contrast, LegalZoom says: "Just answer a few simple online questions and LegalZoom takes over. You get a quality legal document filed for you by real helpful people." [Doc. # 119 at 51.] Thus, LegalZoom's internet portal sells more than merely a good (i.e., a kit for self help) but also a service (i.e., preparing that legal document). Because those that provide that service are not authorized to practice law in Missouri, there is a clear risk of the public being served in legal matters by "incompetent or unreliable persons." * * *

That Defendant's legal document service is delivered through the internet is not the problem. The internet is merely a medium, and LegalZoom's sale of blank forms over the internet does not constitute the unauthorized practice of law. Nor would LegalZoom be engaging in the unauthorized practice of law if it sold general instructions to accompany those blank forms over the internet (as may already be the case).

LegalZoom's legal document preparation service goes beyond self-help because of the role played by its human employees, not because of the internet medium. LegalZoom employees intervene at numerous stages of the so-called "self-help services." First, after the customer has completed the online questionnaire, a LegalZoom employee reviews the data file for completeness, spelling and grammatical errors, and consistency of names, addresses, and other factual information. If the employee spots a factual error or inconsistency, the customer is contacted and may choose to correct or clarify the answer. Later in the process, after the reviewed information is inserted into LegalZoom's template, a LegalZoom employee reviews the final document for quality in formatting—e.g., correcting word processing "widows," "orphans," page breaks, and the like. Next, an employee prints and ships the final, unsigned document to the customer. Finally, customer service is available to LegalZoom customers by email and telephone.

As in *Brumbaugh:*

> Although Marilyn Brumbaugh never held herself out as
> an attorney, it is clear that her clients placed some

reliance upon her to properly prepare the necessary legal forms. . . . To this extent we believe that Ms. Brumbaugh overstepped proper bounds and engaged in the unauthorized practice of law. . . . While Marilyn Brumbaugh may legally sell forms . . . and type up instruments which have been completed by clients, she must not engage in personal legal assistance in conjunction with her business activities, including the correction of errors and omissions.

Furthermore, LegalZoom's branching computer program is created by a LegalZoom employee using Missouri law. It is that human input that creates the legal document. A computer sitting at a desk in California cannot prepare a legal document without a human programming it to fill in the document using legal principles derived from Missouri law that are selected for the customer based on the information provided by the customer. There is little or no difference between this and a lawyer in Missouri asking a client a series of questions and then preparing a legal document based on the answers provided and applicable Missouri law. That the Missouri lawyer may also give legal advice does not undermine the analogy because legal advice and document preparation are two different ways in which a person engages in the practice of law. *See,* Mo.Rev.Stat. § 484.010 (defining law business as giving legal advice for compensation or "assisting in the drawing for a valuable consideration of any paper, document or instrument affecting or relating to secular rights".)

The Missouri Supreme Court cases which specifically address the issue of document preparation, *First Escrow, Mid-America* and *Eisel,* make it clear that this is the unauthorized practice of law. The fact that the customer communicates via computer rather than face to face or that the document is prepared using a computer program rather than a pen and paper does not change the essence of the transaction. As in *Hulse, First Escrow, Mid-America,* and *Eisel,* LegalZoom's customers are rendered passive bystanders after providing the information necessary to complete the form. Yet LegalZoom charges a fee for its legal document preparation service. Unlike *Thompson,* the customer does not have to follow directions to fill in a blank legal form.

The customer merely provides information and "LegalZoom takes over."

## D. Defendant's Constitutional Arguments

Defendant LegalZoom also argues that the application of Missouri law prohibiting the unauthorized practice of law to its conduct would raise constitutional issues.

### 1. First Amendment

First, Defendant argues that an interpretation of Missouri law as prohibiting its conduct would violate the First Amendment of the U.S. Constitution and Article I, § 8 of the Missouri Constitution. However, LegalZoom cites no caselaw from any jurisdiction where the application of law prohibiting the unauthorized practice of law was found to violate the First Amendment, much less Article I, § 8 of the Missouri Constitution.

LegalZoom relies primarily on a Second Circuit case finding that a self-help book containing blank forms and general instructions was protected by the First Amendment's guarantee of free speech. Dacey v. New York County Lawyers' Ass'n, 423 F.2d 188, 193 (2d Cir.1969). However, the Court has already determined that LegalZoom's sale of such merchandise does not constitute the unauthorized practice of law. Thus, it is not the content of speech at issue here, as there is no dispute regarding what speech could be included in any goods sold over the internet. Rather, LegalZoom's conduct in preparing legal documents is at issue.

Moreover, LegalZoom's customers remain free to represent themselves in any court proceeding. LegalZoom has pointed to no court that has held that a right exists to receive legal services from a non-lawyer. The Supreme Court has recognized a First Amendment right to receive legal advice from duly qualified attorneys, consistent with "the State's interest in high standards of legal ethics." United Mine Workers v. Illinois State Bar Ass'n, 389 U.S. 217, 225, 88 S.Ct. 353, 19 L.Ed.2d 426 (1967).

The Supreme Court has explained that a regulation imposed by the Ohio bar affecting speech involved "a subject only marginally affected with First Amendment concerns." Ohralik v. Ohio State

Bar Ass'n, 436 U.S. 447, 459, 98 S.Ct. 1912, 56 L.Ed.2d 444
(1978). There, the Supreme Court held that the bar could
discipline a lawyer for soliciting clients under certain
circumstances, even though it involved speech, noting that "the
State does not lose its power to regulate commercial activity
deemed harmful to the public whenever speech is a component
of that activity." Elsewhere, the Supreme Court has
"recognize[d] that the States have a compelling interest in the
practice of professions within their boundaries," and that "[t]he
interest of the States in regulating lawyers is especially great
since lawyers are essential to the primary governmental
function of administering justice, and have historically been
'officers of the courts.'" * * *

Given the weight of these authorities indicating that states have
a compelling interest in the regulation of professionals for the
protection of the public, as well as the paucity of authority cited
by Defendant, the Court declines to alter Missouri law based on
inarticulate free speech principles.

## 2.  Due Process

LegalZoom also argues that applying Missouri's unauthorized
practice of law statute to its conduct would violate due process.
LegalZoom argues that the statute should be construed under
the rule of lenity because—in addition to providing a private
right of action—it states that any person engaging in the
unauthorized practice of law "shall be guilty of a misdemeanor
and upon conviction therefor shall be punished by a fine not
exceeding one hundred dollars and costs of prosecution. . . ."
Mo.Rev.Stat. § 484.020.2.

Even when a statute is entirely penal in nature, the Eighth
Circuit has explained: "[T]he rule that a penal statute is to be
strictly construed in favor of persons accused, is not violated by
allowing the language of the statute to have its full meaning,
where that construction supports the policy and purposes of the
enactment." Moreover, a statute is presumed constitutional and
is void for vagueness only where it "fails to give a person of
ordinary intelligence fair notice that his contemplated conduct
is forbidden by the statute."

It is often true that past cases have not applied a statute to the particular fact pattern before a court. Here, the statute clearly prohibits the unauthorized "assisting in the drawing for a valuable consideration of any paper, document or instrument affecting or relating to secular rights. . . ." Mo.Rev.Stat. § 484.010.2. As explained above, the application of the statute to LegalZoom's legal document preparation service does not conflict with the Missouri judiciary's regulation of the practice of law. Additionally, cases such as *Hulse, First Escrow, Mid-America,* and *Eisel* put LegalZoom on notice that it could not charge a fee for the preparation of legal documents. Finally, the Missouri Supreme Court rejected a similar argument in Carpenter v. Countrywide Home Loans, Inc., 250 S.W.3d 697 (Mo. 2008) ("Countrywide has not established that sections 484.010 and 844.020 were vague and did not provide it fair notice of the prescribed acts or the penalty associated with those acts."). Here too, LegalZoom's due process argument fails.

### 3.  Preemption

LegalZoom's final constitutional argument is that with respect to patent and trademark applications, Plaintiffs' claims are preempted by federal law permitting non-lawyers to practice before the Patent and Trademark Office ("PTO"). LegalZoom cites Sperry v. Florida ex rel. Florida Bar, 373 U.S. 379, 404, 83 S.Ct. 1322, 10 L.Ed.2d 428 (1963), where the Supreme Court held that Florida could not enjoin a non-lawyer registered to practice before the U.S. Patent Office from preparing and prosecuting patent applications in Florida, even though such activity constituted the practice of law. There, the Supreme Court reasoned that states could not review the "federal determination that a person or agency is qualified" or otherwise "impose upon the performance of activity sanctioned by federal license additional conditions not contemplated by Congress."

Congress has authorized the PTO to prescribe regulations "govern[ing] the recognition and conduct of agents, attorneys, or other persons representing applicants or other parties before the Office." 35 U.S.C. § 2(b)(2)(D). With respect to patents, 37 C.F.R. § 1.31 states that an applicant may file and prosecute his own case or "may give a power of attorney so as to be represented by one or more patent practitioners or joint inventors." A "patent practitioner" is defined to include a registered patent agent. 37 C.F.R. §§ 1.32(a), 11.6(b). The regulations authorize the PTO to allow a non-registered non-lawyer to serve as a patent agent on designated applications. 37 C.F.R. § 11.9(a). With respect to non-patent matters, the regulations also authorize non-lawyers to practice before the PTO under certain limited circumstances. *See* 37 C.F.R. § 11.14.

* * *[T]he Federal Circuit, relying on *Sperry,* [has] stated clearly that "state licensing requirements which purport to regulate private individuals who appear before a federal agency are invalid." Augustine v. Dep't of Veterans Affairs, 429 F.3d 1334, 1340 (Fed.Cir.2005) (also noting that "states cannot regulate practice before the PTO"). * * *

Here, the issue is whether Missouri can prohibit non-lawyers from practicing law before the PTO. Under *Sperry, Kroll,* and *Augustine,* Missouri cannot do so. Even though there is no evidence that LegalZoom is licensed to practice before the PTO, that field of regulation is occupied by federal law. With respect to patent and trademark applications, federal law preempts Plaintiffs' claims. Therefore, the Court grants Defendant's Motion for Summary Judgment with respect to Plaintiffs' claims as they relate to patent and trademark applications. * * *

### III. Conclusion

Accordingly, it is hereby ORDERED that Defendant LegalZoom's Motion for Summary Judgment [Doc. # 100] is GRANTED with respect to Plaintiffs' claims as they relate to patent and trademark applications and DENIED in all other respects. * * *

TEX. GOV'T CODE ANN. § 81.101.
DEFINITION ["PRACTICE OF LAW"]

(a)  In this chapter the "practice of law" means the preparation of a pleading or other document incident to an action or special proceeding or the management of the action or proceeding on behalf of a client before a judge in court as well as a service rendered out of court, including the giving of advice or the rendering of any service requiring the use of legal skill or knowledge, such as preparing a will, contract,

or other instrument, the legal effect of which under the facts
and conclusions involved must be carefully determined.

(b) The definition in this section is not exclusive and does not
deprive the judicial branch of the power and authority under
both this chapter and the adjudicated cases to determine
whether other services and acts not enumerated may
constitute the practice of law.

(c) In this chapter, **the "practice of law" does not include
the design, creation, publication, distribution,
display, or sale, including publication, distribution,
display, or sale by means of an Internet web site, of
written materials, books, forms, computer software,
or similar products if the products clearly and
conspicuously state that the products are not a
substitute for the advice of an attorney** (emphasis
added). * * *

CHAPTER V

# WHEN DOES SELF-REPRESENTATION AMOUNT TO UPL?

■ ■ ■

## A. THE *PRO SE* EXCEPTION TO UPL

RESTATEMENT (THIRD) OF THE LAW
GOVERNING LAWYERS § 4

Comment: * * *

d.  **Every jurisdiction recognizes the right of an individual to proceed "pro se" by providing his or her own representation in any matter, whether or not the person is a lawyer.** Because the appearance is personal only, it does not involve an issue of unauthorized practice. The right extends to self-preparation of legal documents and other kinds of out-of-court legal work as well as to in-court representation. In some jurisdictions, tribunals have inaugurated programs to assist persons without counsel in filing necessary papers, with appropriate cautions that court personnel assisting the person do not thereby undertake to provide legal assistance. * * * **In general, however, a person appearing pro se cannot represent any other person or entity, no matter how close the degree of kinship, ownership, or other relationship** (emphasis added).

———————

This right of self-representation applies only to natural persons and is personal; that is, it cannot be assumed by anyone else, no matter how closely related familiarly or organizationally. And, the right cannot be delegated, assigned, or otherwise bestowed on any agent or other representative, even by power of attorney. Being an agent or otherwise empowered to act for someone else

159

does not allow the agent to engage in the practice of law for a principal. In other words, allowing someone to represent you and your interests—no matter how completely and deliberately— does not allow the person derivably to exercise your right to self-representation in court.

### COLEMAN V. UNNAMED RESPONDENT
2017 WL 619013, at *1 (S.D. Ga. 2017),
*report and recommendation adopted*, 2017 WL 901098 (S.D. Ga. 2017)

[W]hile the law may recognize a party's right to proceed in a representative capacity, that capacity does not entitle the representative to pursue the case pro se. *See Weber [v. Garza],* 570 F.2d 511, 514 [(5th Cir. 1978)] ("[I]ndividuals not licensed to practice law by the state may not use the 'next friend' device as an artifice for the unauthorized practice of law."). Even parents permitted to pursue a claim on behalf of their own minor children may not litigate pro se. * * *

---

Even an agent of God must have a lawyer.

### GARDNER V. POTESTIVO & ASSOCS. P.C.
2016 WL 7494697, at *6–7 (Mich. Ct. App. Dec. 20, 2016)

Plaintiff . . . objects to Judge Kelly's refusal to recognize her as "Agent Nancy" at . . . hearing in the declaratory judgment action. The following exchange occurred at that hearing:

> *Plaintiff.* For the record, Agent Nancy respectfully objects to the following:

> *Trial court.* I don't recognize you as an agent of yourself. I recognize you as a person that has come before this Court and has submitted to the Court's jurisdiction. You may proceed in that fashion.

> *Plaintiff.* Okay. Agent Nancy objects to—

> *Trial court.* Again, you're not an Agent.

> *Plaintiff.* Nancy.

> *Trial court.* You're Mrs. Gardner.

Plaintiff claims that Judge Kelly violated her right to the freedom of speech, U.S. Const, Am I, and Const 1963, art 1, § 5, and her religious beliefs, Const 1963, art 1, § 4. She explains that Agent Nancy is an agent of the Almighty God acting on behalf of "property you refer to as Nancy J. Gardner."

An "agent" is " 'a person having express or implied authority to represent or act on behalf of another person, who is called his principal.' " According to this definition, plaintiff could not serve as an agent for herself, only "another person." And even if plaintiff could serve as an agent for herself, she could not appear in court in that capacity unless she was a licensed attorney.

## OFFICE OF DISCIPLINARY COUNSEL V. COLEMAN
### 724 N.E.2d 402 (Ohio 2000)

During each of the past few years we have decided cases in which it was asserted that a power of attorney gives one the right to appear in court for the person assigning that power.

The argument in each of these cases was similar to that made by respondent in this case. He contends that the client he represented had "every right to file" an action on her own behalf, that she also had "the right to assign her rights to act for herself to another," and that when respondent filed the cases on behalf of his client he also filed "a Limited Power-of-Attorney form assigning [the client's] right to act in this matter to me."

Because the argument appears regularly, its sophistry should be exposed.

In the first place, persons holding powers of attorney have historically not been considered attorneys who can appear in the courts. When a principal through the execution of a "power of attorney" designates another to transact some business that could have been transacted by the principal, he appoints an agent to act for him as an "attorney in fact" or "private attorney." An "attorney in fact" has been consistently distinguished from an "attorney at law" or "public attorney" since at least 1402 when certain attorneys in England were examined by Justices and "their names be entered on the roll" of those permitted to practice in the courts. Thus, a person holding a power of attorney, but whose name is not entered on the roll, is an attorney in fact, but not an attorney at law permitted to practice in the courts.

Secondly, respondent's argument results in an absurd interpretation of our Constitution. Section 2(B)(1)(g), Article IV of the Ohio Constitution gives the Supreme Court power over all matters relating to the practice of law. Pursuant to the Constitution and to secure the public's interest in competent legal representation, we have promulgated rules with respect to admission to the practice of law, rules to govern the conduct of those admitted to the practice, and rules to ensure that those admitted maintain their knowledge and skills through continuing legal education. If accepted, respondent's argument that a person may execute a power of attorney and so enable the grantee to practice law in Ohio would render meaningless the supervisory control of the practice of law given to us by the Ohio Constitution.

Thirdly, the use of a power of attorney as a contract to represent another in court violates the laws of Ohio. [W]e [have] held that among other activities, "[t]he practice of law * * * embraces the preparation of pleadings and other papers incident to actions and special proceedings and the management of such actions and proceedings on behalf of clients before judges and courts."

R.C. 4705.01 provides: "No person shall be permitted to practice as an attorney and counselor at law, or to commence, conduct, or defend any action or proceeding in which the person is not a party concerned, either by using or subscribing the person's own name, or the name of another person, unless the person has been admitted to the bar by order to the supreme court in compliance with its prescribed and published rules."

This law recognizes that a person has the inherent right to proceed *pro se* in any court. But it also prohibits a person from representing another by commencing, conducting, or defending any action or proceeding in which the person is not a party. When a person not admitted to the bar attempts to represent another in court on the basis of a power of attorney assigning *pro se* rights, he is in violation of this statute. A private contract cannot be used to circumvent a statutory prohibition based on public policy.

Finally, courts in other states have all held, as have we, that a non-lawyer with a power of attorney may not appear in court on behalf of another, or otherwise practice law.

Not having been admitted to the bar by our order, respondent, as the previous respondents before him, has engaged in the unauthorized practice of law. Respondent is hereby enjoined from all further activities which constitute the practice of law.
* * *

### A Nonlawyer Who Holds a Power of Attorney May Not Engage in the Practice of Law

NJ Atty. Advert. Op. 50 (N.J. Comm. Atty. Advt.),
211 N.J.L.J. 866, 2013 WL 1281420
New Jersey Supreme Court Committee on Attorney Advertising
Opinion Number 50
March 25, 2013

The Committee on the Unauthorized Practice of Law received a complaint alleging that a nonlawyer attempted to represent a grievant in an attorney discipline matter. The nonlawyer argued that his conduct was permitted because the grievant had executed a power of attorney authorizing him to act as the grievant's agent. The Committee hereby issues this Opinion to clarify that a nonlawyer holding a power of attorney is not authorized to act as a lawyer licensed in the State of New Jersey. A power of attorney does not permit a nonlawyer to provide legal services or advice, or represent the principal in any judicial or quasi-judicial forum. A nonlawyer who acts in this manner engages in the unauthorized practice of law.

"A power of attorney is a written instrument by which an individual known as the principal authorizes another individual . . . known as the attorney-in-fact to perform specified acts on behalf of the principal as the principal's agent." *N.J.S.A.* 46:2B–8.2a. An "attorney-in-fact" is different from an "attorney-at-law"; an "attorney-in-fact" is not a lawyer but, rather, a person who merely has authorization to perform certain acts on behalf of a principal.

A power of attorney cannot authorize an agent to perform acts that would be considered the practice of law.[1] Only the New

---

[1]   Powers of attorney often include provisions empowering the agent to "pursue claims and litigation." This provision permits the agent to act on behalf of the principal

Jersey Supreme Court has the power to regulate the practice of law and to decide who is authorized to practice law. * * *

The Committee considered whether it is in the public interest to permit nonlawyers who hold powers of attorney to provide legal services or represent parties in court or a quasi-judicial forum. Permitting nonlawyers who hold a power of attorney to practice law would expose members of the public to persons who are not bound by the *Rules of Professional Conduct* and who do not have any training in law. It would interfere with the orderly administration of justice and judges' expectations that representatives appearing in court will act ethically. It would abrogate New Jersey's licensing and admission requirements. The Committee finds that it is not in the public interest to permit the practice of law by nonlawyers who have been appointed agent of a principal pursuant to a power of attorney. Such conduct is the unauthorized practice of law.

This decision of the Committee is consistent with the findings of courts in New Jersey and other jurisdictions. In *Kasharian v. Wilentz*, 93 *N.J. Super.* 479 (App. Div. 1967), the court rejected an attempt by an administrator *ad prosequendum* who sought to institute a wrongful death action. "[N]ominal representatives or even active fiduciaries of the persons in beneficial interest, not themselves lawyers, should not be permitted to conduct legal proceedings in court involving the rights or liabilities of such persons without representation by attorneys duly qualified to practice law."

The Ohio Supreme Court recently found that a person holding a power of attorney is not authorized to file papers in court on behalf of the principal. The Ohio Court quoted the findings of its Board on Unauthorized Practice of Law:

> A durable power of attorney, naming a non-attorney as one's agent and attorney-in-fact, does not permit that person to prepare and pursue legal filings and proceedings as an attorney-at-law. Since 1402, the law

---

as the client in a lawsuit. An attorney-in-fact (the holder of a power of attorney) may make decisions concerning litigation for the principal, such as deciding to settle a case, but a nonlawyer attorney-in-fact may not act as lawyer to implement those decisions. See 3 C.J.S. Agency, Paragraph 217, page 499 (2008). Nor may an agent appear on behalf of a principal in court as a pro se party; only the real party in interest—the principal, not a nonlawyer agent—is permitted to appear in court pro se. R. 1:21–1 (a).

has recognized the distinction between an attorney-in-fact and an attorney-at law, and only attorneys-at-law have been permitted to practice in the courts.

*[Ohio State Bar Ass'n v. Jackim, 901 N.E.2d 792, 794 (Ohio 2009).] See also In re Estate of Friedman, 482 N.Y.S.2d 686, 687 (Surr. Ct. NY 1984)* (principal "cannot use a power of attorney as a device to license a layman to act as her attorney in a court of record. To sanction this course would effectively circumvent the stringent licensing requirements of attorneys by conferring upon lay persons the same right to represent others by the use of powers of attorney"); *Ross v. Chakrabarti, 5 A.3d 135, 141 (Ct. Special App. Maryland 2010)* (power of attorney did not give agent right to provide legal advice or appear in court on behalf of principal; to confer such power would be to give a nonlawyer "the right to practice law in this State without meeting the educational, examination, and ethical standards established by the General Assembly and the Court of Appeals"); *In re Conservatorship of Riebel, 625 N. W.2d 480, 482 (Minn. 2001)* (a power of attorney does not authorize a nonlawyer to sign pleadings and appear for principal in court proceedings; "the attorney-in-fact may make decisions concerning litigation for the principal, but a nonlawyer attorney-in-fact is not authorized to act as an attorney to implement those decisions"); *Mosher v. Hiner, 154 P.2d 372, 374 (Ariz. 1944)* (prohibiting attorney-in-fact from filing case in court on behalf of principal; "if an attorney-in-fact could appear in cases in our courts there would be no need for a College of Law at our University"); *Risbeck v. Bon, 885 S. W.2d 749, 750 (Ct. App. Missouri 1994)* (while parties may represent themselves in court, an agent or attorney-in-fact who is not a licensed attorney may not represent another person in court); *State v. MiUiman, 802 N.W. 2d 776, 780 (Ct. Appeals Minn. 2011)* ("a principal of an agent cannot, by executing a power of attorney, authorize the agent to practice law if the agent is not an attorney-at-law"); *Christiansen v. Melinda, 857 P. 2d 345 (Alaska 1993)* (nonlawyer holding a power of attorney cannot bring suit on behalf of another person).

In sum, a nonlawyer holding a power of attorney is not authorized to act as a lawyer licensed in the State of New Jersey, cannot provide legal services or advice, and cannot represent the principal in any judicial or quasi-judicial forum. A nonlawyer who acts in this manner engages in the unauthorized practice of law.

### TODD V. FRANKLIN COLLECTION SERV., INC.
694 F.3d 849 (7th Cir. 2012)

The issue in this appeal is whether the district court properly dismissed the claims purportedly assigned to Michael Todd after determining that he was engaged in the unauthorized practice of law. Todd attempted to purchase claims against Franklin Collection Service, a collection agency, from Vicki Fletcher—who had no relationship to Todd before she assigned her claims to him. He then sued Franklin for violations of the Fair Debt Collection Practices Act, 15 U.S.C. § 1692, and for common law negligence. The district court dismissed the complaint after ruling that the assignment was void because Todd was using it merely to attempt to practice law without a license. * * *

The district court correctly ruled that the assignment was void as against public policy because Todd was using it to attempt to engage in the unauthorized practice of law. Illinois public policy forbids the assignment of legal claims to non-attorneys in order to litigate without a license. As the district court noted, the evidence submitted (the validity of which, again, Todd does not dispute) shows that Todd created a business providing legal advice and repeatedly agreed to purchase claims in order to litigate them in state and federal court. It does not matter whether these claims would be [otherwise] assignable under [under Illinois law] * * * because "a cause of action cannot be assigned if such assignment violates public policy * * *. By attempting to litigate Fletcher's claims through the guise of an assignment, Todd sought to practice law without a license, and therefore the assignment violated public policy. * * *

Accordingly, we AFFIRM the judgment of the district court.

## B. LEGAL ENTITIES AND THE LIKE CANNOT REPRESENT THEMSELVES *PRO SE*

Pro se representation is limited to natural persons. Legally created entities, such as corporations and partnerships, are legal fictions and cannot represent themselves *pro se*. The same rule applies to other, legal creatures such as trusts, estates, and the like.

However, this common statement of the prohibition is, in practice, overbroad. In most states, a more accurate statement is that with some important exceptions, a company cannot be represented in most judicial proceedings by an officer, employee, or other representative of the company who is not a licensed attorney.

The prohibition does not mean that a company's in-house lawyers, who are employees, cannot represent it. They can. The company is not required to retain outside counsel. It means that at least in court, the company's legal representative, whether in-house or outside counsel, must be authorized to practice law in the state.

In many states, the prohibition and exceptions leave considerable space for unlicensed employees to engage in law-related activities for employers without engaging in UPL.

## 1. Applying the General Rule

### SHENANDOAH SALES & SERV., INC. V. ASSESSOR OF JEFFERSON COUNTY
724 S.E.2d 733 (W.Va. 2012)

This is a consolidated appeal of two cases from the Circuit Court of Jefferson County wherein the circuit court dismissed two appeals filed by a corporation, Shenandoah Sales & Services, Inc. ("corporation" or "Shenandoah"), disputing the Jefferson County Assessor's valuation of real estate owned by the corporation. The corporation failed to retain a lawyer to prosecute its appeals to the circuit court, and instead appeared through its vice-president, David C. Tabb. The circuit judge ordered the corporation to appear through a lawyer in circuit court and stated that the court would not accept pleadings or motions from the corporation that were not signed by a lawyer. Despite this order from the circuit court, the corporation failed to retain a lawyer and the circuit court dismissed the corporation's appeals. * * *

Mr. Tabb's . . . argument is that the circuit court erred in ruling that a corporation is required to be represented by a lawyer in a trial court of record. Mr. Tabb [argues] in support of this position that * * * West Virginia does not follow the general rule that a corporation must be represented by a lawyer in a trial court of record. . . .

* * *

By way of background, it is a well-settled legal principle that a corporation must be represented by a lawyer in a court of record.

Courts have offered a number of policy reasons why a corporation must be represented by a lawyer in a court of record. One court observed that, "unlike lay agents of corporations, attorneys are subject to professional rules of conduct and thus amenable to disciplinary action by the court for violations of ethical standards." A lawyer purportedly has the legal expertise necessary to participate in litigation and other proceedings. Conversely, a non-lawyer corporate agent's lack of legal expertise could "frustrate the continuity, clarity and adversity which the judicial process demands." The rule is also intended to preserve the corporation as a legal entity separate from its shareholders. * * *

A corporation is not a natural person. It is an artificial entity created by law. Being an artificial entity it cannot act pro se. It must act in all of its affairs through an agent or representative. Trial Court Rule 4.03 does not contain any provision allowing a corporation to be represented through an agent or representative. Rather, a corporation is required to be "represented by a person admitted to practice before the Supreme Court of Appeals of West Virginia[.]"

Based on all of the foregoing, we conclude that the circuit court did not err when it ruled that Shenandoah was required to be represented by a lawyer in the circuit court. * * *

Mr. Tabb next argues that since Shenandoah is a closely-held corporation, consisting of only two people, the general rule requiring a corporation to be represented by a lawyer in a trial court of record should be relaxed. We find nothing in our jurisprudence exempting a closely-held corporation from the general rule. A number of courts have considered this argument and concluded that closely-held corporations should adhere to the general rule requiring corporations to appear through licensed lawyers. For instance, in Richardson v. Integrity Bible Church, Inc., 897 So.2d 345 (Ala.Civ.App.2004), the court found that a corporation with a sole shareholder and one director could not represent itself in court. In City of Akron v. Hardgrove Enterprises, Inc., 47 Ohio App.2d 196, 353 N.E.2d 628 (1973), the court found that the trial court erred by allowing a small corporation, made up only of a father and son, to represent itself during a trial. The decision to allow the closely-held corporation to represent itself injected "a great deal of error into the trial . . . [t]he net result was a trial replete with improper evidence and collateral issues." Mindful of the problems inherent in allowing non-lawyers to practice law, we decline to exempt Shenandoah from the general rule requiring a corporation to be represented by a lawyer before a court of record.

Based on all of the above, we find that the circuit court did not err when it ruled that the corporation was required to be represented by a lawyer when appearing in the circuit court.

## STEINHAUSEN V. HOMESERVICES OF NEB., INC.
857 N.W.2d 816 (Neb. 2015)

Shelly J. Nitz is a real estate agent affiliated with HomeServices of Nebraska, Inc. (HomeServices). Matthew M. Steinhausen is a home inspector who inspected a house that one of Nitz' clients owned. More than 2 years after the inspection, Nitz sent an e-mail to HomeServices real estate agents and employees stating that Steinhausen was a "[t]otal idiot." Steinhausen, proceeding pro se, sued Nitz and HomeServices, alleging claims of libel, false light invasion of privacy, and tortious interference with a business relationship or expectancy. The district court sustained Nitz' and HomeServices' motions for summary judgment, reasoning that a qualified privilege protected the e-mail and that the evidence failed to show that Steinhausen had a business relationship or expectancy with Nitz or HomeServices. We affirm the court's judgment as it relates to the claims asserted by Steinhausen in his personal capacity. Because Steinhausen's attempt to also prosecute this action for a business entity is a nullity, we reverse, and remand with directions to vacate the judgment as it relates to claims brought for the entity. * * *

HomeServices argues that "Steinhausen's appeal was made on behalf of only one appellant, the business, as opposed to the business and himself individually." HomeServices concedes that Steinhausen could raise on appeal "claims which he holds on behalf of himself individually," but contends that "[h]is Complaint alleges no harm against him personally. . . ." Because Steinhausen is not licensed to practice law in Nebraska, HomeServices concludes that the "appeal is a nullity and should be dismissed." Steinhausen states in his response to the show cause order that he, and not SHI—which he refers to as "the professional identity for individual home inspector Matthew M. Steinhausen"—is the sole party to the appeal. Steinhausen explains that he merely "included his business name on the complaint to clarify his position as the individual owner/operator of Steinhausen Home Inspections, LLC." * * *

Persons not licensed to practice law in Nebraska are prohibited from prosecuting an action or filing papers in the courts of this state on behalf of another. Neb. Rev. Stat. § 7–101 (Reissue 2012) provides:

> [N]o person shall practice as an attorney or counselor at law, or commence, conduct or defend any action or proceeding to which he is not a party, either by using or subscribing his own name, or the name of any other person, or by drawing pleadings or other papers to be signed and filed by a party, in any court of record of this state, unless he has been previously admitted to the bar by order of the Supreme Court of this state. No such paper shall be received or filed in any action or proceeding unless the same bears the endorsement of some admitted attorney, or is drawn, signed, and presented by a party to the action or proceeding.

But, under Neb. Rev. Stat. § 7–110 (Reissue 2012), "[p]laintiffs shall have the liberty of prosecuting, and defendants shall have the liberty of defending, in their proper persons." We have explained that the phrase " 'in their proper persons' " means "in their own persons."

The prohibition of the unauthorized practice of law is not for the benefit of lawyers. Prohibiting the unauthorized practice of law protects citizens and litigants in the administration of justice from the mistakes of the ignorant on the one hand and the machinations of the unscrupulous on the other.

A legal proceeding in which a party is represented by a person not admitted to practice law is a nullity and is subject to dismissal. An individual can represent himself in legal proceedings in his own behalf, but one who is not an attorney cannot represent others. And the rule that a layperson cannot appear in court in a representative capacity cannot be circumvented by subterfuge.

The prohibition on representation by a layperson applies to entities. For example, we have held that a corporation, a partnership, and a trust must be represented by a member of the bar. We have never addressed whether the same rule applies to a limited liability company (LLC), which is "a hybrid of the partnership and corporate forms." But other courts have held that LLC's must also be represented in court by a licensed attorney, including LLC's with a single member.

We conclude that a licensed member of the Nebraska bar must represent an LLC in the courts of this state. An LLC is an entity distinct from its members. It has the capacity to sue and be sued in its own name, but like a corporation, an LLC is an abstraction, and "abstractions cannot appear pro se." Furthermore, the right to conduct business as an LLC confers a significant privilege on its members: limited liability. The Legislature's grace " 'carries with it obligations one of which is to hire a lawyer if you want to sue or defend on behalf of the entity.' "

We decline to recognize an exception for LLC's with a single member. Because Steinhausen is the sole member of SHI, it might be true that no other person's financial interest in SHI would be harmed by Steinhausen's lay representation. But a layperson's lack of professional skills and ethical obligations "imposes undue burdens on opposing parties and the courts," and "[t]hese considerations are just as important when the LLC has only one owner." And the limited liability Steinhausen enjoys is no less limited because he is the sole member of SHI. Put simply, having called into being a new juridical person, Steinhausen cannot ignore SHI's separate existence when it suits him. * * *

## ZAPATA V. MCHUGH
893 N.W.2d 720 (Neb. 2017)

### Nature of Case

The plaintiff, as both an individual and an assignee, filed an action pro se to recover for wrongs allegedly committed against the assignor, a limited liability corporation (LLC). The district court dismissed the action on the grounds that the plaintiff engaged in the unauthorized practice of law and that the pleadings, accordingly, were a nullity. The district court reasoned that an LLC is an entity incapable of self-representation and that the policy reasons requiring representation by an attorney of such entity's interests cannot be circumvented through the assignment of the business entity's cause of action to a layperson. The plaintiff appeals.

### Background

This action was brought pro se by John Zapata. The first pleading in the record is a "Mandatory Disclosure" filed under the caption, "John Zapata, an individual and as an Assignee, Plaintiff, v. Donald McHugh, an individual, et. al., Defendant." The complaint is not in the record, but documents attached to the mandatory disclosure purported to describe $11,100 in lost rent and $21,973.41 in repair costs owed by Lincoln Metal Recycling and Donald McHugh in relation to an address on Saunders Avenue in Lincoln, Nebraska. * * * [T]he claim was based on the fact that McHugh Metal Brokerage, LLC, vacated premises leased to it by Zapata's assignor, Coljo Investments, LLC (Coljo), the owner of the premises. The pretrial order stated that Zapata was "an individual and an assignee" . . . . Zapata alleged that he paid consideration to Coljo in order to collect the alleged debt owed by the defendants. * * *

As to the underlying merits, the parties stated that the legal issues were whether McHugh Metal Brokerage was liable to Zapata or Coljo arising out of the lease agreement, the nature and extent of any unpaid rentals, and the measure of damages for the reasonable cost for repairs to Coljo's premises.

On May 19, 2016, the district court dismissed the action. * * * The court concluded that even if the assignment of any right of action by Coljo to Zapata was effective, Zapata could not proceed pro se with the action on the assigned claims. The court explained that the right to represent oneself pro se * * * does not extend to the representation of any other person or entity. The court cited to several cases setting forth the general propositions that corporate entities cannot be represented pro se and that this rule cannot be circumvented through an assignment of the corporate claims to a pro se plaintiff. * * *

While the district court noted that in this case, Zapata did not list Coljo as a party, it found that such fact was not decisive, stating: "[Zapata] may not escape the fact that what he is attempting to litigate is not his claim. It is the claim of another which has merely been assigned to him. This is true even if [Zapata] is the one who will receive the entirety of any recovery."

As for Zapata's claim that he had a right to proceed pro se under Neb. Rev. Stat. § 25–304,[a] the district court stated that while Zapata had a right to bring an assigned action in his own name, this did not excuse the requirement that an attorney is required when the action derives from a wrong to a corporation. The court concluded that permitting the present action to go forward would unlawfully circumvent § 7–101. The court found the proceedings were a nullity. Zapata appeals. * * *

Analysis

Layperson Cannot Represent LLC

Zapata does not dispute the general rule that a layperson cannot represent a corporation or other distinct business entity existing legally separate from its owner—including an LLC. The rule that such entities may litigate only through a duly licensed attorney is "venerable and widespread." This rule prohibits even presidents, major stockholders, and sole owners from appearing pro se in relation to causes of action involving the entity's status as a business.

---

[a] "An executor, administrator, guardian, trustee of an express trust, a person with whom or in whose name a contract is made for the benefit of another, or a person expressly authorized by statute, may bring an action without joining the person for whose benefit it is prosecuted. Officers may sue and be sued in such name as is authorized by law and official bonds may be sued upon the same way. Assignees of choses in action assigned for the purpose of collection may sue on any claim assigned in writing." [Ed.]

It is well settled that such business entities are artificial persons who cannot appear in their own behalf, but must appear through an agent; thus, they are not their own proper persons who may appear in court without the representation of an attorney. And "because self-representation by unskilled persons usually leads to delay, confusion and other difficulties in the judicial system, the state has no interest in extending the right of self-representation to corporations."

Persons not licensed to practice law in Nebraska are prohibited from prosecuting an action or filing papers in the courts of this state "on behalf of another." Under § 7–101, no such "person" shall practice law in any action or proceeding "to which he is not a party." Neb. Rev. Stat. § 7–110 (Reissue 2012) expands upon the exception to the unauthorized practice of law for persons as a party, stating that plaintiffs shall have the liberty of prosecuting "in their proper persons," which we have said means, " 'in their own persons.' "

We have explained that an entity is an abstraction, not a person. " '[A]bstractions cannot appear pro se.' " Distinct business entities must appear by counsel or not at all.

We applied this rule most recently in *Steinhausen* to affirm the dismissal of causes of action relating to an LLC's status as a business, brought pro se by the sole owner of the LLC. We noted that the prohibition of the unauthorized practice of law protects citizens and litigants in the administration of justice from the mistakes of the ignorant on the one hand and the machinations of the unscrupulous on the other. A layperson's lack of professional skills and ethical obligations imposes undue burdens on opposing parties and the courts.

We reasoned that while an LLC has the capacity to sue and be sued in its own name, the Legislature's grace in conferring the significant privilege of limited liability " ' "carries with it obligations . . . to hire a lawyer . . . to sue or defend on behalf of the entity." ' " This, we said, is no less true for an LLC with a single owner. And we emphasized that "the rule that a layperson cannot appear in court in a representative capacity cannot be circumvented by subterfuge."

May Assignee of Business Entity's Right of Action Proceed With Such Action Pro Se?

We have said that the assignee of a cause of action is the proper and only party who can maintain the suit thereon. But whether the assignee of a corporation's or other distinct legal entity's cause of action may maintain such action pro se is an issue of first impression for our court.

Zapata reasons that if he is the proper party to this action, he must be able to proceed pro se pursuant to §§ 7–101 and 7–110. However, the weight of authority from other jurisdictions is that an assignment does not erase the requirement that the suit arising from the entity's status as a business must be represented by a duly licensed attorney.

In *Shamey v. Hickey*, the court explained that although the action was brought in the name of the assignee, the assignee had essentially assumed the role of a collection agent, and the corporation was thus able to avoid the need for representation by a member of the bar through the device of selling its claim to the assignee. The court stated that it could not sanction such a convenience and remanded the cause with directions to dismiss the action. The court explained that both collection agencies and individuals engage in the unauthorized practice of law when they proceed pro se to recover on claims assigned by a corporation.

Similarly, the court in *Bischoff v. Waldorf* held that an action brought pro se in the name of the layperson assignee, alleging various claims relating to wrongs allegedly committed against the assignor corporation, must be dismissed. The court pointed out the "compelling policy reasons" for the rule requiring representation of distinct business entities by attorneys. These included protection of the court and the public from irresponsible behavior of lay advocates. The court noted that the requirement of attorney representation in such actions also protected the various interests of a corporation's managers, workers, investors, and creditors, which interests may not be aligned with the interests of the layperson assignee making the claim. In light of these important policy reasons for requiring attorney representation of claims relating to corporations, the court held that a nonlawyer may not circumvent those policy reasons through an assignment of corporate claims to an individual.

In *Biggs v. Schwalge*, the court affirmed the dismissal of an action brought in the name of the sole stockholder of a corporation and legal assignee of the corporation's cause of action. The record showed that the stockholder had regularly appeared pro se by virtue of his status as assignee. The stockholder attempted to convince the court of his competence in legal representation despite the fact that he was not an admitted member of the bar. The court held that the stockholder was prohibited from proceeding pro se despite the exception to the prohibition of the practice of law by laypersons that allows plaintiffs and defendants to defend "in their own proper person." The court noted that "[i]t is a compliment to the profession that it should have this irresistible attraction for some laymen. . . ." Nevertheless, "[a]n assignment cannot be used as a subterfuge to enable plaintiff to indulge his overwhelming desire to practice law, without complying with the requirements for admission to the bar."

One case reaching a different result is *Traktman v. City of New York*, wherein the court held that an action by an assignee to recover damages for breach of contract with the assignor corporation did not violate a statute that prohibited a corporation from appearing pro se, despite the fact that the assignment may have been made to circumvent it. The court did not explain its reasoning. This case has been limited by subsequent case law and cited by other jurisdictions as an outlier.

We agree with those cases that hold an assignment of a distinct business entity's cause of action to an assignee who then brings such suit requires that the assignee must be represented by counsel and cannot bring such action pro se. The important policy reasons supporting the rule that corporations and other related legal entities must be represented by an attorney should not be easily circumvented. To permit a distinct business entity to maintain litigation through the device of an assignment would destroy the salutary principle that a corporation cannot act in legal matters or maintain litigation without the benefit of an attorney.

An assignee stands in the shoes of the assignor and accepts it subject to all available defenses. The assignment transfers to an assignee only the rights of the assignor. When an assignee brings suit in his or her own name, the assignee is still bound by the business entity's limitation that any legal action arising out of its interests must be represented by counsel. * * *

## Zapata Engaged In Unauthorized Practice Of Law

Zapata engaged in the practice of law in bringing this action, and he is a "nonlawyer," as defined by Neb. Ct. R. § 3–1002(A). By bringing the assigned claim of Coljo pro se, Zapata engaged in the unauthorized practice of law. We regard the unauthorized practice of law as a serious offense and consider any unauthorized practice a nullity. The district court was correct in dismissing Zapata's action. * * *

## Conclusion

For the foregoing reasons, we affirm the judgment of the district court. * * *

## TEHUTI V. ZIENTZ

2016 WL 1238605, at *1, *report and recommendation adopted,*
2016 WL 1223320 (N.D. Tex. 2016)

The party plaintiffs are identified as Sheik Tehuti as Executor for the Fahamme Nation of Nations a Non-Profit Church and Foundation. The first listed defendant is Michael W. Zientz.

* * *[T]his suit was filed by Sheik Tehuti as "Executor for the Fahamme Nation of Nations a Non-Profit Church and Foundation," and the complaint purports to make claims on behalf of such an entity. Since Sheik Tehuti has not shown that he is a licensed attorney, he may not represent the Fahamme Nation of Nations a Non-Profit Church and Foundation in court. And, an organization cannot proceed pro *se* in this litigation.

## MAYER V. LINDENWOOD FEMALE COLL.

453 S.W.3d 307 (Mo. App. 2014)

D. Wayne Mayer, acting in his capacity as trustee of the John J. Stock Trust, and Ronald A. Nolle, acting in his capacity as trustee of the Oscar A. Nolle Trust (collectively, "Trusts"), appeal the trial court's judgment in favor of Lindenwood University on its action for a judgment declaring that the proposed redevelopment of the Trusts' property would not constitute a breach of the lease or waste. The Trusts also appeal the trial court's judgment in favor Lindenwood on the Trusts' action seeking damages for breach of the lease and waste. Because Mr. Mayer and Mr. Nolle, who are not licensed attorneys, filed the notice of appeal as trustees on behalf of the Trusts, and thereby engaged in the unauthorized practice of law, we dismiss the appeal. * * *

Missouri limits the practice of law, both in and out of its courts, to "persons with specific qualifications and duly licensed as attorneys." Although our courts have struggled to formulate a "precise and comprehensive definition of the practice of law," it is clear that "the act of appearing in court to assert or defend claims on behalf of another lies at the very heart of the practice of law." Because Missouri prohibits the unauthorized practice of law, "actions constituting the unauthorized practice of law must not be recognized or given effect." "The normal effect of a representative's unauthorized practice of law is to dismiss the cause or treat the particular actions taken by the representative as a nullity." Importantly, our courts have held that a notice of appeal filed on behalf of another by a nonattorney is null and void.

Missouri courts have not directly addressed the question of whether a nonattorney trustee representing the interests of a trust engages in the unauthorized practice of law when he or she appears pro se. However, we find the Supreme Court's recent decision in Naylor [Senior Citizens Hous., LP v. Side Const. Co., 423 S.W.3d 238 (Mo. 2014)] instructive. There, the nonattorney managing partner of two partnerships signed and filed a petition seeking damages in negligence on behalf of himself and the partnerships. The defendants moved to dismiss the action on the grounds that the partner who signed the petition could not represent the partnerships because he was not a licensed attorney. The partner and partnerships responded through a licensed attorney, but did not file or seek leave to file a "corrected" signature page for the original petition pursuant to Rule 55.03(a). The trial court dismissed the partnerships' claims on the grounds that the nonattorney partner's filing of the petition constituted the unauthorized practice of law.

The *Naylor* Court affirmed the trial court's dismissal of the partnerships' claims and held that, unlike a natural person who is generally entitled to appear and assert claims on his or her own behalf in Missouri courts, a statutory entity, such as a corporation or limited partnership, may appear only through a licensed attorney. The Court reasoned that "[w]hen an individual appears pro se, i.e., for himself, that person is not engaging in the practice of law because he is not representing **another** in court (emphasis in original)." In contrast, a statutory entity or "legal fiction" cannot "be anywhere or do anything— including, but not limited to, appearing in court—unless some individual does so on its behalf." Such an individual, acting on behalf of the statutory entity "by definition is 'representing another' in court and, therefore, necessarily is engaging in the practice of law." Because Missouri courts restrict the practice of law to licensed attorneys, a statutory entity's representative must be a licensed attorney.

The Trusts assert that the rule requiring statutory entities to appear only through counsel does not apply to trusts because "a trust is unlike a statutory business entity, because a trustee has a special . . . interest in the trust." Under Missouri law, "[t]he trustee is the legal owner of the trust property, in which the beneficiaries have equitable ownership." In contrast to a corporation, a trust is not a legal entity and lacks the capacity to sue or be sued.

Even though a trust is not considered a legal entity, "in practice trustees act on behalf of their trusts and are sued as trust representatives." Pursuant to Missouri law governing a trustee's duty to administer the trust, "the trustee shall administer the trust in good faith, in accordance with its terms and purposes and the interests of the beneficiaries." Additionally, Missouri Revised Statute Section 456.8–802 mandates that "[a] trustee shall administer the trust solely in the interests of the beneficiaries."

Numerous courts have held that a non-attorney trustee may not appear pro se in a representative capacity. Although it has no precedential value, we find persuasive the reasoning of In re

Guetersloh, 326 S.W.3d 737 (Tex.App.2010). In that case, James Guetersloh was trustee and beneficiary of a trust. The other beneficiaries filed suit against Guetersloh, in his capacity as trustee, seeking termination of the trust and distribution of the trust property. When Guetersloh, acting pro se, filed an answer and motion to transfer, the trial court sua sponte "found that the trustee of a trust cannot appear in court pro se because to do so would amount to the unauthorized practice of law."

Guetersloh did not obtain legal counsel, but instead sought a writ of mandamus ordering the trial court to allow him to appear pro se on behalf of the trust because, as trustee, "he is the actual party to the suit[.]" The Texas Court of Appeals held that the trial court did not err in prohibiting Guetersloh, in his capacity as trustee, from appearing without legal representation "because in that role he is appearing in a representative capacity rather than in propia persona." The court explained: "Because of the nature of trusts, the actions of the trustee affect the trust estate and therefore affect the interests of the beneficiaries." Accordingly, "if a non-attorney trustee appears in court of behalf of the trust, he or she necessarily represents the interests of others, which amounts to the unauthorized practice of law."

In the instant case, Mr. Mayer and Mr. Nolle, as trustees, managed the Property for the benefit of the Trusts' beneficiaries. Indeed, Mr. Mayer testified, that "as a trustee, that's one of my responsibilities is to—to the grandchildren that I represent. . . . I represent thirteen grandchildren who are on my side. . . ." As trustees, Mr. Mayer and Mr. Nolle did not represent their own interests alone, but rather the interests of all the Trusts' beneficiaries. Thus, when the Trustees appeared on behalf of the Trusts, they were necessarily representing the interests of others in court, which constitutes the unauthorized practice of law. * * *

The Trusts' appeal is dismissed.

### KELLY V. SAINT FRANCIS MED. CTR.
889 N.W.2d 613 (Neb. 2017)

*[In this case, which is reprinted in Chapter VII, infra, Ann Kelly filed, in her own behalf and on behalf of the estate of Stephen Kelly, a pro se wrongful death action against Saint Francis*

*Medical Center (Saint Francis), Dr. Jeff S. Burwell, and other "fictitious entities." Saint Francis and Burwell filed a motion to dismiss, alleging that Ann was engaged in the unauthorized practice of law. The court had to determine whether the filing of the pro se complaint by Ann on behalf of the estate was the unauthorized practice of law.]*

### 2. Exceptions and Limits on the Rule

#### KY. ST. S. CT. R. 3.020.
##### PRACTICE OF LAW DEFINED

The practice of law is any service rendered involving legal knowledge or legal advice, whether of representation, counsel or advocacy in or out of court, rendered in respect to the rights, duties, obligations, liabilities, or business relations of one requiring the services. But nothing herein shall prevent any natural person not holding himself out as a practicing attorney from drawing any instrument to which he is a party without consideration unto himself therefor. ***An appearance in the small claims division of the district court by a person who is an officer of or who is regularly employed in a managerial capacity by a corporation or partnership which is a party to the litigation in which the appearance is made shall not be considered as unauthorized practice of law*** (emphasis added).

#### JAMES V. TOP OF THE HILL RENOVATIONS
61 N.E.3d 734 (Ohio 2016)

[A]ppellant argues that the trial court erred when it determined that appellant, as a non-attorney, had engaged in the unauthorized practice of law by filing a motion for relief from judgment on behalf of [his business]. We agree.

Under Ohio law, a corporation can maintain litigation or appear in court only through an attorney admitted to the practice of law and may not do so through an officer of the corporation or some other appointed agent. The trial court determined that because Top of the Hill is a corporation and Hill is not an attorney, Hill engaged in the unauthorized practice of law when he filed the July 17, 2015 motion on behalf of Top of the Hill. The record, however, does not support the trial court's determination that Top of the Hill is a corporation.

A "corporation" is defined generally as "[a]n entity (usu[ally] a business) having authority under law to act as a single person distinct from the shareholders who own it and having rights to issue stock and exist indefinitely." Conversely, the Supreme Court of Ohio has defined a "sole proprietorship" as an individual doing business under a fictitious name while remaining "one person, personally liable for all his obligations."

In the affidavit of mechanics' lien and throughout this litigation, Hill has identified himself as "owner" of Top of the Hill. Hill has never referred to himself by any title or designation that would suggest that he is an officer, agent, employee, or shareholder of a corporation known as Top of the Hill. Additionally, in referring to Top of the Hill, neither party has included a corporate designation or any other designation identifying Top of the Hill as a legal entity separate and apart from its owner.

On this record, we find that the trial court erred when it determined that Top of the Hill is a corporation having a separate legal identity from its owner, Hill. As a consequence, the trial court erred when it determined that Hill had engaged in the unauthorized practice of law when he filed the . . . motion.
* * *

### AULISIO V. BANCROFT
230 Cal.App.4th 1516, 1519–20, 179 Cal.Rptr.3d 408, 410–11 (2014)

Anthony Aulisio, Jr., appeals from a jury verdict that found defendants, consisting of his homeowners association's management company (Optimum Professional Property Management and Debra Kovach), the patrol service it employed (BLB Enterprises, Inc., doing business as Patrol One, and Bill Bancroft), and a towing company (PD Transport, doing business as Southside Towing, and John Vach), did not wrongfully tow and convert his Jeep vehicle, or convert the personal property it contained. CAAJ Leasing Trust (CAAJ), which Aulisio created as sole grantor, trustee, and trust beneficiary, owned legal title to the Jeep and also appeals. Specifically, CAAJ appeals the trial court's ruling at the outset of trial that CAAJ "can't participate in the proceedings" with Aulisio appearing in propria persona as the trust's sole trustee and sole beneficiary.

The trial court relied on precedent that an executor or personal representative may not appear in propria persona in court proceedings outside the probate context on behalf of a decedent's estate because representing another person or entity's interest in a lawsuit constitutes the unauthorized practice of law. Similarly, in actions involving the trust corpus, a trustee generally may not appear in propria persona " 'because in this capacity [he or she] would be representing *interests of others* and would therefore be engaged in the unauthorized practice of law.' " But if a sole trustee is also the trust's sole settlor and beneficiary, the rationale of these cases ceases to apply: no interests are at stake except those of one person.

The purpose of the State Bar Act and its prohibition against the unauthorized practice of law (§ 6125) is to protect the public, the courts, and litigants who rely on attorneys by " 'assur[ing] the competency of those performing [legal] services.' " It may be advantageous to a litigant, the courts, the public, and even lawyers to hire legal representation; indeed, the adage that "a self-represented attorney has a fool for a client" is too often proven true. But nothing in the State Bar Act since its enactment in 1927 has abrogated the right to represent one's own interests in court. That right of self-determination applies equally to nonlawyers like Aulisio.

Consequently, we conclude that a sole trustee of a revocable living trust who is also the sole settlor and beneficiary of the trust assets he or she is charged to protect does not appear in court proceedings concerning the trust in a representative capacity. Instead, he or she properly acts in propria persona and does not violate the bar against practicing law without a license. (§ 6125.) We therefore reverse the judgment as to CAAJ, and remand so Aulisio may appear in propria persona to assert his interest as the sole beneficial owner of the Jeep as a trust asset. As we explain, however, we affirm the judgment against Aulisio in his individual capacity concerning his personal property in the Jeep.

## BASS V. LEATHERWOOD

788 F.3d 228, 229–31 (6th Cir. 2015)

Karen P. Mobley and Lawrence Everett Reed filed a pro se complaint on behalf of the Karen Mobley Gunn Estate and the Lawrence Everett Reed Estate, respectively. They contended that various financial institutions fraudulently transferred real estate properties in Shelby County, Tennessee, and failed to follow proper procedures for selling properties encumbered by outstanding liens. The district court dismissed the complaint on the ground that a nonattorney cannot appear in court on behalf of an artificial entity such as an estate, even though Mobley and Reed claimed that they were the sole beneficiaries of their respective estates. On appeal, the financial institutions have again moved to dismiss the case for lack of jurisdiction because Mobley and Reed each signed the notice of appeal as the "Authorized Representative" of the estates.

Federal law allows parties to "plead and conduct their own cases personally or by counsel." In 1997, the Second Circuit interpreted this language to impose a barrier on pro se litigants wishing to appear on behalf of "another person or entity," including a corporation, a partnership, a minor child, or "an estate . . . when the estate has beneficiaries or creditors other than the litigant." The court reasoned that "appearance pro se denotes (in law latin) appearance for one's self," but "when an estate has beneficiaries or creditors other than the administratrix or executrix, the action cannot be described as the litigant's own." This court adopted the Second Circuit's reasoning in *Shepherd v. Wellman,* 313 F.3d 963 (6th Cir.2002), prohibiting a litigant from proceeding pro se "because he is not the sole beneficiary of the decedent's estate."

Although the above cases imply that the sole beneficiary of an estate without creditors may represent the estate pro se, this court has never resolved the issue directly. We now hold that he or she may do so. "The rule against non-lawyer representation 'protects the rights of those before the court' by preventing an ill-equipped layperson from squandering the rights of the party he purports to represent." The purpose of the rule, then, is to protect third parties. But that purpose has no role to play when

the only person affected by a nonattorney's representation is the
nonattorney herself.

The Second Circuit has reached the same conclusion. "[T]he
administrator and sole beneficiary of an estate with no
creditors," it has concluded, "may appear *pro se* on behalf of the
estate." *Guest v. Hansen,* 603 F.3d 15, 21 (2d Cir. 2010). Writing
for the court, Judge Calabresi reasoned:

> It is only a legal fiction that assigns the sole
> beneficiary's claims to a paper entity—the estate—
> rather than the beneficiary himself. Accordingly, *pro se*
> representation is consistent with our jurisprudence
> both on the right to self-representation and on the
> prohibition of appearances by non-attorneys on behalf
> of others. Because the administrator is the only party
> affected by the disposition of the suit, he is, in fact,
> appearing solely on his own behalf. This being so, the
> dangers that accompany lay lawyering are outweighed
> by the right to self-representation. . . .

In this case, the appellants have stipulated that they are the sole
beneficiaries of their respective estates and that their estates
lack creditors. The appellees have not contested either point.
Although the record does not reveal why the appellants are
litigating on behalf of estates and not on behalf of themselves as
individuals, § 1654 does not bar this appeal.

The appellees insist that we have misread *Shepherd,* which in
their view held that non-attorneys may not represent *any*
artificial entities, including estates in which the pro se litigants
are the sole beneficiaries. The district court read the case the
same way. It is true that, under longstanding tradition, "a
*corporation* can only appear by attorney," perhaps because by
definition another person—natural or artificial—is involved.
But we have never extended the logic of this rule to estates. In
*Shepherd* and similar cases we held only that § 1654 "does not
permit plaintiffs to appear *pro se* where interests other than
their own are at stake,"—a situation distinct from the one here.

For these reasons, we deny the appellees' motion.

## HARKNESS V. UNEMPLOYMENT COMP. BD. OF REVIEW
### 920 A.2d 162 (Pa. 2007)

In this appeal . . . we consider whether an employer may be represented at an unemployment compensation hearing before a referee of the Unemployment Compensation Board of Review by an individual who is not an attorney. A majority of the Commonwealth Court determined that an employer may not be so represented. We respectfully disagree, and thus, for the reasons set forth below, reverse the order of the Commonwealth Court. * * *

The Pennsylvania Constitution vests with our Court the exclusive authority to regulate the practice of law, which includes the power to define what constitutes the practice of law. What constitutes the practice of law, however, is not capable of a comprehensive definition. For this reason, our Court has not attempted to provide an all-encompassing statement of what activities comprise the practice of law. Thus, we have determined what constitutes the practice of law on a case-by-case basis.

While our Court has addressed the question of what constitutes the practice of law on an individualized basis, we have made clear that paramount to the inquiry is consideration of the public interest. Consideration of the public interest has two related aspects: protection of the public and prudent regulation so as not to overburden the public good.

Regarding the protection of the public, then Justice, later Chief Justice Stern perhaps best summarized this aspect of the Court's concern in *Shortz* [Shortz et al. v. Farrell, 327 Pa. 81, 193 A. 20, 21 (1937)], "While in order to acquire the education necessary to gain admission to the bar and thereby become eligible to practice law, one is obliged to 'scorn delights, and live laborious days,' the object of the legislation forbidding practice to laymen is not to secure to lawyers a monopoly, however deserved, but, by preventing the intrusion of inexpert and unlearned persons in the practice of law, to assure to the public adequate protection in the pursuit of justice, than which society knows no loftier aim."

While the public interest is certainly served by the protection of the public, it is also achieved by not burdening the public by too broad a definition of the practice of law, resulting in the overregulation of the public's affairs. As stated by our Court in *Dauphin Cty.* [Bar Ass'n v. Mazzacaro, 465 Pa. 545, 351 A.2d 229 (1976)],

> "The threads of legal consequences often weave their way through even casual contemporary interactions. There are times, of course, when it is clearly within the ken of lay persons to appreciate the legal problems and consequences involved in a given situation and the factors which should influence necessary decisions. No public interest would be advanced by requiring these lay judgments to be made exclusively by lawyers. . . . Each case must turn on a careful analysis of the particular judgment involved and the expertise which must be brought to bear on its exercise."

Thus, our Court, in determining what constitutes the practice of law, must keep the public interest of primary concern, both in terms of the protection of the public as well as in ensuring that the regulation of the practice of law is not so strict that the public good suffers.

When considering the public interest, our Court has focused on the character of the activities at issue. In *Shortz,* our Court set forth three broad categories of activities that may constitute the practice of law: (1) the instruction and advising of clients in regard to the law so that they may pursue their affairs and be informed as to their rights and obligations; (2) the preparation of documents for clients requiring familiarity with legal principles beyond the ken of ordinary laypersons; and (3) the appearance on behalf of clients before public tribunals in order that the attorney may assist the deciding official in the proper interpretation and enforcement of the law.

More recently, our Court expressed that the practice of law is implicated by the holding out of oneself to the public as competent to exercise legal judgment and the implication that he or she has the technical competence to analyze legal problems and the requisite character qualifications to act in a representative capacity. Thus, the character of the actions taken by the individual in question is a significant factor in the determination of what constitutes the practice of law.

Finally, we have cautioned that the tribunal before which the individual is before is not determinative in deciding what comprises the practice of law, viz., "whether or not the tribunal is called a 'court' or the controversy 'litigation'. . . ." Yet, the nature of the proceedings in which the individual is acting is not to be wholly discounted. Indeed, the nature of such proceedings certainly is relevant in determining the needs of the public, both in terms of protection and overregulation.

Cognizant that a determination of the practice of law is made on a case-by-case basis, focusing primarily on protection of the public and the public weal, and in doing so, considering the character of the activities engaged in, as well as the nature of the proceedings at issue, we turn to the facts at issue in this appeal.

First, we find that the activities performed by an employer representative in an unemployment compensation proceeding are largely routine and primarily focus upon creating a factual basis on which a referee will award or deny unemployment compensation benefits. As a general proposition, providers of services such as the management of payroll, tax, and employee benefit operations will also attend unemployment compensation proceedings to provide appropriate personnel records and other documents and assist in the fact-finding process so as to aid the referee in his or her determination. These individuals are more akin to facilitators rather than legal practitioners. The purpose of their presence is not to engage in the analysis of complex and intricate legal problems, but rather as an adjunct to the employer (or claimant) in offering their respective viewpoints concerning the events at issue.

In terms of the three broad categories of activities that our Court has suggested may constitute the practice of law, there is scant advising as to legal rights and responsibilities and few instances of the preparation of documents requiring familiarity with legal principles. Furthermore, while as noted by the Commonwealth Court, non-attorney representatives certainly appear on behalf of an employer before public tribunals, their role in assisting the deciding official in the proper interpretation and enforcement of the law is lacking. As noted above, the role of the non-attorney representative is more as a facilitator rather than an advocate engaging in an analysis of the law.

Second, we take note of the nature of unemployment compensation proceedings. The Unemployment Compensation Law is remedial in nature. The fundamental purpose of the Law is to provide economic security to those unemployed through no fault of their own. * * *

To this end, the unemployment compensation system must operate quickly, simply, and efficiently. The proceedings are "by design, brief and informal in nature." Thus, the claims for benefits are not intended to be intensely litigated. Unemployment compensation proceedings are not trials. The rules of evidence are not mandated; there is no pre-hearing discovery; the parties have no right to a jury trial; indeed there is no requirement that the referee be a lawyer. Also, and importantly, there are only minimal amounts of money in controversy. Issues arising in these matters are generally questions of fact not requiring complex legal analysis. Requiring employers to be represented by counsel will not only undermine the informal, speedy and low cost nature of these proceedings, it may dissuade many employers from defending claims for benefits leading to the possibility of an unwarranted drain on the system.

Simply stated, the character of the activities performed by representatives at unemployment hearings coupled with the informal nature of these proceedings, the minimal amounts at issue, and the long history of participation by non-lawyer representatives suggest that the public does not need the protection that serves as the basis for classifying certain activities to constitute the practice of law and that indeed, finding non-lawyer representatives to be engaging in the practice of law by acting in unemployment compensation proceedings would impose an unnecessary burden on the public.[5]

---

[5] These activities and type of proceedings can be contrasted with the situation in *Shortz*, relied upon by the Commonwealth Court in this matter, in which our Court found non-lawyer representation during workers' compensation proceedings to constitute the practice of law. The formality and complexity of workers' compensation proceedings, however, stand in sharp contrast to the informal, straightforward proceedings that serve as the vehicle to determine unemployment compensation benefits. The hallmarks of

Based upon the above considerations, we hold that a non-attorney representing an employer before a referee of the Board is not engaging in the practice of law. * * *

## VT. STAT. ANN. TIT. 11A, § 3.02.
### GENERAL POWERS [OF BUSINESS CORPORATIONS]

Unless its articles of incorporation provide otherwise, every corporation has perpetual duration and succession in its corporate name and has the same powers as an individual to do all things necessary and convenient to carry out its business and affairs, including without limitation power:

(1) to sue and be sued, complain and defend in its corporate name. A court or other adjudicative body shall permit a corporation to appear through a nonattorney representative if:

(A) the proposed nonattorney representative is authorized to represent the corporation;

(B) the proposed nonattorney representative demonstrates adequate legal knowledge and skills to represent the organization without unduly burdening the opposing party or the court; and

(C) the proposed nonattorney representative shares a common interest with the corporation. * * *

## RESTATEMENT (THIRD) OF THE LAW GOVERNING LAWYERS § 4

Comment: * * *

e. Unauthorized practice for and by entities. A limitation on pro se representation (see Comment d) found in many jurisdictions is that a corporation cannot represent itself in litigation and must accordingly always be represented by counsel. The rule applies, apparently, only to appearances in litigated matters. Thus a nonlawyer officer of a

---

workers' compensation proceedings include pre-trial investigation and discovery, the filings of pleadings, testimony by experts, and the potentiality of significant benefit amounts at issue. None of these hallmarks, however, are present in unemployment compensation proceedings.

corporation may permissibly draft legal documents, negotiate complex transactions, and perform other tasks for the employing organization, even if the task is typically performed by lawyers for organizations. With respect to litigation, several jurisdictions except representation in certain tribunals, such as landlord-tenant and small-claims courts and in certain administrative proceedings (see Comment c hereto), where incorporation (typically of a small owner-operated business) has little bearing on the prerogative of the person to provide self-representation. * * *

## GARDNER V. N.C. STATE BAR
341 S.E.2d 517, 520 (N.C. 1986)

The practice of law is defined in North Carolina as "performing any legal service for any other person, firm or corporation, with or without compensation. . . ." N.C.G.S. § 84–2.1 (1985). A corporation may not perform legal services for others; N.C.G.S. § 84–5 forbids it to do so. * * * [However,] [w]hen a corporation's employees perform legal services for the corporation in the course of their employment, their acts have been held to be the acts of the corporation so that in law, the corporation itself is performing the acts [for itself, not others] . . . [and, to the extent provided by] State v. Pledger, 257 N.C. 634, 127 S.E.2d 337 [1962][,] [the employees themselves are not engaging in the practice of law].

## STATE V. PLEDGER
127 S.E.2d 337 (N.C. 1962)

Defendant is charged in eight criminal cases . . . with unauthorized practice of law in violation of G.S. § 84–4.

The indictments allege that defendant prepared directly 'and through others' eight deeds of trust for other persons and corporations, he not being a member of the North Carolina Bar and not being licensed to practice as an attorney at law. The beneficiary in the deeds of trust referred to in the indictments in cases 5773, 5774 and 5775 is Designed for Living, Inc. The beneficiary in the deeds of trust referred to in the indictments in cases 5776, 5777, 5778, 5779 and 5780 is Century Home Builders, Inc.

The evidence tends to show: Century Home Builders, Inc., is engaged in the sale and construction of 'shell' homes. Its principal office is in Lumberton, North Carolina, and it has a branch office in New Bern. At the times mentioned in the indictment defendant was its employee and was in charge of the New Bern office. He solicited sales, and when time sales were made deeds of trust were prepared by him or under his direction for his corporate employer. Printed forms were used and preparation consisted in inserting in blank spaces the names of the parties to the instrument, the description of the land, and the terms of the instruments. Defendant also saw to the execution, acknowledgment and recordation of the deeds of trust.

The eight deeds of trust referred to in the indictment were prepared by defendant or under his supervision by his secretary. He is not a member of the North Carolina Bar and is not a licensed attorney at law. Designed for Living, Inc., has its principal office in Atlanta, Georgia.

The cases were consolidated for trial. Defendant pleaded not guilty in each case. The jury returned a verdict of 'Guilty as charged.' * * *

Defendant appeals.

**Moore**, Justice. It is charged that defendant engaged in unauthorized practice of law. The bills of indictment are grounded on G.S. § 84–4 which, in pertinent part, provides: '* * * (I)t shall be unlawful for any person or association of persons except members of the Bar, for or without a fee or consideration, to * * * prepare for another person, firm or corporation, any * * * legal document.'

A deed of trust is a legal document. Practice of law embraces the preparation of legal documents and contracts by which legal rights are secured. G.S. § 84–2.1.

The evidence for the State tends to show that the deeds of trust in question were prepared by defendant directly or under his supervision, and that he is not a member of the North Carolina Bar and is not a licensed attorney at law. The crucial question on this appeal is: Did he prepare the documents 'for another person, firm or corporation' within the intent and meaning of the statute?

It was not the purpose and intent of the statute to make unlawful all activities of lay persons which come within the general definition of practicing law. G.S. § 84–2.1. Any adult person desiring to do so may prepare his own will. A person involved in litigation, though not a lawyer, may represent himself and either defend or prosecute the action or proceeding in a tribunal or court, even in Supreme Court, and may prepare and file pleadings and other papers in connection with the litigation.

A person, firm or corporation having a primary interest, not merely an incidental interest, in a transaction, may prepare legal documents necessary to the furtherance and completion of the transaction without violating G.S. § 84–4. The statute was not enacted for the purpose of conferring upon the legal profession an absolute monopoly in the preparation of legal documents; its purpose is for the better security of the people against incompetency and dishonesty in an area of activity affecting general welfare.

Automobile, furniture, and appliance dealers prepare conditional sale contracts. Banks prepare promissory notes, drafts and letters of credit. Many lending institutions prepare deeds of trust and chattel mortgages. Owner-vendors and purchasers of land prepare deeds. Almost all business concerns prepare contracts in one form or another. All such activities are legal and do not violate the statute so long as the actor has a primary interest in the transaction. For example, the grantor or the beneficiary in a deed of trust may prepare the instrument with impunity if the latter is extending credit to the former; the named trustee may not do so, for his interest is only incidental. A corporation can act only through its officers, agents and employees. A person who, in the course of his employment by a corporation, prepares a legal document in connection with a business transaction in which the corporation has a primary interest, the corporation being authorized by law and its charter to transact such business, does not violate the statute, for his act in so doing is the act of the corporation in the furtherance of its own business.

Century Home Builders, Inc., is in the business of selling houses. In this connection it extends credit to purchasers and takes deeds of trust as security. Defendant at the times in question was its employee and manager of its New Bern office, and was charged with the prosecution of its business. His acts in preparing deeds of trust, to secure the indebtedness of buyers incurred in the purchase of houses from Century, were not violative of G.S. § 84–4. As to the defendant, Century was not 'another * * * corporation.' In cases 5776, 5777, 5778, 5779 and 5780, the court below erred in denying defendant's motion for nonsuit.

Designed for Living, Inc., is a foreign corporation with its principal office in Atlanta, Georgia. In his argument in Supreme Court defendant's counsel stated that this corporation is a finance company. The evidence in the record, considered as a whole, permits the inference that defendant was not such agent or employee of Designed for Living, Inc., as to allow him to prepare deeds of trust on its behalf without being liable to the penalty of the statute. As to defendant, this corporation was 'another * * * corporation' within the meaning of the statute, so far as the present record discloses. In cases 5773, 5774 and 5775 the motion for nonsuit was properly overruled. * * *

CHAPTER VI

# WHO REGULATES UPL?

■ ■ ■

QUINTIN JOHNSTONE, UNAUTHORIZED PRACTICE OF LAW
AND THE POWER OF STATE COURTS: DIFFICULT
PROBLEMS AND THEIR RESOLUTION
39 Willamette L. Rev. 795, 823–30 (2003)

## II. The Scope of State Court Legal Power Over Unauthorized Law Practice

The source of legal power of each branch of state government over any matters, unauthorized law practice matters included, is the state's constitution. What power is allocated to each branch often depends on interpretations of the amorphous constitutional concept of separation of powers and how that concept is amplified and interpreted in each state. Unlike the Federal Constitution, most state constitutions have express separation of powers provisions, usually phrased in very general terms. Ten states have no explicit separation of powers clause in their constitution, but separation of powers is inferred from the constitutional power allocation to each branch, analogous to the approach taken in interpreting the United States Constitution. Most state constitutions are much more detailed than the United States Constitution, and some states supplement separation of powers as the source of judicial power by adding more explicit provisions.

Courts often rely on the concept of inherent power in determining the scope of their authority. In very general terms, this power includes the authority to carry out the courts' essential operations and to fulfill their responsibilities. More particularly, this includes the power over court governance, implementation of adjudication, logistical support of the courts and enforcement procedures. Some judicial opinions expressly declare that the inherent power concept is constitutionally based and use the concept to interpret and delimit the state constitution's separation of powers requirement as applied to the courts. In many other judicial opinions in which the courts rely on the inherent power concept in their reasoning, no reference to the concept's constitutional source is made, apparently assuming that it is constitutionally based. But whatever the conceptual reasoning applied, it is generally recognized that state courts have the last word in interpreting their state's constitution.

The latest interpretation of a state constitution's meaning by the state's supreme court is considered binding law. Some may consciously violate what the court's interpretation requires. Others may try to have the interpretation reversed by subsequent court action, but the final interpretive authority of the state supreme court as to the meaning of the state's constitution is rarely challenged. But can courts exert their power only through litigated case determinations? Or can they also do so through legislative-type rules issued independently of any litigated matter? Quite universally courts, in some states only the state's highest court, have the power to adopt court rules on at least some aspects of court administration, practice and procedure. Judicial rule-making is expressly authorized by the state constitutions in a majority of states and, in others, is an incident of other judicial constitutional powers. The legislative-type rule-making power of state courts is separate and distinct from the courts' power to declare authoritative rules as binding legal principles when deciding cases in litigation before them. Unauthorized law practice is one of the many matters expressly dealt with by court rules in a number of states.

Although state courts obviously have the power to determine what is and is not the unauthorized practice of law, to what extent do they share this power with the other two branches of government? There are several possible answers to this question with authoritative support in prevailing law in at least some states. One is that the courts' power over unauthorized practice of law matters is exclusive. Only the courts have law-making power in this field of law. This position has been adopted in a few states. Another, the majority position, is that the power is concurrent, shared by all three governmental branches, but that the courts have ultimate power. The courts' determinations prevail if their position differs from that of one of the other branches. A third position, and one that also has authoritative support in a few states, is that power over unauthorized practice of law matters is concurrent but that the courts' power is subordinate to that of either of the other two branches when their positions differ. However, the position of some states on the power allocation issue is unclear, either because there are no reported opinions on the matter or because reported opinions on the issue are vague or inconclusive. In justifying their declared position on court power over unauthorized law practice matters, whatever that position is, state courts typically have relied on brief references to state constitutional texts as to judicial authority or have referred in general terms to their inherent powers. They rarely, if ever, have asserted policy arguments to further justify whatever power position they adopt.

### IN RE TOWN OF LITTLE COMPTON
37 A.3d 85, 88 (R.I. 2012)

"It has long been the law of this state that the definition of the practice of law and the determination concerning who may practice law is exclusively within the province of this court * * *." We recognize that the General Assembly has, from time to time, enacted statutes that to some extent codified and regulated the practice of law with little interference by this Court. Although this legislative effort may be beneficial in protecting our citizenry from unqualified persons promoting themselves as skilled practitioners of the law, we pause to reiterate that the Supreme Court reserves to itself the ultimate and exclusive authority to determine what does and does not constitute the practice of law within the state and to regulate those people qualified to engage in the practice.

### BINKLEY V. AM. EQUITY MORTG., INC.
447 S.W.3d 194, 196–97 (Mo. 2014)

Missouri restricts the practice of law solely to licensed attorneys to "protect the public from being advised or represented in legal matters by incompetent or unreliable persons." This Court, as the "sole arbiter of what constitutes the practice of law," is the final authority on issues of who may practice law or engage in law business in this state. While there are statutes concerning the "practice of law" and "law business," such as sections 484.010 and 484.020, these statutes "are merely in aid of, and do not supersede or detract from, the power of the judiciary to define and control the practice of law." These statutes do, however, provide guidance for the courts in determining the scope of the practice of law.

### CAMPBELL V. ASBURY AUTO., INC.
381 S.W.3d 21 (Ark. 2011)

[*Part of this case is reprinted in Chapter II of this book, supra. There, the issue highlighted is whether a car dealer, Asbury, engaged in the authorized practice of law by charging Plaintiffs, including Campbell, an illegal document preparation fee for preparing the vehicle installment contract (a legal instrument) for the purchase of a vehicle. The court answered yes. Here, the issue is whether the consequences can include liability under the Arkansas Deceptive Trade Practices Act ("ADTPA"). Asbury essentially argued that applying this statute, which is a legislative remedy, is unconstitutional in violation of the judicial branch's exclusive power to regulate the practice of law.*]

Campbell argues that the circuit court erred in granting Asbury summary judgment on the class's ADTPA claim involving the documentary fee. He contends that the circuit court's [was wrong in holding] that the legislature cannot prohibit nonlawyer corporations from providing legal services. He urges this court to * * * hold that * * * the ADTPA [is not] inapplicable to car dealers and nonlawyer corporations rendering legal services.

Asbury responds that the circuit court [was correct], arguing that the ADTPA does not provide a private right of action for the unauthorized practice of law. It claims that only this court may regulate the practice of law, authorized or unauthorized, and, therefore, the General Assembly may not create a statutory cause of action, such as under the ADTPA, for the unauthorized practice of law.

[W]e must determine whether the General Assembly is precluded from creating a cause of action for the unauthorized practice of law by a nonlawyer, such as under the ADTPA. We hold that it is not.

Amendment 28 of the Arkansas Constitution provides that "[t]he Supreme Court shall make rules regulating the practice of law and the professional conduct of attorneys at law," and this court has recognized that amendment 28 "put to rest for all time any possible question about the power of the courts to regulate the practice of law in the state." We have also recognized, however, that "[s]tatutes which provide a penalty for unauthorized practice of law by a nonresident of the forum state have been held to be cumulative to the powers of the courts to punish."

Statutes relating to the practice of law are merely in aid of, but do not supersede or detract from the power of the judicial department to define, regulate, and control the practice of law, and the legislative branch may not, in any way, hinder, interfere with, restrict, or frustrate the powers of the courts. Moreover, we have "chosen to recognize and apply certain statutes which are not necessarily inconsistent with, or repugnant to, court rules, and do not hinder, interfere with, frustrate, pre-empt or usurp judicial powers, at least when the statutes were, at the time of enactment, clearly within the province of the legislative branch and when the courts have not acted in the particular matter covered by the statute."

Based on the foregoing, it is clear that . . . amendment 28 has [not] foreclosed any and all legislative foray into the unauthorized practice of law *by a nonlawyer,* such as under the ADTPA, despite Asbury's contention to the contrary. There can be no doubt that the power of the judicial department, acting through this court to regulate the practice of law, is "exclusive and supreme" under amendment 28. Yet, nonlawyers engaging in what we exclusively define as the practice of law are currently beyond its purview for purposes of meaningful sanction.[3]

---

[3] While this court does have a committee that was created to deal with the unauthorized practice of law, we have observed that the rules creating the Supreme Court Committee on the Unauthorized Practice of Law (CUPL) make it plain that, although the Committee is vested with the authority to investigate claims relating to the unauthorized practice of law, the CUPL itself has no power to enforce whatever decision it may reach regarding any given investigation. American Abstract & Title Co. v. Rice, 358 Ark. 1, 186 S.W.3d 705 (2004).

Plainly, the CUPL is without either the authority or the ability to take any affirmative action on its own—other than issuing a nonbinding advisory opinion—to see to it that a party ceases engaging in the unauthorized practice of law. Without this ability to enforce its own rules, the Committee clearly cannot be vested with exclusive jurisdiction to consider allegations that a

Therefore, we hold that, where the General Assembly has seen fit to provide a cause of action when warranted for such activity by a nonlawyer, such as under the ADTPA, . . . amendment 28 [does not] precludes such action, as long as the legislation in no way hinders, interferes with, restricts, or frustrates the powers of the judiciary to define, regulate, and control the practice of law. We, therefore, reverse the circuit court's grant of summary judgment on this issue and remand.

## SHENANDOAH SALES & SERV., INC. V. ASSESSOR OF JEFFERSON COUNTY

724 S.E.2d 733 (W.Va. 2012)

This is a consolidated appeal of two cases from the Circuit Court of Jefferson County wherein the circuit court dismissed two appeals filed by a corporation, Shenandoah Sales & Services, Inc. ("corporation" or "Shenandoah"), disputing the Jefferson County Assessor's valuation of real estate owned by the corporation. The corporation failed to retain a lawyer to prosecute its appeals to the circuit court, and instead appeared through its vice-president, David C. Tabb. The circuit judge ordered the corporation to appear through a lawyer in circuit court and stated that the court would not accept pleadings or motions from the corporation that were not signed by a lawyer. Despite this order from the circuit court, the corporation failed to retain a lawyer and the circuit court dismissed the corporation's appeals.

The corporation's vice-president, David C. Tabb, argues that the circuit court erred by: (1) ruling that a corporation cannot be represented by a non-lawyer corporate agent in a circuit court;
* * *

---

person or entity has engaged in the unauthorized practice of law. In other words, CUPL does not have the authority to enforce its opinions without filing a complaint in circuit court, where it can obtain a declaration finding a person is unlawfully practicing law and an injunction to force that person to stop the unauthorized practice. The CUPL, at most, shares jurisdiction in these matters; most certainly, the Committee does not have exclusive authority in these matters.

Id. at 7, 186 S.W.3d at 708.

After thorough consideration of the briefs, the record submitted on appeal, and the oral arguments of the parties, we affirm the circuit court's orders dismissing the two appeals. * * *

David C. Tabb, the vice-president of Shenandoah Sales & Services, Inc., disputed the Jefferson County Assessor's 2010 and 2011 real estate tax assessment of property owned by the corporation. The first case before us (No. 11–0248) is Mr. Tabb's appeal of the 2010 real estate tax assessment. The second case (No. 11–0701) is Mr. Tabb's appeal of the 2011 real estate tax assessment.

After objecting to the 2010 assessment, the corporation was given a hearing and presented arguments and evidence before the Jefferson County Board of Review and Equalization. The corporation did not retain legal counsel for this hearing before the board; instead it was represented by Mr. Tabb. The board denied Mr. Tabb's objections to the real estate tax assessment and approved the assessor's valuation of the subject property. Mr. Tabb appealed the board's ruling to the Circuit Court of Jefferson County.

Mr. Tabb sought to represent the corporation as its "agent" in the appeal to the circuit court. By letter dated March 18, 2010, the circuit court informed the corporation that:

> It is a long-standing legal notion that corporations must be represented by a licensed attorney in courts of law. The State of West Virginia recognizes corporations as a separate and distinct person and a non-lawyer representing a corporation constitutes the unauthorized practice of law . . .

> If you wish to continue filing motions and pleadings with this Court, an attorney must enter an appearance on behalf of your corporation and sign all pleadings and motions. Any filings made by a non-attorney will not be accepted or reviewed.

The circuit court sent the corporation another letter on April 8, 2010, again stating that the corporation must retain a lawyer to proceed with the appeal of the 2010 real estate tax assessment. The corporation failed to retain a lawyer after receiving these letters from the circuit court and continued filing motions through Mr. Tabb.

Five months after informing the corporation that it must retain a lawyer to appeal the board's ruling, the circuit court dismissed the appeal of the 2010 tax assessment by order entered on September 14, 2010. The circuit court's order stated that it was dismissing the appeal because of the corporation's failure to retain a lawyer. * * *

The corporation also failed to retain a lawyer when it appealed the 2011 real estate tax assessment to the circuit court. The appeal concerning the 2011 tax assessment was also preceded by a hearing before the Jefferson County Board of Review and Equalization, in which Mr. Tabb was given the opportunity to present evidence and argue on behalf of the corporation. As with the 2010 hearing, the board denied Mr. Tabb's objections and approved the 2011 tax assessment on the subject property.

The circuit court dismissed the 2011 appeal by order entered on March 23, 2011, stating "[a] corporation may not represent itself *pro se* in the circuit court. It appearing to the Court that an attorney has not filed a notice of appearance on behalf of the Plaintiff Corporation, this matter is hereby DISMISSED, *sua sponte*. No further action will be taken by this Court since the appeal has not been properly filed." * * *

Mr. Tabb . . . argues that despite the general rule requiring a corporation to be represented by a lawyer in a trial court of record, W. Va. Code § 11–3–25(b) [2010] permits a corporation to be represented by a non-lawyer corporate agent when appealing a decision of the board of equalization and review. W. Va. Code § 11–3–25(b) states:

> The right of appeal from any assessment by the board of equalization and review or order of the board of assessment appeals as provided in this section, *may be taken either by the applicant or by the state, and in case the applicant, by his or her agent or attorney,* or the state, by its prosecuting attorney or Tax Commissioner, desires to take an appeal from the decision of the either board, the party desiring to take an appeal shall have the evidence taken at the hearing

of the application before either board, including a transcript of all testimony and all papers, motions, documents, evidence and records as were before the board, certified by the county clerk and transmitted to the circuit court as provided in section four, article three, chapter fifty-eight of this code, except that, any other provision of this code notwithstanding, the evidence shall be certified and transmitted within thirty days after the petition for appeal is filed with the court or judge, in vacation (emphasis added).

Mr. Tabb argues that according to the plain language of this statute, he has the authority to represent the corporation as its agent in the circuit court.

The respondent argues that the phrase "by his or her agent" contained in W. Va. Code § 11–3–25(b) renders the statute void and unconstitutional because "the Legislature may not permit a layman to practice law through a statutory grant as the regulation of the practice of law is exclusively within the jurisdiction of the judiciary."

Before examining whether the "by his or her agent" language in W. Va. Code § 11–3–25(b) is a legislative encroachment on this Court's power to define, regulate and control the practice of law, we will examine Mr. Tabb's actions before the circuit court and consider whether these actions constitute the practice of law. This Court, in the exercise of its constitutionally granted power to promulgate rules regulating the practice of law, has formulated the following definition of the practice of law:

> In general, one is deemed to be practicing law whenever he or it furnishes to another advice or service under circumstances which imply the possession of [or] use of legal knowledge and skill.

> More specifically but without purporting to formulate a precise and completely comprehensive definition of the practice of law or to prescribe limits to the scope of that activity, one is deemed to be practicing law whenever (1) one undertakes, with or without compensation and whether or not in connection with another activity, to advise another in any matter involving the application

of legal principles to facts, purposes or desires; (2) one undertakes, with or without compensation and whether or not in connection with another activity, to prepare for another legal instruments of any character; or (3) one undertakes, with or without compensation and whether or not in connection with another activity, to represent the interest of another before any judicial tribunal or officer, or to represent the interest of another before any executive or administrative tribunal, agency or officer otherwise than in the presentation of facts, figures or factual conclusions as distinguished from legal conclusions in respect to such facts and figures.

In the instant case, Mr. Tabb's actions in the circuit court clearly constitute the practice of law under our definition. In Mr. Tabb's petition for appeal, he states that in his capacity as the corporation's agent in the circuit court, he "has filed hundreds of pages of briefs, motions, requests and orders" on behalf of the corporation. These include summary judgment motions, a motion for default judgment, and a motion to recuse the circuit judge. These motions cite to legal authority and make legal arguments.

Based on the plain language of W. Va. Code § 11–3–25(b), Mr. Tabb, acting as a corporate agent, contends that he was authorized to prosecute this appeal to the circuit court. We will therefore examine the constitutionality of W. Va. Code § 11–3–25(b) and consider whether the "by his or her agent" language contained in the statute, purportedly allowing a non-lawyer agent to appeal a ruling of the board of equalization and review to the circuit court, is a legislative encroachment on this Court's authority to define, regulate and control the practice of law.

In deciding the constitutionality of W. Va. Code § 11–3–25(b), we are mindful that

> In considering the constitutionality of a legislative enactment, courts must exercise due restraint, in recognition of the principle of the separation of powers in government among the judicial, legislative and executive branches. Every reasonable construction must be resorted to by the courts in order to sustain constitutionality, and any reasonable doubt must be

resolved in favor of the constitutionality of the legislative enactment in question. Courts are not concerned with questions relating to legislative policy. The general powers of the legislature, within constitutional limits, are almost plenary. In considering the constitutionality of an act of the legislature, the negation of legislative power must appear beyond reasonable doubt.

Furthermore, "[a]cts of the Legislature are always presumed to be constitutional, and this Court will interpret legislation in any reasonable way which will sustain its constitutionality." With these rules of statutory construction in mind, we turn to our previous decisions addressing the Court's power to define, regulate and control the practice of law.

In Syllabus Point 1 of *State ex rel. Askin v. Dostert,* 170 W.Va. 562, 295 S.E.2d 271 (1982), we stated, "[t]he exclusive authority to define, regulate and control the practice of law in West Virginia is vested in the Supreme Court of Appeals." The Court's power to regulate the practice of law exists inherently and by express recognition in our Constitution. We acknowledged the inherent authority courts possess to define, regulate and control the practice of law in Syllabus Point 10 of *West Virginia State Bar v. Earley, supra,* wherein we held, "[i]n the exercise of their inherent power the court may supervise, regulate and control the practice of law by duly authorized attorneys and prevent the unauthorized practice of law by any person, agency or corporation."

The West Virginia Constitution provides that this Court has "the power to promulgate rules for all cases and proceedings, civil and criminal, for all of the courts of the State relating to writs, warrants, process, practice and procedure, which shall have the force of law." *W. Va. Const.* art. 8, § 3. The power embodied in this constitutional provision extends to supervision of the practice of law, as directly stated in Syllabus Point 1 of *Lane v. West Virginia State Board of Law Examiners,* 170 W.Va. 583, 295 S.E.2d 670 (1982), "[a]rticle eight, section one et seq. of the West Virginia Constitution vests in the Supreme Court of Appeals the authority to define, regulate and control the practice of law in West Virginia."

This Court considered a similar issue to the one in the instant case in *State ex rel. Frieson v. Isner*, 168 W.Va. 758, 285 S.E.2d 641 (1981). In *Frieson*, the Court considered whether W. Va. Code § 50–4–4a [1981], which authorizes a party to appear by a lay agent in *magistrate court*—not a court of record—was an unconstitutional legislative encroachment on this Court's power to define, regulate and control the practice law. The Court stated in *Frieson* that "it cannot be questioned that the Legislature cannot restrict or impair the power of the judiciary to regulate the practice of law by enacting a statute permitting or authorizing laymen to practice law . . . [w]here, however, the intrusion upon the judicial power is minimal and inoffensive, and is consistent with and intended to be in aid of the aims of the Court with respect to the regulation of the practice of law, such legislation may be upheld as being in aid of the judicial power."

Unlike *Frieson*, we find that the phrase "by his or her agent" contained in *W. Va. Code* § 11–3–25(b), allowing a non-lawyer agent to appeal a ruling of the board of equalization and review to the *circuit court* and engage in activities which constitute the practice of law, is not in aid of the aims of this Court. This statute allows either a corporation or a natural person to retain a non-lawyer representative to act as an agent on their behalf and engage in activities which constitute the practice of law in a *circuit court*. This is a clear violation of this Court's inherent and constitutional authority to define, regulate and control the practice of law. "Any enactment by the Legislature which undertakes or attempts to authorize the practice of law by a person not duly licensed by the courts or to permit laymen to engage in the practice of law, is void and of no force and effect as an attempt to exercise judicial power by the legislative branch of the government."

Based upon our review of our prior case law and our Constitution, we hold that the phrase "by his or her agent" contained in *W. Va. Code* § 11–3–25(b) [2010], allowing a non-lawyer agent to appeal a ruling of the board of equalization and review to the circuit court and engage in activities which constitute the practice of law, is a legislative encroachment on this Court's exclusive authority to define, regulate and control the practice of law. * * *

We therefore hold that *W. Va. Code* § 11–3–25(b) is unconstitutional [but] only insofar as the word "agent" allows an applicant's non-lawyer representative to appeal a decision of the board of equalization and review to a circuit court. The remainder of *W. Va. Code* § 11–3–25(b), is constitutional and remains fully enforceable. * * *

# CHAPTER VII

# WHAT ARE THE CONSEQUENCES OF UPL?

■ ■ ■

## A. IN GENERAL

### SUSAN D. HOPPOCK, ENFORCING UNAUTHORIZED PRACTICE OF LAW PROHIBITIONS: THE EMERGENCE OF THE PRIVATE CAUSE OF ACTION AND ITS IMPACT ON EFFECTIVE ENFORCEMENT
20 Geo. J. Legal Ethics 719, 730 (2007)

[J]urisdictions employ different sanctions and strategies to enforce restrictions against UPL. The enforcement goal of UPL prohibitions is to deter the lawyer from engaging in UPL to prevent harm to the public. The most common sanctions employed by states include criminal prosecutions, civil injunctions, restitution, disbarment or other ethical sanction, contempt of court, sanctions in the current legal proceedings, and a private cause of action. * * *

### MATHEW ROTENBERG, STIFLED JUSTICE: THE UNAUTHORIZED PRACTICE OF LAW AND INTERNET LEGAL RESOURCES
97 Minn. L. Rev. 709, 716–17 (2012)

Each state's highest court has the inherent power to regulate the practice of law within the state. This authority is typically delegated to state bar associations or unauthorized practice committees, who act as the primary interpretive, investigative, and enforcement mechanisms in most jurisdictions. In some jurisdictions, multiple authorities enforce unauthorized practice rules, including state attorneys general, private individuals, state bar committees, supreme court committees, and local county attorneys. States have implemented a variety of sanctions and strategies to enforce unauthorized practice regulations. The most common include civil injunctions, restitution, disbarment, suspension, criminal and civil contempt, sanctions in the current legal proceedings, private cause of action, and criminal prosecutions. Although a number of remedies are available, states vary dramatically in method and vigor of unauthorized practice enforcement[.]

### LISA H. NICHOLSON, ACCESS TO JUSTICE REQUIRES ACCESS TO ATTORNEYS: RESTRICTIONS ON THE PRACTICE OF LAW SERVE A SOCIETAL PURPOSE

82 Fordham L. Rev. 2761, 2788–89 (2014)

[E]nforcement efforts [to deter UPL] are not uniform across the states. Thirty-two states reported some level of active enforcement of UPL restrictions, with several states permitting multiple entities (e.g., state supreme court, state bar counsel, state bar committee, and county prosecutor) to enforce UPL restrictions. Authority to enforce UPL restrictions is established by statute in twenty-nine states and by court rules in twenty-three states. Despite overlapping grants of authority, however, insufficient funding or staff resources challenge many of the states' ability to bring enforcement actions.

Penalties for UPL violations also vary from state to state, some with overlapping sanctions: civil injunctions in thirty-two states; criminal fines in twenty-four; prison sentences in twenty; civil contempt in twenty-two; restitution in sixteen; and civil fines in thirteen. The spotty enforcement effort, coupled with the varied designations of wrongdoing and the resulting penalties from UPL violations, can impede the deterrent effect on nonattorneys. Criminal prosecutions, for example, are not widespread, because such cases typically fall on the overburdened state attorney general, and where designated as misdemeanors, the time and costs of prosecution are outweighed. Though prosecutorial power may be delegated to a state bar committee, the number of UPL enforcement actions generally does not improve given the budget constraints of many state bar committees. Civil injunctions, though useful against the threat of repeat offenders, similarly are not wholly effective to deter noncompliance given the insufficient level of accompanying monetary sanctions.

## B. PRIVATE ENFORCEMENT

Enforcement of UPL rules by prosecutors and regulators is usually underfunded and, as a result, spotty and unreliable.

This "public" enforcement, however, is supplemented by private enforcement; that is, victims of UPL personally complaining and seeking remedies themselves.

A very common example is a person who defends against the enforcement of a contract for the provision of services that amounted to the unauthorized practice of law. Such a contract is unlawful and void. And the victim can recover any money already paid based on unjust enrichment or a similar theory.

Less common and still developing is a theory of further recovery of additional damages for consequential harm resulting from UPL. The common law does not provide for a cause of action based strictly on UPL itself, but facts showing negligence or intentional tort may allow a plaintiff to state a claim that is fundamentally based on the defendant's UPL.

Also, some states have legislatively created private causes of action for the unauthorized practice of law. Caselaw seems clear that UPL, or the facts underlying it, can be used to establish liability under existing statutes that sometimes provide private causes of action against deceptive practices or similar conduct.

### ARMSTRONG V. BROWN SERV.
### FUNERAL HOME WEST CHAPEL
700 So.2d 1379 (Ala. 1997)

The plaintiffs appeal from the dismissal of their **claims of the unauthorized practice of law and of fraud by suppression** (emphasis added).

In December 1995 Nora Armstrong and Clarence Rowlins (plaintiffs) filed a complaint against Brown Service Funeral Home West Chapel (defendant), alleging that the defendant had engaged in the unauthorized practice of law, pursuant to Ala.Code 1975, § 34–3–6. Specifically, the plaintiffs alleged that they entered into a contract with the defendant for the burial of Robert Louis Armstrong; that the defendant charged them a fee of $175 in connection with the assistance of preparing certain legal forms; that the preparation of the forms constituted the unauthorized practice of law, as well as fraud by suppression; and that the contract between the parties is void as a result thereof. * * *

On January 26, 1996, the defendant filed a motion to dismiss the plaintiffs' claims. . . . On February 16, 1996, the trial court granted the defendant's motion. Thereafter, the plaintiffs filed a post-judgment motion, which was denied.

The plaintiffs appeal. * * *

The dispositive issue on appeal is whether the trial court erred in granting the defendant's motion to dismiss. We find that it did.

* * * [W]e are not convinced that the plaintiffs would be unable to recover against the defendant under any cognizable theory of law or under any given set of facts. The contract between the plaintiffs and the defendant clearly indicates that the plaintiffs were charged a fee of $175 for "ASSISTANCE WITH SOCIAL SECURITY, LEGAL & INSURANCE FORMS."

The defendant argues that the only forms it prepared for the plaintiffs were the Social Security form and the death certificate which, it says, is a service that it is allowed to perform under Alabama law. The defendant also contends that the plaintiffs did not pay any consideration under the contract. The plaintiffs did present evidence, however, that they gave the defendant a burial policy and a vault policy which, they say, constituted some consideration. The plaintiffs also contend that the defendant may have completed other forms. Based on the language contained in the contract, we conclude that there exists a question of fact as to what type of "legal" forms the defendant actually prepared for the plaintiffs. * * *

It is apparent that the Legislature's purpose in the enactment of § 34–3–6, Ala.Code 1975, was to ensure that "laymen would not serve others in a representative capacity in areas requiring the skill and judgment of a licensed attorney."

Based on the foregoing, we are also not convinced that the plaintiffs would be unable to recover against the defendant under their suppression claim. This court, in *LaCoste v. SCI Alabama Funeral Services, Inc.*, 689 So.2d 76 (Ala.Civ.App.1996), stated the following:

> "To make out a suppression claim, a plaintiff must show that the defendant had a duty to disclose a material fact

and failed to do so, that the concealment or failure to disclose induced the plaintiff to act, and that the plaintiff suffered actual damage as a result. One may be liable for suppression only if he has knowledge of the fact allegedly suppressed and only if he is under a duty to disclose. A duty to disclose may arise from a confidential relationship, from a request for information, or from the circumstances of the case. If the plaintiff offers evidence of particular circumstances creating an inference that the defendant should have disclosed certain material facts, then whether the defendant had a duty to communicate those facts is for the jury to determine."

The plaintiffs stated in their complaint that the suppression of the material fact proximately damaged them because, they say, they believed that they were responsible for, and did pay for, the charges imposed by the defendant, which stemmed from the defendant's unauthorized practice of law. We find that any duty of the defendant to disclose or to communicate any such information is a question of fact, which is directly related to the plaintiffs' **unauthorized practice of law claim** (emphasis added).

Accordingly, we conclude that the complaints set forth by the plaintiffs present **cognizable theories of law** which may, upon proof of the proper facts, entitle the plaintiffs to recover against the defendant. Therefore, we reverse and remand the case for proceedings consistent with this opinion (emphasis added). * * *

## TORRES V. FIOL
### 441 N.E.2d 1300 (Ill. App. 3d 1982)

Plaintiffs appeal from a dismissal of that portion of their amended complaint seeking damages against defendant, Lorenzo Fiol, Jr., a non-attorney for his alleged practice of law involving a business transaction. On appeal plaintiffs contend that the trial court erred in concluding that in this State an action for compensatory damages is not cognizable for the negligent practice of law by a non-attorney. * * *

The 2-count amended complaint recited that plaintiffs owned a certain parcel of real estate and managed a grocery and liquor store situated thereon. In 1979 they agreed to lease the store to Octavio Serrano who assumed certain contractual obligations to the mortgage holder. Plaintiffs alleged that they contacted defendant, who held himself out to the public for the purpose of rendering legal services, to prepare the necessary documents for the transaction. Plaintiffs claimed that defendant rendered a legal opinion and advice on the transaction and also prepared the documents for the transaction, although they averred he performed the latter in an improper and careless manner.

The parties then filed memorandums of law following defendant's motion to dismiss the complaint. The trial court, citing *Rathke v. Lidiya* (1978), 59 Ill.App.3d 560, 16 Ill.Dec. 764, 375 N.E.2d 871 and Ill.Rev.Stat.1979, ch. 13, par. 1, held that no private cause of action for damages for the unauthorized practice of law is recognized in Illinois.

In *Rathke* a real estate buyer sought damages against several realtors for their unauthorized practice of law when one or more allegedly inserted a provision into a printed sales contract. The appellate court opinion recited that plaintiff had not alleged that defendants were negligent or that they had represented themselves as attorneys. Rather plaintiff's claim was predicated upon section 1 of "An act to revise the law in relation to attorneys and counselors" dealing with the unauthorized practice of law, and plaintiff apparently asserted that a mere violation of this statute gave rise to a cause of action for damages. The court held that this statute did not permit a claim for damages.

The statute in question provides a contempt sanction against a person for the unauthorized practice of law. In addition, the statute recites:

> "The provisions of this Act <u>shall be in addition to other remedies permitted by law</u> and shall not be construed to deprive courts of this State of their inherent right to punish for contempt or to restrain the unauthorized practice of law." Ill.Rev.Stat.1979, ch. 13, par. 1. (emphasis added).

The underscored language of the statute plainly evidences a legislative intent not to circumscribe other theories of recovery against a non-attorney who is retained to perform legal duties and who then mishandles the matter. We therefore conclude that the statute and *Rathke,* which interpreted that provision, do not preclude this action.

While not extensive there appear several reported decisions allowing for the recovery against a non-attorney for the unauthorized and negligent practice of law. In *Biakanja v. Irving* (1958), 49 Cal.2d 647, 320 P.2d 16 a non-attorney was charged with improperly preparing a will. The court commented that "such conduct should be discouraged and not protected by immunity from civil liability, as would be the case if plaintiff, the only person who suffered a loss, were denied a right of action."
* * *

Similar to the *Biakanja* case is *Latson v. Eaton* (Okl.1959), 341 P.2d 247, where a non-attorney was held liable for the preparation of legal documents. Further, in *Mattieligh v. Poe* (1960), 57 Wash.2d 203, 356 P.2d 328, the court remarked that the undertaking involving the practice of law by a real estate broker, who was not an attorney, may render him liable if the work is negligently performed. See also *Wright v. Langdon* (Ark.1981), 623 S.W.2d 823, 827.

Because of the above authorities and the lack of contrary precedent in this State we conclude that plaintiffs are not prevented from proceeding against defendant upon a negligence theory for his alleged improper activity. The judgment of the circuit court is reversed, and the cause is remanded.

Reversed and remanded.[b]

### N.C. GEN. STAT. ANN. § 84–10.1.
#### PRIVATE CAUSE OF ACTION FOR THE
#### UNAUTHORIZED PRACTICE OF LAW

If any person knowingly violates any of the provisions of [state law prohibiting the unauthorized practice of law], fraudulently holds himself or herself out as a North Carolina certified paralegal by use of the designations set forth in G.S. 84–37(a), or knowingly aids and abets another person to commit the unauthorized practice of law, in addition to any other liability imposed pursuant to this Chapter or any other applicable law,

---

b   Illinois has since created by statute a private cause of action for UPL. [Ed.]

any person who is damaged by the unlawful acts set out in this section shall be entitled to maintain a private cause of action to recover damages and reasonable attorneys' fees and other injunctive relief as ordered by court. No order or judgment under this section shall have any effect upon the ability of the North Carolina State Bar to take any action authorized by this Chapter.

## CAMPBELL V. ASBURY AUTO., INC.
### 381 S.W.3d 21 (Ark. 2011)

*[Parts of this case are reprinted in Chapters II and VI of this book,* supra. *The issue highlighted in Chapter II is whether a car dealer, Asbury, engaged in the authorized practice of law by charging Plaintiffs, including Campbell, an illegal document preparation fee for preparing the vehicle installment contract (a legal instrument) for the purchase of a vehicle. The court answered yes. In Chapter VI, the issue is whether the consequences can, as a constitutional matter, include liability under the Arkansas Deceptive Trade Practices Act ("ADTPA"). The answer is yes. Here, the issue is whether Asbury is also liable for breach of fiduciary duty, which raises an issue that transcends this case and applies in other private actions for UPL: what is the standard of care of a non-lawyer who engages in the unauthorized practice of law.]*

B.    Finding of a Fiduciary Relationship

Asbury argues * * * that the circuit court erred in finding that car dealers that prepare or complete legal documents are held to the same standards as a licensed attorney. Specifically, it claims that the unauthorized practice of law in no way creates a fiduciary relationship. Asbury maintains, instead, that it is the circumstances of the interaction between one engaged in the unauthorized practice of law and a "client" that form the nature of the duties that arise.

Campbell responds that Asbury must be held to have had the same fiduciary duties as an attorney when it engaged in the unauthorized practice of law, because to hold a nonlawyer corporation to any lower standard would condone and encourage the unauthorized practice of law. He urges that Arkansas law makes clear that attorneys are required to meet the standards of full disclosure, fair dealing, good faith, honesty, and loyalty, and they are strictly prohibited from representing opposing or conflicting interests; these same duties, he asserts, applied to Asbury when it engaged in the same conduct as attorneys.

Asbury challenges the circuit court's grant of Campbell's motion, which requested the circuit court to determine questions of law regarding the duties imposed on nonlawyers engaged in the unauthorized practice of law. \* \* \* Here, the circuit granted Campbell's motion requesting the following determinations of law:

1.   Car dealers that prepare or complete legal documents for pay are held to the same standard as a licensed attorney.

. . . .

2.   Because car dealers that prepare or complete legal documents for pay are held to the same standard as a licensed attorney, they are required to meet the requisite standards of full disclosure, fair dealing, good faith, honesty and loyalty.

. . . .

3.   Because car dealers that prepare or complete legal documents for pay are held to the same standard as a licensed attorney, they are prohibited from representing opposing or conflicting interests.

. . . .

4.   Car dealers that prepare or complete legal documents for pay, and that represent opposing or conflicting interests, are barred from receiving a fee, no matter how successful their labors.

. . . .

5.   Car dealers that prepare or complete legal documents for pay are prohibited from arguing or proving that in fact their conflict of loyalties had no influence upon their conduct.

The question presented is whether, in being held to the same standards as a licensed attorney, Asbury stood in a fiduciary relationship with its consumers, and we conclude that it did. A person is ordinarily not liable for the acts of another unless a special relationship exists between the two parties. A person standing in a fiduciary relationship with another is subject to liability to the other for harm resulting from a breach of the duty imposed by the relationship. It follows that, regardless of the express terms of an agreement, a fiduciary may be held liable for conduct that does not meet the requisite standards of fair dealing, good faith, honesty, and loyalty. The guiding principle of the fiduciary relationship is that self-dealing, absent the consent of the other party to the relationship, is strictly proscribed.

As already set forth, Asbury engaged in the unauthorized practice of law when it completed legal forms for its customers and charged a fee for doing so. This court has previously held that the standard of care to be applied to one who improperly assumes the function of a lawyer shall be, at a minimum, no less than that required of a licensed attorney. We have further held that a fiduciary relationship exists between attorney and client, and the confidence that the relationship begets between the parties makes it necessary for the attorney to act in utmost good faith. Here, Asbury, by virtue of its unauthorized practice of law, was held to the same standard of care as a licensed attorney, and that would include having a fiduciary relationship with its customers. Accordingly, we cannot say that the circuit court erred in so concluding.

### SANDE L. BUHAI, ACT LIKE A LAWYER, BE JUDGED LIKE A LAWYER: THE STANDARD OF CARE FOR THE UNLICENSED PRACTICE OF LAW
2007 Utah L. Rev. 87, 88–89 (2007)

Given the extensive attention that has been given to regulation of the practice of law ex ante, it is remarkable how little attention has been given to the problem of protecting consumers from the provision of substandard legal services by non-lawyers ex post—that is, through the tort system after injury has occurred. Legal scholars have largely ignored the question. The case law is sparse and apparently not well-settled.

A majority of courts have held that one who provides legal services, regardless of whether licensed or authorized, should be held to the standard of care applicable to attorneys providing those same services. On this basis, courts have imposed an attorney's standard of care on insurance claim adjusters, real estate brokers, paralegals, persons assisting in divorce, and escrow agents, when such non-lawyers provide legal advice or render other legal services.

Other courts have imposed liability for negligence in the course of the unlicensed practice of law without specifying a standard of care. One court held that its state legislature, in authorizing non-lawyers to represent claimants before its state's Industrial Accident Commission, must have been "aware of the dangers of non-lawyer practice" and therefore must have contemplated a lower standard—on the facts of the case, a significantly lower standard. Another held, without any analysis or citation of authority, that a paralegal, not being an attorney, cannot be charged with legal malpractice.

## C. NULLIFICATION

### KELLY V. SAINT FRANCIS MED. CTR.
889 N.W.2d 613 (Neb. 2017)

## I. INTRODUCTION

Ann Kelly filed, in her own behalf and on behalf of the estate of Stephen Kelly, a pro se wrongful death action against Saint Francis Medical Center (Saint Francis), Dr. Jeff S. Burwell, and other "fictitious entities." Ann later filed, through counsel, a motion for leave to file an amended complaint. The district court concluded that an amended complaint could not relate back to the date of the original filing and dismissed the action as untimely. Ann appeals. We affirm.

## II. BACKGROUND

On March 9, 2013, Stephen suffered a fall in his home. He was transported to Saint Francis' emergency department on March 10. Burwell attended to Stephen and ordered an x ray of Stephen's shoulder, a CT scan of his head, and an injection of pain medication. Based on the results of the tests, Burwell prescribed Toradol and discharged Stephen. Two days later, on March 12, Ann found Stephen unresponsive. Stephen was transported to Saint Francis, where he died on March 16.

On March 10, 2015, Ann filed a pro se complaint in her own behalf and on behalf of the estate of Stephen against Saint Francis, Burwell, "John and Jane Does I-X; ABC Corporations; and XYZ Partnerships." In Ann's complaint, she alleged that (1) Burwell provided negligent medical care to Stephen, which was the direct cause of his death, and (2) Saint Francis provided negligent medical care to Stephen, which was the direct cause of his death. Ann signed the complaint as a "Pro Se Plaintiff." A law firm located in Arizona assisted Ann in drafting the complaint. It is undisputed that at the time of filing, Ann was not a licensed attorney.

On April 22, 2015, Saint Francis filed its answer, denying Ann's allegations seeking dismissal of her complaint. On August 12, Saint Francis and Burwell filed a motion to dismiss, alleging that (1) the complaint fails to state facts sufficient to state a cause of action, (2) Ann was engaged in the unauthorized practice of law, and (3) the complaint showed on its face that any claim was barred by the statute of limitations.

Ann subsequently retained counsel. On August 28, 2015, counsel entered an appearance. On that same date, Ann, through counsel, filed a motion to continue. On September 1, Ann filed a motion for leave to file an amended complaint. In the motion, Ann stated that she was the special administrator of the estate of Stephen when the complaint was filed. Ann further stated that she filed her pro se complaint within the 2-year statute of limitations, that she had retained counsel for her amended complaint, and that she sought leave to file an amended complaint that would relate back to the date of the original complaint and cure any defects in the original complaint, including any unauthorized practice of law. Ann argued that an amended complaint should relate back to the date of the original complaint, because it would change only her capacity as the personal representative of the estate of Stephen, or, in the alternative, it should relate back, because all defendants received notice of this action and would not be prejudiced by the filing of an amended complaint.

Following a hearing, the district court denied Ann's motion for leave to file an amended complaint and dismissed the motions filed against Saint Francis and Burwell. The court reasoned that "any pleadings filed by nonattorneys are of no effect." They are a "nullity" and "because they are a nullity, it is as if they never existed and therefore no amendment can relate back to them or save an action from a valid statute of limitations defense." Applying this reasoning to the facts of the case, the court held that the original complaint filed by Ann was a nullity and that "an amended complaint cannot relate back to something that never existed, nor can a nonexistent complaint be corrected."

Ann appeals.

\* \* \*

## V. ANALYSIS

## 1. WHETHER PRIOR COMPLAINT WAS NULLITY

### (a) Unauthorized Practice of Law

First, to find whether the prior complaint was a nullity, we must determine whether the filing of the pro se complaint by Ann on behalf of the estate was the unauthorized practice of law, as was found by the district court.

No nonlawyer shall engage in the practice of law in Nebraska or in any manner represent that such nonlawyer is authorized or qualified to practice law in Nebraska except as may be authorized by published opinion or court rule. The term " '[n]onlawyer' " is defined by the rules as "any person not duly licensed or otherwise authorized to practice law in the State of Nebraska," including "any entity or organization not authorized to practice law by specific rule of the Supreme Court whether or not it employs persons who are licensed to practice law." The term " 'practice of law' " is defined as "the application of legal principles and judgment with regard to the circumstances or objectives of another entity or person which require the knowledge, judgment, and skill of a person trained as a lawyer." This includes, but is not limited to, "[s]election, drafting, or completion, for another entity or person, of legal documents which affect the legal rights of the entity or person. . . ."

In *Waite v. Carpenter*, the Nebraska Court of Appeals held that a nonattorney was engaged in the unauthorized practice of law when he filed a wrongful death action on behalf of the estate for which he was a personal representative. The court noted that under Neb. Rev. Stat. § 30–2464(a) (Reissue 1989), a personal representative " 'is a fiduciary who shall observe the standards of applicable trustees . . .' " and "one who seeks to represent the legal interests of the personal representative must be an attorney." In addition, "[Neb. Rev. Stat.] § 7–101 prevents the filing of any paper in any action 'unless the same bears the endorsement of some admitted attorney, or is drawn, signed, and presented by a party to the action or proceeding.' " The court reasoned that

> the pleadings were not signed by an admitted attorney, but, rather, by [the personal representative], and it is only where a party acts in a nonrepresentative capacity that he may file his own pleadings. There can be no question that [the personal representative] was engaged in the practice of law in violation of § 7–101.11

Similarly, this court held in *Back Acres Pure Trust v. Fahnlander* that the trustees of a trust were engaged in the unauthorized practice of law when they filed complaints pro se on behalf of the trust. This court reasoned that

> a trustee's duties in connection with his or her office do not include the right to present argument pro se in courts of the state, because in this capacity such trustee would be representing interests of others and would therefore be engaged in the unauthorized practice of law.

> Because [the nonlawyer] had no authority to file a brief in this matter, either in his own behalf or on behalf of appellants, appellants' briefs are ordered stricken, and the appeal is dismissed.

In the present case, both parties agree that Ann was a nonattorney at the time she filed a complaint on behalf of the estate. In her complaint, Ann sought to represent the interests of the estate. Ann drafted the complaint and signed it as a pro se plaintiff, though she apparently had the help of Arizona counsel in doing so. With this legal document, Ann is seeking to "affect the legal rights" of the estate. This constitutes the unauthorized practice of law.

(b) Dismissal of Ann's Unauthorized Practice of Law Because It Was "nullity"

Ann argues that her pro se complaint should not have been dismissed as a "nullity" because (1) there was no flagrant and persistent unauthorized practice of law, (2) the basis for the prohibition against unauthorized practice is not promoted by dismissal in this case, and (3) dismissal should not be required based on the harsh consequences to litigants. Saint Francis and Burwell argue that the district court did not abuse its discretion when it dismissed Ann's complaint, because a legal proceeding in which a party is represented by a person not admitted to practice law is a nullity and is subject to dismissal.

(i) Flagrant and Persistent Unauthorized Practice

Ann contends that the term "nullity" has a technical definition of " 'legally void,' " but that it has been applied in similar Nebraska cases with discretionary language. Furthermore, Ann argues that courts have consistently premised dismissal only on flagrant and persistent unauthorized acts.

In *Niklaus v. Abel Construction Co.*, this court held that "[t]he flagrant and persistent unlawful practice of law" committed by a disbarred attorney "require[d] that the proceedings be held to be a nullity and the action dismissed." The disbarred attorney prepared and filed the summons, submitted the documents to the court, and was "actively, openly, and persistently performing the duties and exercising the powers of a member of the bar of this state." We stated that " '[p]roceedings in a suit by a person not entitled to practice are a nullity, and the suit may be dismissed.' " This court reasoned that "[t]he dismissal of a proceeding for such a cause is a drastic remedy and may not be required in all cases. The extent of the unlawful practice . . . in this case requires that it be done."

This court subsequently decided *Steinhausen v. HomeServices of Neb.*, in which the plaintiff, a nonlawyer, filed a pro se complaint to the district court in his own behalf and on behalf of the limited liability company of which he was the sole member. The complaint was dismissed on summary judgment, and he filed a brief on appeal. This court ruled that a licensed member of the Nebraska bar must represent a company in the courts of this state. Therefore, this court held that the pro se complaint filed by the plaintiff in his own behalf and on behalf of the company he owned was a nullity to the extent that he had appealed on behalf of the company, but was valid as to the errors assigned in his own behalf. In its analysis, this court did not discuss whether the acts constituted flagrant and persistent unauthorized acts in determining that the complaint as to the company was a nullity. Rather, the unauthorized practice of law was sufficient to find that the pro se complaint on behalf of the company was a nullity.

Ann argues that the opinion in *Niklaus* indicates that this court has the discretion to hold that an unauthorized practice of law is a nullity depending on the extent of the unlawful practice. However, this court's more recent decision in *Steinhausen* shows that the extent of the unauthorized practice of law is not a consideration in a court's determination of whether the unauthorized filing of a legal document is a nullity.

Similarly to *Steinhausen*, Ann drafted and filed a complaint that constituted the unauthorized practice of law. While she later obtained counsel to file her motion for leave to file an amended complaint and her subsequent appeal of the court's ruling on the motion, the single act constituting the unauthorized practice of law was sufficient for the court to rule that her complaint was a nullity, as we found in *Steinhausen*. The court was not required to find that Ann's acts constituted flagrant and persistent unauthorized acts.

(ii) Whether Basis for Prohibition Against Unauthorized Practice of Law Is Promoted by Dismissal

Ann contends that the policy supporting the prohibition against the unauthorized practice of law is not promoted by dismissal in this case. Burwell argues that any other result would not serve the policy considerations at issue, because this protects the estate and discourages the unauthorized practice of law. Saint Francis does not address this issue.

In *Waite*, the Court of Appeals held that policy considerations for the rule against nonattorneys practicing law for others was not "to perpetuate a professional monopoly," but, rather,

> (1) to protect citizens from injury caused by the ignorance and lack of skill on the part of those who are

untrained and inexperienced in the law, (2) to protect the courts in their administration of justice from interference by those who are unlicensed and are not officers of the court, and (3) to prevent the unscrupulous from using the legal system for their own purposes to the harm of the system and those who may unknowingly rely upon them.

The court further stated in *Waite* that in wrongful death actions, "one who seeks to represent the legal interests of the personal representative must be an attorney" and "[t]his rule protects the estate, its heirs, and its creditors." By dismissing the case based on the unlawful filing of a wrongful death complaint by a nonlawyer on behalf of the estate, the lower court clearly promoted the policy reasons behind the prohibition against the unlawful practice of law and essentially sought to protect the estate. The policy considerations behind the prohibition of the unauthorized practice are furthered by the lower court's decision that the prior complaint was a nullity.

(iii) Whether Dismissal Should Not Be Required Based on Harsh Consequences to Litigants

Ann contends that in cases such as this, in which the unauthorized practice of law was minimal and the party has taken steps to cure the unauthorized practice, the court should be permitted to allow the party to cure the unauthorized practice.

There is a split of authority on the question of whether the unauthorized practice of law renders a proceeding a nullity or merely amounts to an amendable defect. Some courts hold that the unauthorized practice of law amounts to a nullity and find that the "proscription on the unauthorized practice of law is of paramount importance in that it protects the public from those not trained or licensed in the law." Other jurisdictions find that it merely amounts to an amendable defect in "an attempt to avoid what they deem to be the unduly harsh result of dismissal on technical grounds."

In *Steinhausen*, this court did not address any harsh consequences that would result from dismissing the plaintiff's claims as related to his limited liability company. Rather, this court reasoned:

> The prohibition of the unauthorized practice of law is not for the benefit of lawyers. Prohibiting the unauthorized practice of law protects citizens and litigants in the administration of justice from the mistakes of the ignorant on the one hand and the machinations of the unscrupulous on the other.

This court then simply held that "because [the plaintiff] is not licensed to practice law in Nebraska, his appeal . . . is a nullity." Thus, while we have not explicitly addressed the issue of whether the harsh consequence to litigants should be taken into account, we have shown that our paramount concern in such cases is to protect the public from the unauthorized practice of law.

In order to sufficiently address this paramount concern, it is not necessary for this court to engage in a calculation as to whether the consequences for the unauthorized practice of law are proportional to the gravity of the harm done to the public. We regard the unauthorized practice of law as a serious offense, and we therefore favor the approach of those jurisdictions that have found that any unauthorized practice is a nullity.

Under a de novo standard of review, the district court correctly held that Ann's complaint was a nullity and the district court was not required to find flagrant and persistent unauthorized acts. Ann's first assignment of error is without merit.

## 2.   WHETHER AMENDED COMPLAINT COULD RELATE BACK AND CURE DEFECTS OF INITIAL COMPLAINT

Ann contends that * * * an amended complaint filed by counsel could have related back to her pro se complaint and cured any defects. * * *

Burwell * * * cites the Arkansas Supreme Court's decision in *Davenport v. Lee*, mentioned above, in which a nonattorney personal representative filed a pro se complaint in a wrongful-death action on behalf of the decedent's estate. The Arkansas Supreme Court found that the defect "rendered the complaint a nullity" and held that "the original complaint, as a nullity never existed, and thus, an amended complaint cannot relate back to something that never existed, nor can a nonexistent complaint be corrected." * * *

Similarly to the Arkansas Supreme Court's reasoning in *Davenport*, Ann's amended complaint, which would be filed by counsel after the statute of limitations had run, cannot relate back to her pro se complaint. The pro se complaint constituted an unauthorized practice of law; thus, it was "something that never existed," and, as a nonexistent complaint, it cannot be corrected.

Ann's second assignment of error is without merit.

## VI. CONCLUSION

The district court did not err in holding that (1) the prior complaint was a nullity and (2) an amended complaint could not relate back to the filing of the original pro se complaint.

The decision of the district court is affirmed.

**DOWNTOWN DISPOSAL SERVS.,
INC. V. CITY OF CHICAGO**
979 N.E.2d 50 (Ill. 2012)

In this case, we must determine whether a complaint for administrative review filed by a corporation's president, on behalf of the corporation, is a nullity because the president is not an attorney. For the reasons that follow, we conclude that the complaints are not void.

## BACKGROUND

Between December 2007 and March 2008, the City of Chicago's department of transportation issued plaintiff, Downtown Disposal Services, Inc., four notices for violating City ordinances pertaining to several of its dumpsters. The notices required Downtown Disposal to appear at administrative hearings on various dates between February and April 2008. When Downtown Disposal failed to appear at any of the hearings, the department of administrative hearings entered default judgments against Downtown Disposal requiring it to pay costs and penalties.

On August 18, 2008, Peter Van Tholen, president of Downtown Disposal, filed four motions to set aside the default judgments, alleging the company did not receive notice of the hearings. On September 19, 2008, at a consolidated hearing, Van Tholen advised the administrative law officer that for the previous five years, Downtown Disposal had made several attempts to change its address on file with the City, but the City had not made the change in its records. Because of the City's failure, Downtown Disposal did not receive the violation notices. Following Van Tholen's testimony, the administrative law officer denied Downtown Disposal's motions, finding that the City sent the notices to the address on file for Downtown Disposal and that Downtown Disposal failed to provide any evidence it had changed its address before the violations were mailed. Thereafter, the following colloquy occurred:

> Administrative Law Officer Harris: However, you do have a right to appeal the decision—
>
> Mr. Van Tholen: I will.
>
> Administrative Law Officer Harris: —to the Circuit Court.
>
> That's fine, sir. You have a right to appeal the decision to the Circuit Court within 35 days of today's date, and you would do that in Room 602 of the Daley Center.

On October 16, 2008, Van Tholen filled out four blank pro se complaints for administrative review. On the preprinted form supplied by the clerk's office, Van Tholen filled in plaintiff's name, its address, the date of the administrative decision, and the docket number. Van Tholen signed the forms. Service was then made upon the City by certified mail. On April 19, 2009, attorney Richard D. Boonstra filed appearances on behalf of plaintiff in each of the cases.

On July 29, 2009, the City moved to dismiss the complaints pursuant to section 2–619(a)(9) of the Code of Civil Procedure (735 ILCS 5/2–619(a)(9) (West 2008)), arguing that because a nonattorney, Van Tholen, filed the complaints on behalf of Downtown Disposal, a corporation, they were null and void. On September 23, Boonstra filed motions for leave to file amended complaints, arguing that the lack of an attorney's signature was a technical defect which could be cured by filing an amended complaint signed by an attorney. In addition, in January of 2010, Downtown Disposal filed a motion for summary judgment, arguing that because the City was a municipal corporation, the violations had to be signed by an attorney and, since they were not, the underlying actions filed by the City were null and void ab initio.

Following a hearing on January 29, 2010, the circuit court of Cook County granted the City's motions to dismiss, finding it was compelled to follow authority from the First District of the appellate court holding that actions filed by nonattorneys on behalf of a corporation are null and void. Based on this ruling, the court declared Downtown Disposal's motions for leave to amend the complaints and motion for summary judgment moot.

In ruling on the question before it, the trial court found "this is a troubling issue" because, in administrative review cases, the trial courts are "confronted with nonattorneys filing pleadings" on a daily basis. After pointing out that the appellate court had held that filling in a form was the unauthorized practice of law, the trial court stated as follows:

> "If you review the Complaint that's filed in the Administrative Review cases, it is just that. It is a prepared form. It is handed to anyone who walks into the Clerk's office. They merely have to fill in names and fill in the date that the Findings and Decision was entered against them, and it has form language as to why they are appealing the matter and it initiates this process."

After again stating it was compelled to follow the decisions of the appellate court, the trial judge identified certain issues he believed should be revisited. Specifically:

> "The actual issue in this case as to the filing of this form, is it the unauthorized practice of law?
>
> And then there is [sic] other considerations, such as here where the refiling of an action is not available to the party that it would be time barred by dismissal of the pending action, is that too severe a sanction to impose?

> Coupled with the clearly erroneous legal instructions
> which are being given by the administrative law officers
> at the City of Chicago Department of Administrative
> Hearings, where they inform nonattorneys who appear
> before them representing corporations that you,
> quotation marks, 'You have the right to appeal this,' and
> they direct these people to the 6th Floor of Daley Center
> to file an appeal in these matters."

The trial court further questioned whether a nonattorney representing a corporate entity before the administrative hearings in the City might not also be engaged in the unauthorized practice of law. Plaintiff appealed.

The appellate court reversed and remanded. * * * The court noted that "appellate court decisions have differed in their adherence to the automatic application of the nullity rule," and held that, in the case at bar, the purposes underlying the nullity rule, protection of litigants and the public as well as the integrity of the court system, would not be furthered by its application. Accordingly, the appellate court reversed the trial court's decision and remanded for further proceedings.

We granted the City's petition for leave to appeal (Ill. S.Ct. R. 315 (eff. Feb. 26, 2010)), and allowed the Illinois State Bar Association to file an amicus brief on behalf of the City.

ANALYSIS

Unauthorized Practice of Law

We must first determine whether Van Tholen engaged in the unauthorized practice of law when he filed the complaints for administrative review on behalf of plaintiff corporation.

This court has the inherent power to define and regulate the practice of law in this state. Our rules are intended to safeguard the public from individuals unqualified to practice law and to ensure the integrity of our legal system.

There is no mechanistic formula to define what is and what is not the practice of law. Rather, we examine the character of the acts themselves to determine if the conduct is the practice of law and each case is largely controlled by its own peculiar facts.

Plaintiff contends that there was no unauthorized practice of law because Van Tholen merely filled in blanks on a simple form that did not require the use of any legal expertise. We disagree. It is not the simplicity of the form that is important but the fact that an appeal was pursued on behalf of a corporation by a nonattorney.

A corporation must be represented by counsel in legal proceedings. This rule arises from the fact a corporation is an artificial entity that must always act through agents and there may be questions as to whether a particular person is an appropriate representative. For example, while an officer of a corporation, i.e., an individual such as Van Tholen, may believe review of an administrative decision is in the best interests of a company, it may, in fact, not be. The interests of the corporate officers and that of the corporation, a distinct legal entity, are separate. It is not every case where the views or interests of a principal and the corporation mesh. By requiring an attorney to represent a corporation in legal proceedings, this problem is mitigated.

A complaint for administrative review is essential to preserve one's right to appeal an administrative decision and invokes the appellate review mechanism. The filing of the complaint affects the substantial legal rights of the party seeking administrative review, in this case, Downtown Disposal. As such, only an individual representing the corporation itself can ascertain whether it is best for a corporation to pursue review of an administrative decision and invoke the appellate mechanism.

Accordingly, when Van Tholen filed the complaints for administrative review, he engaged in the unauthorized practice of law. He was not an attorney representing the interests of the corporation and could not file for administrative review on behalf of Downtown Disposal.

Having reached this conclusion, we must now determine the consequences of Van Tholen's conduct and decide whether the complaints for administrative review were a nullity.

Nullity Rule

Courts in this country, including this court, unanimously agree that a corporation must be represented by counsel in legal proceedings. However, courts disagree on the consequences the lack of representation has on actions taken by nonlawyers on behalf of a corporation. Some courts, including our appellate court, have held that such actions are a nullity and warrant dismissal, the entry of a default judgment against the corporation, or vacatur of any judgment rendered. The defect is deemed incurable and goes to the court's power to exercise subject matter jurisdiction.

Other jurisdictions take the approach that actions by nonattorneys on behalf of a corporation are curable defects, allowing the corporation a reasonable time to obtain counsel and make any necessary amendments. These courts liberally construe the rules of civil procedure and emphasize substance over form to advance the policy favoring resolution of cases on the merits.

This court has recently discussed the nullity rule on two occasions wherein we declined to apply it. However, as the City maintains, these two cases are distinguishable. Neither involved a nonattorney representing a corporation in a legal proceeding. The City urges us to follow the line of authority holding that any unauthorized practice of law by a nonattorney is a nullity. We decline to do so.

A recent decision of the Seventh Circuit, *In re IFC Credit Corp.*, 663 F.3d 315 (7th Cir.2011), authored by Judge Posner, provides insight. The question before the court was whether a corporate bankruptcy petition, signed only by the president of the company who was not an attorney, rendered the proceedings void or, in state court terms, a nullity. If so, the court lacked jurisdiction over the matter and the error could not be cured by amending the petition, signed by an attorney, even one day after the original petition had been filed. The Seventh Circuit held that the proceedings were not void.

First, the court concluded that the rule prohibiting corporations from litigating without counsel could not be deemed a rule of subject-matter jurisdiction. In so finding, the court noted that the United States Supreme Court has "taken a sharp turn toward confining dismissals for want of subject-matter jurisdiction to cases in which the federal tribunal has been denied by the Constitution or Congress or a valid federal regulation the authority to adjudicate a particular type of suit." The court stated that "[t]he primary distinction is thus between classes of case that the Constitution or legislation declares off limits to the federal courts and errors in the conduct of cases that are within limits." The court reasoned that bankruptcy proceedings are "the type[s] of proceeding[s] that Congress has authorized federal courts to handle, while the rule barring lay representation of a corporation concerns the conduct of cases that are within that authority."

The court then further found that the consequences which result from a finding that the court lacks jurisdiction can be severe. In some cases, the statute of limitations may have run, thus depriving the corporation of access to the courts. Where the statute of limitations has not run, requiring a "do over" is costly, particularly if the lack of representation is discovered late in a protracted litigation. The court concluded that these consequences "are not appropriate punishments for pro se litigation by a corporation." Finally, the court posited there was "no danger that litigation by unrepresented corporations will flourish" because judges dislike pro se litigation and "will be vigorous enforcers of the rule that bars it, except in cases like this where the violation was utterly inconsequential."

The court reasoned that the rule against nonattorneys representing corporations "should be enforced, but sanctions for its violation should be proportioned to the gravity of the violation's consequences." In *In re IFC Credit Corp.*, there were no adverse consequences by the filing error. As such, there was no reason to impose any sanction, let alone dismissal.

We find the reasoning of *In re IFC Credit Corp.* sound. This court's definition of subject matter jurisdiction is similar to that of the supreme court precedent. In this case, as in *In re IFC Credit Corp.*, our constitution has authorized the legislature to provide the circuit court with the power to review administrative proceedings. Thus, in this case, as in *In re IFC Credit Corp.*, the rule prohibiting lay representation concerns the conduct of cases and the orderly administration of justice, not subject matter jurisdiction.

Further, we agree with the Seventh Circuit that a per se nullity rule is unreasonable and that sanctions for violating the rule against the unauthorized practice of law "should be proportioned to the gravity of the violation's consequences." * * * [B]ecause the consequences of applying the nullity rule to a case can be harsh, it should be invoked only where it fulfills the purposes of protecting both the public and the integrity of the court system from the actions of the unlicensed, and where no other alternative remedy is possible.

We hold there is no automatic nullity rule. Instead, the circuit court should consider the circumstances of the case and the facts before it in determining whether dismissal is proper. The circuit court should consider, inter alia, whether the nonattorney's conduct is done without knowledge that the action was improper, whether the corporation acted diligently in correcting the mistake by obtaining counsel, whether the nonattorney's participation is minimal, and whether the participation results in prejudice to the opposing party. The circuit court may properly dismiss an action where the nonlawyer's participation on behalf of the corporation is substantial, or the corporation does not take prompt action to correct the defect.

In the instant case, the trial court should have allowed Downtown Disposal to amend its complaints for administrative review. It is evident that Van Tholen was unaware he could not prepare and sign the complaints on behalf of the corporation. In fact, the administrative law officer advised Van Tholen that: "You have a right to appeal the decision to the Circuit Court within 35 days of today's date, and you would do that in Room 602 of the Daley Center." Even though the corporation was the party before the administrative hearing, Van Tholen appeared on its behalf and he, as a layperson, could reasonably have interpreted the "you" to mean him personally. Likewise, Van Tholen's participation was minimal. Van Tholen filled in a preprinted blank form with plaintiff's name, address, the date of the administrative decision, and the docket numbers. Van Tholen made no unscrupulous attempt to litigate on behalf of the corporation. Downtown Disposal retained counsel prior to any involvement by the City in the case other than having been served. As this case demonstrates, the absence of counsel at the threshold stage of the lawsuit—filing the complaint for administrative review—could not have prejudiced the City. As such, Downtown Disposal's commencement of the proceedings without the assistance of counsel was essentially inconsequential. For all practical purposes, Downtown Disposal was represented by counsel before the City became a player in the action, so neither the City nor the trial court was ever in the position of having to deal with a corporation unrepresented by counsel.

Further, deeming the complaints a nullity would be harsh: it "would yield the ironic result of prejudicing the constituents of the corporation, the very people sought to be protected by the rule against the unauthorized practice of law." Thus, rather than protecting the litigant (Downtown Disposal), application of the nullity rule would prejudice it. Downtown Disposal would lose its right to appeal and, thus, any remedy as might be provided for by law.

Moreover, there is clearly an alternative remedy to dismissal—allowing amendment of the complaints to add counsel's signature. Thus, it would indeed be a very harsh consequence to the corporation to apply the nullity rule to the case at bar.

We further disagree with the City that, if we affirm the appellate court, nonattorney representation of corporations will become commonplace. We agree with the Seventh Circuit that circuit court judges will be vigorous enforcers of the rule prohibiting nonattorneys from representing corporations.

Based on the foregoing principles, we reject the City's contention that any act of legal representation undertaken by a nonattorney on behalf of a corporation renders the proceedings void ab initio. We hold that the lack of an attorney's signature on a complaint for administrative review filed on behalf of a corporation does not render the complaint null and void or mandate dismissal in all instances. In situations where a nonattorney signs a complaint for administrative review on behalf of a corporation, the trial court should afford the corporation an opportunity to retain counsel and amend the complaint if the facts so warrant.

CONCLUSION

We conclude that the trial court erred in dismissing Downtown Disposal's complaints for administrative review based on the fact they were signed by Van Tholen because the lack of an attorney's signature was not jurisdictional and, therefore, did not render the proceedings null and void. Moreover, in the instant case, application of the nullity rule would be a harsh result since neither of the purposes underlying the rule are implicated and an alternative remedy was available. Accordingly, we affirm the appellate court's judgment, which reversed the circuit court's dismissal of Downtown Disposal's complaints and remanded for further proceedings. Appellate court judgment affirmed.

# CHAPTER VIII

# ARE THERE SYSTEMIC EXCEPTIONS OR REFORMS TO UPL?

■ ■ ■

## A. THE NARROWING COMMON-LAW DEFINITION OF THE PRACTICE OF LAW

### IN RE MORALES
151 A.3d 333 (Vt. 2016)

*[This case is reprinted in Chapter I, supra. It is referenced here because the court and the state attorney general admit that although past cases:*

> *articulate[ ] an expansive definition of the practice of law, as the Attorney General has argued in this case, "This decades-old definition does not reflect the reality of practice in Vermont and does not provide sufficient guidance to prosecutors, practitioners, and the public."*

*In re Morales, 2016 VT 85, ¶ 12, 151 A.3d 333, 337 (Vt. 2016). The opinion shows how the definition how narrowed in modern cases and "suggest[s] that the general scope of the prohibition against the unauthorized practice of law may not be solely a function of the tasks an individual performs but also reflects a balancing of the risks and benefits to the public of allowing or disallowing such activities. Id., 2016 VT at ¶ 18, 151 A.3d at 339.]*

## B. FEDERAL ADMINISTRATIVE AGENCIES

DREW A. SWANK, NON-ATTORNEY SOCIAL SECURITY
DISABILITY REPRESENTATIVES AND THE
UNAUTHORIZED PRACTICE OF LAW
36 S. Ill. U. L.J. 223, 234–35 (2012)

Certain exceptions to the unauthorized practice of law doctrine exist, including * * * representing others in federal * * * administrative proceeding. How non-attorney representatives came to practice before federal agencies involves the growth of administrative agencies, the Administrative Procedure Act, and, most importantly, a man named Sperry.

The Industrial Revolution was the creative force behind the creation of many administrative agencies in the United States. As administrative agencies were designed without the formalities and rules of the courts, they were ideally suited for non-attorney representatives. As the number of administrative agencies increased, so too did the opportunities for non-attorneys to practice law.

Historically, non-attorneys have routinely appeared before certain federal administrative agencies. Non-attorneys represent claimants ranging from eleven to fourteen percent of the more than 700,000 cases heard by the Social Security Administration each year. This equates to a minimum of 77,000 to 98,000 cases per year. As the Social Security Administration is the largest adjudicatory system in the world, more non-attorney representatives likely appear before it than in any other forum. Besides the Social Security Administration, non-attorney representatives appear before other federal agencies such as the Department of Health and Human Services, Immigration and Naturalization Service, Department of Labor, Patent and Trademark Office, and Merit Systems Protection Board.

This approach of allowing—or at least tolerating—non-attorney representation was codified in the Administrative Procedure Act. Enacted in 1946, the Administrative Procedure Act has been referred to as one of the most important pieces of legislation ever created. Among other things, the Administrative Procedure Act sets the framework for federal administrative agency adjudication, including the hearings conducted by the Social Security Administration and other federal agencies.

With the exception of the Internal Revenue Service, the Administrative Procedure Act neither grants nor denies non-attorneys permission to represent others before federal administrative agencies. Rather, it allows each federal agency to determine who may, and who may not, represent others before it.

While both the historical precedent and the Administrative Procedure Act allowed for non-attorney representation before federal administrative agencies, it was not until 1963 that the Supreme Court of the United States announced the basis as to why the states are unable to challenge who may represent others before federal administrative agencies.

### SPERRY V. STATE OF FLA. EX REL. THE FLA. BAR
373 U.S. 379 (1963)

Petitioner is a practitioner registered to practice before the United States Patent Office. He has not been admitted to practice law before the Florida or any other bar. Alleging, among other things, that petitioner 'is engaged in the unauthorized practice of law, in that although he is not a member of The Florida Bar, he nevertheless maintains an office * * * in Tampa, Florida, * * * holds himself out to the public as a Patent Attorney * * * represents Florida clients before the United States Patent Office, * * * has rendered opinions as to patentability, and * * * has prepared various legal instruments, including * * * applications and amendments to applications for letters patent, and filed same in the United States Patent Office in Washington, D.C.,' the Florida Bar instituted these proceedings in the Supreme Court of Florida to enjoin the performance of these and other specified acts within the State. Petitioner filed an answer in which he admitted the above allegations but pleaded as a defense 'that the work performed by him for Florida citizens is solely that work which is presented to the United States Patent Office and that he charges fees solely for his work of preparing and prosecuting patent applications and patent assignments and determinations incident to preparing and prosecuting patent applications and assignments.' Thereupon, the court granted the Bar's motion for a summary decree and permanently enjoined the petitioner from pursuing the following activities in Florida until and unless he became a member of the State Bar:

'1.  using the term 'patent attorney' or holding himself out to be an attorney at law in this state in any field or phase of the law (we recognize that the respondent according to the record before us has already voluntarily ceased the use of the word 'attorney');

'2.  rendering legal opinions, including opinions as to patentability or infringement on patent rights;

'3.  preparing, drafting and construing legal documents;

'4.  holding himself out, in this state, as qualified to prepare and prosecute applications for letters patent, and amendments thereto;

'5.  preparation and prosecution of applications for letters patent, and amendments thereto, in this state; and

'6.  otherwise engaging in the practice of law.'

The Supreme Court of Florida concluded that petitioner's conduct constituted the unauthorized practice of law which the State, acting under its police power, could properly prohibit, and that neither federal statute nor the Constitution of the United States empowered any federal body to authorize such conduct in Florida.

In his petition for certiorari, petitioner attacked the injunction 'only insofar as it prohibits him from engaging in the specific activities * * * (referred to above), covered by his federal license to practice before the Patent Office. He does not claim that he has any right otherwise to engage in activities that would be regarded as the practice of law.' We granted certiorari, to consider the significant, but narrow, questions thus presented.

We do not question the determination that under Florida law the preparation and prosecution of patent applications for others constitutes the practice of law. Such conduct inevitably requires the practitioner to consider and advise his clients as to the

patentability of their inventions under the statutory criteria, 35
U.S.C. §§ 101—103, 161, 171, as well as to consider the
advisability of relying upon alternative forms of protection
which may be available under statute law. It also involves his
participation in the drafting of the specification and claims of
the patent application, 35 U.S.C. § 112, which this Court long
ago noted 'constitute(s) one of the most difficult legal
instruments to draw with accuracy,' And upon rejection of the
application, the practitioner may also assist in the preparation
of amendments, 37 CFR §§ 1.117—1.126, which frequently
requires written argument to establish the patentability of the
claimed invention under the applicable rules of law and in light
of the prior art. 37 CFR § 1.119. Nor do we doubt that Florida
has a substantial interest in regulating the practice of law
within the State and that, in the absence of federal legislation,
it could validly prohibit nonlawyers from engaging in this
circumscribed form of patent practice.

But 'the law of the State, though enacted in the exercise of
powers not controverted, must yield' when incompatible with
federal legislation. Gibbons v. Ogden, 9 Wheat. 1, 211, 6 L.Ed.
23. Congress has provided that the Commissioner of Patents
'may prescribe regulations governing the recognition and
conduct of agents, attorneys, or other persons representing
applicants or other parties before the Patent Office,' 35 U.S.C.
§ 31, and the Commissioner, pursuant to § 31, has provided by
regulation that '(a)n applicant for patent * * * may be
represented by an attorney or agent authorized to practice
before the Patent Office in patent cases.' 37 CFR § 1.31. The
current regulations establish two separate registers 'on which
are entered the names of all persons recognized as entitled to
represent applicants before the Patent Office in the preparation
and prosecution of applications for patent.' 37 CFR § 1.341. One
register is for attorneys at law, 37 CFR § 1.341(a), and the other
is for nonlawyer 'agents.' 37 CFR § 1.341(b). A person may be
admitted under either category only by establishing 'that he is
of good moral character and of good repute and possessed of the
legal and scientific and technical qualifications necessary to
enable him to render applicants for patents valuable service, and
is otherwise competent to advise and assist them in the

presentation and prosecution of their applications before the
Patent Office.' 37 CFR § 1.341(c).

The statute thus expressly permits the Commissioner to
authorize practice before the Patent Office by non-lawyers, and
the Commissioner has explicitly granted such authority. If the
authorization is unqualified, then, by virtue of the Supremacy
Clause, Florida may not deny to those failing to meet its own
qualifications the right to perform the functions within the scope
of the federal authority. A State may not enforce licensing
requirements which, though valid in the absence of federal
regulation, give 'the State's licensing board a virtual power of
review over the federal determination' that a person or agency
is qualified and entitled to perform certain functions, or which
impose upon the performance of activity sanctioned by federal
license additional conditions not contemplated by Congress. 'No
State law can hinder or obstruct the free use of a license granted
under an act of Congress.'

Respondent argues, however, that we must read into the
authorization conferred by the federal statute and regulations
the condition that such practice not be inconsistent with state
law, thus leaving registered practitioners with the unqualified
right to practice only in the physical presence of the Patent
Office and in the District of Columbia, where the Office is now
located. * * *

Bereft of support in the regulations, respondent directs us to the
legislative history of the statute to confirm its understanding
that § 31 and its predecessor provisions were not designed to
authorize practice not condoned by the State. Insofar as this
history provides any insight into the intent of Congress,
however, we are convinced that the interpretation which
respondent asks us to give the statute is inconsistent with the
assumptions upon which Congress has acted for over a century.

Examination of the development of practice before the Patent
Office and its governmental regulation reveals that: (1)
nonlawyers have practiced before the Office from its inception,
with the express approval of the Patent Office and to the
knowledge of Congress; (2) during prolonged congressional study
of unethical practices before the Patent Office, the right of
nonlawyer agents to practice before the Office went

unquestioned, and there was no suggestion that abuses might be curbed by state regulation; (3) despite protests of the bar, Congress in enacting the Administrative Procedure Act refused to limit the right to practice before the administrative agencies to lawyers; and (4) the Patent Office has defended the value of nonlawyer practitioners while taking steps to protect the interests which a State has in prohibiting unauthorized practice of law. We find implicit in this history congressional (and administrative) recognition that registration in the Patent Office confers a right to practice before the Office without regard to whether the State within which the practice is conducted would otherwise prohibit such conduct.

The power of the Commissioner of Patents to regulate practice before the Patent Office dates back to 1861, when Congress first provided that 'for gross misconduct he may refuse to recognize any person as a patent agent, either generally or in any particular case * * *. The 'Rules and Directions' issued by the Commissioner in 1869 provided that '(a)ny person of intelligence and good moral character may appear as the attorney in fact or agent of an applicant upon filing proper power of attorney.' From the outset, a substantial number of those appearing in this capacity were engineers or chemists familiar with the technical subjects to which the patent application related. 'Many of them were not members of the bar. It probably never occurred to anybody that they should be.'

Moreover, although a concentration of patent practitioners developed in Washington, D.C., the regulations have provided since the reorganization of the Patent Office in 1836 that personal attendance in Washington is unnecessary and that business with the Office should be transacted in writing. The bulk of practitioners are now scattered throughout the country, and have been so distributed for many years. As a practical matter, if practitioners were not so located, and thus could not easily consult with the inventors with whom they deal, their effectiveness would often be considerably impaired. Respondent's suggestion that practice by nonlawyers was intended to be confined to the District of Columbia thus assumes either congressional ignorance or disregard of long-established practice. * * *

Hence, during the period the 1922 statute was being considered, and prior to its re-adoption in 1952, we find strong and unchallenged implications that registered agents have a right to practice before the Patent Office. The repeated efforts to assure Congress that no attempt was being made to limit this right are not without significance. Nor is it insignificant that we find no suggestion that the abuses being perpetrated by patent agents could or should be corrected by the States. To the contrary, reform was effected by the Patent Office, which now requires all practitioners to pass a rigorous examination 37 CFR § 1.341(c), strictly regulates their advertising, 37 CFR § 1.345, and demands that '(a)ttorneys and agents appearing before the Patent Office * * * conform to the standards of ethical and professional conduct generally applicable to attorneys before the courts of the United States.' 37 CFR § 1.344.

Moreover, the extent to which specialized lay practitioners should be allowed to practice before some 40-odd federal administrative agencies, including the Patent Office, received continuing attention both in and out of Congress during the period prior to 1952. The Attorney General's Committee on Administrative Procedure which, in 1941, studied the need for procedural reform in the administrative agencies, reported that '(e)specially among lawyers' organizations there has been manifest a sentiment in recent years that only members of the bar should be admitted to practice before administrative agencies. The Committee doubts that a sweeping interdiction of nonlawyer practitioners would be wise * * *.'

Ultimately it was provided in § 6(a) of the Administrative Procedure Act that '(e)very party shall be accorded the right to appear in person or by or with counsel or other duly qualified representative in any agency proceeding. * * * Nothing herein shall be construed either to grant or to deny to any person who is not a lawyer the right to appear for or represent others before any agency or in any agency proceeding.' 60 Stat. 240, 5 U.S.C. § 1005(a). Although the act thus disavows any intention to change the existing practice before any of the agencies, so that the right of nonlawyers to practice before each agency must be determined by reference to the statute and regulations applicable to the particular agency, the history of § 6(a) contains further recognition of the power of agencies to admit nonlawyers, and again we see no suggestion that this power is in any way conditioned on the approval of the State. * * *

It is also instructive to note that shortly after the adoption of the Administrative Procedure Act, the American Bar Association proposed the adoption of an 'Administrative Practitioners Act.' Though limiting the powers of nonattorneys in respects not here relevant, the bill did provide that 'authorized participation in agency proceedings' was permissible, without regard to whether the conduct constituted the practice of law in the State where performed.

Indicative of this same general understanding, we note that every state court considering the problem prior to 1952 agreed that the authority to participate in administrative proceedings conferred by the Patent Office and by other federal agencies was either consistent with or pre-emptive of state law.

Finally, regard to the underlying considerations renders it difficult to conclude that Congress would have permitted a State to prohibit patent agents from operating within its boundaries had it expressly directed its attention to the problem. The rights conferred by the issuance of letters patent are federal rights. It is upon Congress that the Constitution has bestowed the power 'To promote the Progress of Science and useful Arts, by securing for limited Times to Authors and Inventors the exclusive Right to their respective Writings and Discoveries,' Art. I, § 8, cl. 8, and to take all steps necessary and proper to accomplish that end, Art. I, § 8, cl. 18, pursuant to which the Patent Office and its specialized bar have been established. The Government, appearing as amicus curiae, informs the Court that of the 7,544 persons registered to practice before the Patent Office in November 1962, 1,801 were not lawyers and, 1,687 others were not lawyers admitted to the bar of the State in which they were practicing.

Hence, under the respondent's view, one-quarter of the present practitioners would be subject to disqualification or to relocation in the District of Columbia and another one-fourth, unless reciprocity provisions for admission to the bar of the State in which they are practicing are available to them, might be forced to relocate, apply for admission to the State's bar, or discontinue practice. The disruptive effect which this could have upon Patent Office proceedings cannot be ignored. On the other hand, the State is primarily concerned with protecting its citizens from unskilled and unethical practitioners, interests which, as we have seen, the Patent Office now safeguards by testing applicants for registration, and by insisting on the maintenance of high standards of integrity. Failure to comply with these standards may result in suspension or disbarment. 35 U.S.C. § 32; 37 CFR § 1.348. So successful have the efforts of the Patent Office been that the Office was able to inform the Hoover Commission that 'there is no significant difference between lawyers and nonlawyers either with respect to their ability to handle the work or with respect to their ethical conduct.'

Moreover, since patent practitioners are authorized to practice only before the Patent Office, the State maintains control over the practice of law within its borders except to the limited extent necessary for the accomplishment of the federal objectives.

We have not overlooked respondent's constitutional arguments, but find them singularly without merit. We have already noted the source of Congress' power to grant patent rights. It has never been doubted that the establishment of the Patent Office to process patent applications is appropriate and plainly adapted to the end of securing to inventors the exclusive right to their discoveries, nor can it plausibly be suggested that by taking steps to authorize competent persons to assist in the preparation of patent applications Congress has exceeded the bounds of what is necessary and proper to the accomplishment of this same end.

Congress having acted within the scope of the powers 'delegated to the United States by the Constitution,' it has not exceeded the limits of the Tenth Amendment despite the concurrent effects of its legislation upon a matter otherwise within the control of the State. 'Interference with the power of the States was no constitutional criterion of the power of Congress. If the power was not given, Congress could not exercise it; if given, they might exercise it, although it should interfere with the laws, or even the Constitution of the States.' II Annals of Congress 1897 (remarks of Madison). The Tenth Amendment 'states but a truism that all is retained which has not been surrendered.' The authority of Congress is no less when the state power which it displaces would otherwise have been exercised by the state judiciary rather than by the state legislature. Finally, § 31 contains sufficient standards to guide the Patent Office in its admissions policy to avoid the criticism that Congress has improperly delegated its powers to the administrative agency.

It follows that the order enjoining petitioner must be vacated since it prohibits him from performing tasks which are incident to the preparation and prosecution of patent applications before the Patent Office. The judgment below is vacated and the case is remanded for further proceedings not inconsistent with this opinion. It is so ordered.

Judgment vacated and case remanded.

## C. STATE ADMINISTRATIVE AGENCIES

### HARKNESS V. UNEMPLOYMENT COMP. BD. OF REVIEW
920 A.2d 162 (Pa. 2007)

*[This case is reprinted in Chapter I, supra. Balancing concern for the protection of the public against concern for "ensuring that the regulation of the practice of law is not so strict that the public good suffers," the court held that "the activities performed by an employer representative in an unemployment compensation proceeding" before a referee are not the unauthorized practice of law. Other courts have reached the same conclusion, see, e.g., Grafner v. Dep't of Employment Sec., 393 Ill. App. 3d 791, 914 N.E.2d 520 (2009); Unauthorized Practice of Law Comm. of Supreme Court of Colorado v. Employers Unity, Inc., 716 P.2d 460 (Colo. 1986); and the same reasoning has convinced courts in some states to allow non-lawyer representation before certain other administrative agencies. Other courts remain unconvinced. Florez v. City of Glendale, 105 Ariz. 269, 463 P.2d 67 (1969) (practice before an administrative agency is the practice of law).]*

BARBARA ALLISON CLAYTON, ARE WE OUR BROTHER'S
KEEPERS? A DISCUSSION OF NONLAWYER
REPRESENTATION BEFORE TEXAS
ADMINISTRATIVE AGENCIES AND
RECOMMENDATIONS FOR THE FUTURE
8 Tex. Tech. Admin. L.J. 115 (2007)

\* \* \*

## C. Changing the Legal Scene: The Industrial Revolution

The relationship between lawyers and s, delineated by the Bar,
remained essentially unchanged until the Industrial Revolution.
Coupled with the ensuing explosion of business growth was a
corresponding boom in governmental regulation, which resulted
in "the tremendous increase in the practice of law outside the
courtroom." Administrative agencies were created to help
manage and enforce the many new governmental regulations of
the Industrial Revolution. These agencies represented the hope
that the average citizen would have greater access to, and
success with, administrative law.

Congress exercised its constitutionally granted right to establish
these new agencies along with "legislative courts," to decide
matters "which from their nature do not require judicial
determination." These legislative courts, however, had a
"radically different" psychology than judicial courts. The change
was not unintentional. Congress purposefully sought a different
system because it distrusted the ability of the judicial process to
handle the thousands of new claims resulting from the increase
in governmental regulation. It viewed the formality of judicial
procedure as a major weakness; one it sought to remedy in the
legislative courts. With the formalities and restrictions removed,
nonlawyers began to practice in the roles of lawyers, and while
judicial courts demanded those who practiced before them were
certified to do so, legislative courts did not.

## D. Finding the Solution in Administrative Agencies

The Industrial Revolution set off a juggernaut of agency
creation. By the mid-nineteenth century, administrative
agencies had permeated every area of legal practice.
Administrative agencies had tremendous influence over areas
where highly valued individual rights were at stake. As Justice

Jackson said, administrative agency adjudications "have serious impact on private rights."

More people, it is believed, are directly affected by the processes of administrative boards . . . than by adjudications of the courts. Justice, to the majority of our population, is more apt to mean the fairness of an old age pension or unemployment insurance board than the soundness of a judicial pronouncement . . . of the Supreme Court.

In Texas, "the individual is affected daily by the rules, rates, and orders of the administrative agencies of the state." While relatively few individuals ever engage in a judicial trial, hundreds of thousands of Texans will claim some right that an administrative agency has control over. "In Texas, agencies are responsible for the regulation and supervision of railroads and trucks, banking, finance, taxation, securities, corporations, insurance, labor, occupational and professional licensing, civil service, liquor control, highways, conservation, fisheries, water resources, public health and public welfare." This ability to impact important areas for a large amount of the population created an attendant need to regulate.

Although federal administrative agencies had begun to form prior to the Civil War with the predecessors of the Bureau of Customs and the Veterans Administration, significant regulation governing agencies' procedures was not passed until the Federal Administrative Procedure Act in 1946. In reality, "[c]oncern over administrative impartiality and response to growing discontent was reflected in Congress as early as 1929." The discontent started a series of inquiries on the "need for procedural reform in the field of administrative law." At the same time, "[i]nquiries into the practices of state agencies, which tended to parallel or follow the federal pattern, were instituted in several states." The result of the investigations cumulated in the 1941 Attorney General's Report on the Administrative Procedure Act. The report recommended that Congress pass sweeping legislation to impose a new set of procedures for agencies to follow. Congress, in 1946, took the suggestion of the Attorney General's Committee and passed the Administrative Procedure Act (APA).

Shortly after the federal government passed the APA, Texas judges, attorneys, and scholars began debating whether Texas should adopt the Model State APA, based on the Federal APA, and regulate its own administrative agencies' procedures. Texas was experiencing the same problem the federal government had experienced—"[p]ractices var[ied] greatly from agency to agency; and the procedures followed within each agency [were] often a source of bewilderment to outsiders." The confused state of administrative law was blamed squarely on the "failure of the legislature to adopt an administrative procedure act applicable to all the state agencies."

Of particular interest to the Texas Bar in discussing the proposed APA was "[t]he question of whether practice before administrative boards and bureaus should be limited to duly licensed attorneys of the Bar, or whether provision should be made for the admission of certain enumerated personnel." Ultimately, the majority of Bar members who joined the discussion thought that a provision should be included in the act to allow certain qualified nonlawyers to practice before administrative agencies.

The debate raged for almost thirty years before Texas passed its own APA. Despite decades of debate yielding a consensus from the Bar on nonlawyer practice before administrative agencies, the Texas legislature left the decision of whether to allow such representation to the individual agencies. Most chose to allow nonlawyer representation as an option for a claimant.

In 1991, the Texas legislature voted to create a new agency, the State Office of Administrative Hearings (SOAH) "to serve as an independent forum for the conduct of adjudicative hearings in the executive branch of state government." "Originally, SOAH's jurisdiction was limited to . . . state agencies that did not employ an individual whose only duty was to preside as hearings officer over matters related to contested cases before the agencies." SOAH grew, however, and is now the fountainhead of administrative hearings in Texas-hearing cases from sixty-six state administrative agencies and governmental entities. SOAH specifically provides that an individual appearing in a proceeding "may represent himself or herself, or may appear by authorized representative." The only requisite qualification of these representatives is that they "must show authority to appear as the party's representative," but even that minimal proof is required only if they are challenged.

## D. LIMITED LICENSE FOR BANKRUPTCY PREPARERS

### MICHAEL D. SOUSA, LEGITIMIZING BANKRUPTCY PETITION PREPARERS: A SOCIOLEGAL PRESCRIPTION FOR CHANGE
#### 89 Am. Bankr. L.J. 269 (2015)

I argue that bankruptcy petition preparers should be authorized to provide limited legal services to debtors that at present would constitute the unauthorized practice of law. More precisely, I contend that bankruptcy petition preparers should be authorized in consumer no asset Chapter 7 cases to provide legal advice to debtors during the preparatory stages of the bankruptcy petition and schedules, and further be permitted to accompany their debtor clients to and represent them at the § 341 meeting of creditors. I recognize that in practice it can be difficult to distinguish between an asset and a no asset case, particularly because what appears at first blush to be a no asset case can morph into an assert case due to avoidance proceedings, valuation disputes or lien avoidance actions. But as I contend herein, if what appears to be a simple, no asset case becomes complicated, the bankruptcy petition preparer can then step aside and permit the debtor to retain counsel. Importantly, many consumer debtor lawyers would not necessarily be dissuaded by such an unbundled representation because their legal fees would arise post-petition, and would therefore not be subject to discharge under § 523 of the Code (although the dictates of § 329 of the Code would still apply).

Shifting to a limited legal services model for non-lawyer practitioners will necessitate a congressional amendment to § 110 of the Bankruptcy Code. But most importantly, I argue that in order for bankruptcy petition preparers to offer legal advice that would otherwise constitute the unauthorized practice of law, a federal program should be implemented through the United States Trustee's Office whereby interested petition preparers could voluntarily receive licensure and their practices thereby regulated in consumer bankruptcy cases. Any segment of the petition preparer population that chooses not to become licensed and regulated would remain subject to the prohibitions presently contained in § 110. In addition to licensure, regulation and accreditation, any established program should also impose educational requirements upon all licensed bankruptcy petition preparers and mandate the payment of fees by petition preparers towards a general insurance fund to offset any negligence or professional malpractice claims. In lieu of a general fund, the developed Trustee program could require that all petition preparers procure private malpractice insurance.

The creation of such a program would serve two very significant sociolegal purposes. First, because petition preparer fees are much lower than attorneys' fees generally, access to the bankruptcy system would become much more affordable for financially-desperate consumers. Second, the licensure and regulation of bankruptcy petition preparers would help root out many of the reported abuses currently present in the system; with licensing and regulation, consumers could be confident that not only are the bankruptcy petition preparers they retain competent to represent their interests, but that ramifications exist and recovery would be possible in the event of an act of negligence or professional malpractice. * * *

Beyond the sphere of bankruptcy law, non-lawyer practitioners have made inroads in offering their services to the public that would ordinarily constitute the unauthorized practice of law. This is effectuated either by judicial decision or specific authorization by statute or administrative regulation. In certain jurisdictions real estate brokers can prepare standard form agreements, mortgage lenders can complete printed loan documents, laypersons can represent school boards in unfair labor practice hearings before a state Public Employee Relations Commission, certified public accountants can prepare tax returns and offer tax advice, title insurance companies can prepare documents and offer legal opinions, and non-lawyers can render legal advice and services in immigration and naturalization matters.

Although courts possess the inherent authority to regulate the practice of law, this responsibility can be, and often is, shared with the legislature. Most questions regarding the boundaries of what constitutes the unauthorized practice of law occur at the state level. However, state law determinations regarding the scope of the unauthorized practice of law must yield when incompatible federal legislation exists as a result of the Supremacy Clause. In other words, Congress, by federal statute or through a regulation promulgated by a federal administrative agency, can authorize non-lawyers to engage in conduct that would ordinarily be considered the unauthorized practice of law at the state level. And as the United States Supreme Court held in *Sperry v. State of Florida*, so long as the non-lawyer practitioner is authorized by federal law and is confining his or her services to federal law matters, a state cannot "deny to those failing to meet its own qualifications the right to perform the functions within the scope of the federal authority." Some examples of non-lawyer practitioners already exist at the federal level. The Department of Treasury permits non-lawyers, such as enrolled agents, certified public accountants and actuaries, to act on behalf of taxpayers before the Internal Revenue Service; non-attorney agents may practice in patent matters before the United States Patent and Trademark Office; and non-lawyers may represent individuals in immigration matters before the Department of Homeland Security.

From a sociological perspective, the practice of law "touches upon virtually every economic and social facet of our lives today." However, the practice of what amounts to "law" need not remain the province of those admitted to a state bar. An individual does not need three years of law school classes to understand basic bankruptcy law principles in order to competently represent a consumer on a limited basis in the garden-variety no asset Chapter 7 case. "The minimum level of competence that lawyers are expected to maintain in order to continue to practice law does not necessarily mean that nonlawyers are unable to achieve a similar level of competence." In fact, in the standard Chapter 7 case, only occasionally will the debtor require legal representation beyond the § 341 meeting. It is precisely because most no asset Chapter 7 cases are routine and formulaic that attorneys can make a living representing consumer debtors: it is a matter of volume and speed. At the risk of generalizing, the same issues will arise for consumers in every Chapter 7 case: i) whether to file for bankruptcy at all; ii) chapter choice; iii) the continued collection efforts by creditors and the impact of the automatic stay; iv) the characterization of debts (*i.e.*, secured, unsecured, priority); v) whether the debtor will be able to retain personal and real property; vi) the choice of available exemptions; vii) the meaning of a discharge; viii) the general bankruptcy process; ix) the expectations of the court and the trustee; x) the valuation of assets; and xi) the possibility of reaffirming debts. It is precisely on such matters that have heretofore been characterized as the unauthorized practice of law. While I do not downplay the seriousness and importance of these legal issues to consumer debtors, there is no reason why a layperson with knowledge and training cannot become versed in adequately counseling debtors on these limited matters. As one commentator has noted, a consumer bankruptcy case at its core "involves properly filling out forms so as to ensure that the debtor's case is processed seamlessly and ultimately results in discharge."

Given that some debtors' financial situations leave them no choice but to represent themselves pro se, with no alternative for some level of legal guidance, it makes little sense to retain the present lawyer monopoly over the practice of Chapter 7 consumer bankruptcy law in cases where all of the significant decision-making occurs through the completion of routine forms.
* * *

A program to license and regulate the conduct of bankruptcy petition preparers could be accomplished in one of two ways. On one hand, Congress could amend § 110 of the Bankruptcy Code to specifically authorize by statute that petition preparers may offer what would today constitute the unauthorized practice of law by assisting debtors in completing the bankruptcy petition and schedules in Chapter 7 cases. As previously noted, a statutory grant of authority to engage in legal practice would preempt any state unauthorized practice prohibitions. If political momentum is not forthcoming to amend § 110, the Executive Office of the United States Trustee, as the administrative agency responsible for bankruptcy oversight, could be directed by the United States Department of Justice to craft regulations (much like other federal administrative agencies) authorizing bankruptcy petition preparers to engage in limited legal practice by assisting individuals in completing a bankruptcy petition and schedules. In addition to the process of petition completion, licensed and regulated bankruptcy petition preparers should also be authorized to represent Chapter 7 debtors at the § 341 meeting of creditors.

Any statutory amendment or regulation must take into consideration the recent decision by the United States Court of Appeals for the District of Columbia Circuit in *Loving v. IRS*. In *Loving*, the Court of Appeals held that the statutory authority of the Internal Revenue Service to "regulate the practice of representatives of persons before the Department of Treasury" did not include the ability to regulate paid tax-return preparers by requiring them to pass an initial certification exam, pay annual fees, and complete at least fifteen hours of continuing education courses each year. Importantly for present purposes, the circuit court implied that it was not beyond an administrative agency's powers to regulate practitioners in such a way, just that the manner in which the federal statute was worded prevented the Internal Revenue Service from doing so because "practice" did not encompass the preparation of income tax returns. Applying this rationale to the bankruptcy context, any statutory amendment to § 110 or regulatory scheme established by the Executive Office of the United States Trustee should make it clear that "practice" includes the preparation of bankruptcy petitions and schedules in addition to representing a debtor at the § 341 hearing.

The legal assistance offered by bankruptcy petition preparers should be limited to no asset Chapter 7 cases because they are generally straightforward and much less complex than a consumer Chapter 13 case. In the unusual case where significant assets are discovered during the course of the Chapter 7 case or issues of law arise such as dischargeability litigation, it may be then that a debtor would need to retain the services of an attorney. Retaining an attorney in these instances may still prove beneficial overall because a debtor would have saved money on the front end by retaining the services of a less-costly bankruptcy petition preparer and the retained attorney could simply focus on the legal issue that develops during the case, and not charge the debtor for much of the routine background work. The prospective attorney should be enticed by this unbundled representation because his or her legal fee would arise post-petition and therefore not be subject to discharge under § 523 of the Bankruptcy Code.

Any program to license and regulate bankruptcy petition preparers should begin as a pilot program, perhaps limited to a few judicial districts before adopting any program nationwide. The program should be made available to bankruptcy petition preparers on a voluntary basis; preparers that choose not to undergo the process of licensing and accreditation would still be bound by the prohibitions contained in current § 110 and by a forum state's unauthorized practice of law rules.

Individuals seeking licensing by the United States Trustee's Office to operate as bankruptcy petition preparers would first need to register with the agency and apply for licensure and accreditation. A licensed bankruptcy petition preparer would be given an individual registration number which would be required to be included on each document prepared by the petition preparer; this would enable the Trustee's Office to trace and link problem petitions with the preparers who filed them with the court.

The process of licensure and regulation should start with an educational or field experience requirement. In order to be eligible for such a program, the individual bankruptcy petition preparer would need to possess a paralegal certificate or demonstrate practical experience working as a paralegal in a law office (or a similar setting) for a certain number of years. An individual who graduated from law school, but is not a member of any state bar, would satisfy this educational component. If the individual possesses the requisite educational or experience background, he or she should be administered a competency examination on consumer bankruptcy practice to ensure a level of familiarity and understanding of this area of the law when advising a debtor. The examination should test issues and matters that will likely arise in the garden-variety Chapter 7 bankruptcy case when completing the petition and schedules, namely: i) the benefits and differences between bankruptcy chapters; ii) the general process of a Chapter 7 case; iii) the automatic stay; iv) the characterization and nature of certain debts; v) the selection of available exemptions; vi) what property can be retained and how; vii) the process of reaffirming debts; viii) the discharge of debts; ix) the treatment of executory leases; x) the treatment of priority debts such as taxes and spousal/child support awards; and xi) the operation and applicability of the means test. Such a competency examination could be administered by the local United States Trustee's Office in each judicial district or by a non-profit organization such as the American Board of Certification, which currently serves as a nationwide agency certifying attorneys in the specialty areas of consumer bankruptcy, creditors' rights law, and business bankruptcy.

Further, licensed bankruptcy petition preparers should be guided by ethical concerns similar to those of attorneys or, alternatively, a code of professional conduct could be established for licensed bankruptcy petition preparers. For example, a bankruptcy petition preparer should refrain from accepting any bankruptcy case which he or she cannot handle competently or which raises serious legal concerns at the beginning of the case, such as foreseeable automatic stay motions or dischargeability litigation. For these types of cases, the bankruptcy petition preparer should be ethically driven to refer debtors to an attorney. In addition, licensed bankruptcy petition preparers "should be granted client confidentiality privileges similar to those held by attorneys." As a further prophylactic measure, each bankruptcy petition preparer should be required to obtain a signed informed consent form from each debtor that specifically acknowledges that the preparer is not a licensed attorney and that the petition preparer can only offer limited legal services.

To ensure that a licensed bankruptcy petition preparer keeps current with the rapidly developing changes in consumer bankruptcy law, the licensing program should require that petition preparers undergo a certain number of continuing legal education classes or hours each year that specifically deal with developments in consumer bankruptcy law as it pertains to Chapter 7 practice. These courses should not be difficult to find as most every state bar association sponsors continuing legal education classes in bankruptcy law and the American Bankruptcy Institute offers multiple conferences on bankruptcy law each year in cities all around the country. As alternatives, the United States Trustee's Office could develop continuing education courses which could be offered live in local jurisdictions or online through a regional or national classroom environment, or a non-profit organization such as the American Board of Certification could offer continuing education classes for bankruptcy petition preparers.

Finally, and perhaps most importantly, licensed bankruptcy petition preparers should be required to possess adequate malpractice insurance (and verify as much to the United States Trustee's Office) or, as an alternative (or even in addition thereto), the United States Trustee's Office should develop a client protection fund (either nationwide or by each judicial district) that would be used to offset any damages awards arising from a particular petition preparer's negligence or malpractice in the event the petition preparer refuses to pay or cannot do so financially. This client protection fund can be funded through required annual fees to be paid by the bankruptcy petition preparer. Beyond just the client fund, the program developed by the United States Trustee's Office can be funded (in whole or in part) by additional annual fees paid by the licensed bankruptcy petition preparers. * * *

In addition to these requirements, any program established by the United States Trustee's Office should draft and publish a bankruptcy law and procedure manual to be distributed to every licensed bankruptcy petition preparer across the country. This would hopefully serve to standardize the level of knowledge about Chapter 7 bankruptcy law and procedure possessed by each licensed bankruptcy petition preparer and would hopefully promote uniformity in representation across jurisdictions. Because most no asset Chapter 7 debtors would satisfy the means test, together with the fact that most attorneys and bankruptcy petition preparers currently utilize their bankruptcy software programs to complete this aspect of the schedules and forms, there should not be widespread concern that a petition preparer will provide erroneous advice on this complex legal issue under BAPCPA.

Because licensed bankruptcy petition preparers would be enabled to offer limited legal advice and be required to pay annual fees to fund the program and to procure malpractice insurance (or finance a client protection fund), the level of fees a petition preparer could charge may become an issue. That is, on one hand, the underlying impetus for this entire endeavor is to offer an affordable alternative to legal counsel for the neediest bankruptcy debtors; on the other hand, I doubt that a licensed bankruptcy petition preparer could operate a business, pay annual fees, and procure malpractice insurance while being limited in the amount of fees that could be reasonably charged as currently dictated by bankruptcy court decisions and local bankruptcy court rules. That is, bankruptcy petition preparers would need to charge more than the $50–$150 amount that most courts presently allow. In order to keep fees down while accounting for the associated increased liability and overhead, it may be the case that licensed bankruptcy petition preparers would need to somewhat increase the fees charged for their services, but because even these heightened fees would presumptively be much less expensive than the legal fees charged by an attorney, this would still be a victory for needy Chapter 7 debtors while providing them with a level of comfort and protection that does not presently exist in the bankruptcy system. One benefit of starting as a pilot program would be to establish some parameters for fee scales for licensed bankruptcy petition preparers in light of the adopted program's requirements and costs.

Several positive effects may result from the adoption of such a program. First, and most obviously, debtors who could not afford legal representation for the simplest of Chapter 7 cases would have a lower-cost alternative in the form of a trained and licensed bankruptcy petition preparer. Second, a program of regulation and licensing would serve as a signaling function for consumer debtors insofar as debtors would know that a bankruptcy petition preparer possessing a license has a certain level of expertise to handle their bankruptcy case, whereas a debtor would know that he or she is acting at his or her own peril by hiring a petition preparer without these credentials. In other words, a system of licensing may be able to assist debtors in evaluating the quality of services they are being provided by the non-lawyer practitioner. Third, and related to this signaling function, a program of licensing and regulation could deter the truly incompetent practitioner or those set on making money irrespective of any fraudulent, deceptive or predatory behavior. Fourth, it is possible that the increased competition from bankruptcy petition preparers would result in lawyers making their own services more affordable to lower-income consumers in Chapter 7 cases. In fact, one access to justice scholar argues that in the face of competition from non-lawyer practitioners, lawyers may be more inclined to offer their services on a pro bono basis in order "to maintain jurisdictional closure. . . ." * * *

I concede that licensing and regulation will not cure all the evils regarding every element of the bankruptcy petition preparer population. Bad faith actors will continue to exist and resources will continue to be needed to prosecute those who decide not to participate in the regulatory program or comply with its requirements. However, a licensing and regulation program may go far in weeding out the bad actors from those non-lawyer practitioners who are truly interested in serving consumers in a competent and professional manner, while at the same time being able to make a living doing so. * * *

## E.  STATE LIMITED LICENSING

STEPHEN R. CROSSLAND & PAULA C. LITTLEWOOD,
THE WASHINGTON STATE LIMITED LICENSE
LEGAL TECHNICIAN PROGRAM: ENHANCING
ACCESS TO JUSTICE AND ENSURING THE
INTEGRITY OF THE LEGAL PROFESSION
65 S.C. L. Rev. 611, 611–17 (2014)

In June of 2012, the Supreme Court of the State of Washington adopted Admission and Practice Rule (APR) 28—the Limited Practice Rule for Limited License Legal Technicians. The Supreme Court voted 6–3 to approve APR 28, which allows individuals who meet certain education, training, and certification requirements to provide technical help and advice on legal matters—such as selecting and completing court forms, informing clients of procedures and timelines, explaining pleadings, and identifying additional documents that may be needed in a court proceeding. Although limited license legal technicians (LLLTs) will not be allowed to represent clients in court or to contact and negotiate with an opposing party on a client's behalf, they will be able to give legal advice within a defined scope of authority.

As the first licensed, independent paraprofessionals in the legal profession, it is not surprising that the licensing requirements for LLLTs are not unlike those of lawyers. The legal technicians will need to pass an examination, engage in continuing education, adhere to rules of professional conduct, and show proof of financial responsibility—among other stringent requirements. Such requirements serve to protect the public.

\* \* \*

## III. The Rule

\* \* \* APR 28 allows persons authorized by the state supreme court who meet certain education, training, and certification requirements to provide technical help on legal matters. The rule also created a thirteen-member LLLT Board comprised of attorneys, four nonattorney members, and at least one legal educator. The purpose of the board is to pick practice areas to which the rule should be applied, define the scope of practice in those practice areas, design a program to educate LLLTs on the scope of practice authorized, create rules of professional conduct, create an examination, create a continuing education program, and create a discipline system.

In its first official act, the board recommended family law as the area to which the rule should be first applied because it is one of the areas of highest need in the civil law arena. The supreme court approved that recommendation in March 2013. From there, the board undertook the significant work of defining the scope of practice authorized in the family law arena. The work involved members of the LLLT Board, as well as expert family law practitioners, who first outlined the universe of family law issues and then carefully outlined the authorized practice areas for LLLTs.

The scope of practice is codified in Regulation 2 in the appendix to APR 28. Subject to some limitations, the scope of practice generally includes the following areas: child support modification actions, dissolution and legal separation actions, domestic violence actions, committed intimate relationship actions, parenting and support actions, major parenting plan modifications, paternity actions, and relocation actions.

## IV. The Education

One of the most critical aspects of planning the LLLT program was delineating the educational requirements for LLLT candidates to complete. Training the LLLTs in what they are allowed to do—consistent with the scope outlined in Regulation 2—was, of course, the starting point for the training. But exposing the LLLTs to areas beyond their scope of authority is just as important—this way, they understand when they tread into these areas and know when they need to refer clients to a lawyer.

The education component has two main parts: (1) a core education component to be completed at the community college level and (2) a practice area component for each area of law in which the LLLT would like to have a license. The minimum level of education required for an LLLT is an associate-level degree, and it is envisioned that half of the associate-level education will be comprised of the core education requirements. The core education requires forty-five quarter credits, including the following: introduction to law and legal process; civil procedure; legal research, writing, and analysis; contracts; professional responsibility or ethics; law office procedures and technology; interviewing and investigation techniques; and legal studies electives. Currently, candidates must take these courses at an ABA-approved paralegal program; however, representatives from the Washington community college system and the board are working together to define criteria for certifying other paralegal programs in the state to increase accessibility to the education for students.

The second component of the education requirement, the practice area education, must be completed in a curriculum developed by an ABA-approved law school. Interestingly, all three ABA-approved law schools in Washington—University of Washington, Seattle University, and Gonzaga University—came to the table and volunteered to work together in developing the curriculum. The resulting requirement calls for fifteen family law credits: five credits in basic family law and ten credits in

advanced and Washington law-specific topics. The original
vision was for the curriculum to be taught at the local
community colleges by a law professor, practitioner, or
community college instructor, but at the close of developing the
curriculum, the law schools asked to deliver the practice area
education. * * *

## F. LICENSING INTERNET
## LEGAL PROVIDERS

MATHEW ROTENBERG, STIFLED JUSTICE:
THE UNAUTHORIZED PRACTICE OF LAW
AND INTERNET LEGAL RESOURCES
97 Minn. L. Rev. 709, 711–12, 736–40 (2012)

* * *

Advances in computer technology are effectively commoditizing
the law and revolutionizing the ways in which individuals seek
and receive legal services. ILPs [Internet legal providers]
present tremendous potential for increased access to legal
services. Efficient and low-cost legal information is vital to an
increasing number of unrepresented litigants and to combat the
shrinking amounts of legal aid available to them. Technology
has the potential to benefit a court system significantly
burdened by unprepared and uninformed litigants. Seen in this
light, the vague and outmoded language of the unauthorized
practice statutes, and their uneven application, is a more serious
problem than ever before. It decreases confidence in the legal
system, and prevents millions of potential users who stand to
benefit significantly from the growth of ILPs. * * *

## III. PROPOSED SOLUTIONS

Fundamental changes are needed to create safe and valuable
ILP alternatives to insufficient and inadequate traditional legal
services. However, an outright elimination of unauthorized
practice statutes is neither a prudent nor a likely solution.
Instead, a two-part proposal should be implemented which
requires action by the ABA, states, and ILPs: (a) states should
adopt a new ABA Model Rule that relaxes unnecessary
regulation and advances free-market principles; and (b) ILPs

should be required to comply with reasonable state licensing, disclosure, and accreditation requirements.

## A. States Should Adopt an ABA Model Rule That Relaxes Unnecessary Regulation and Advances Free Market Principles

The ABA should create a new model rule defining the practice of law over the Internet. The rule should, first and foremost, separate the jurisdictional regulation of attorneys from the regulation of multi-jurisdictional ILPs. Establishing specific rules for ILPs will eliminate confusion for attorneys, consumers, and courts, and provide incentives for investment by companies currently reluctant to invest in this highly uncertain legal terrain. Specifically, the new ABA rule should legalize document preparation, diagnostic mechanisms, and reactive legal information provided by ILPs, assuming those ILPs comply with reasonable state accreditation and licensure requirements. Authorizing the sale of non-personalized ILP products, as is now permitted in Texas, is an important first step to achieve this clarity. The current reality of allowing these products is that while many providers can sell legal software, they cannot instruct the consumer on how to use it most effectively. New ABA unauthorized practice provisions should thus relax restrictions on personalized features of ILPs as well. For example, diagnostic structures that apply facts to law serve as a linchpin between the individual and Internet legal resources. As in medicine, this feature is critically important to enable consumers to direct intelligibly their research. A relaxed rule will likely spur innovation, creating more advanced, interactive, consumer-friendly systems. This cascading phenomenon is exemplified in the online healthcare industry, where personalized information already helps large numbers of consumers, which in turn spurs more investment. There is strong reason to believe this would also take place with free market ILPs, as companies will increasingly enter the legal market "where value is being counted in billions and the current working practices seem antiquated or inefficient." Allowing the market to drive innovation will also balance these services in many respects, as useful products thrive while ineffective or harmful providers wither.

States should adopt a new ABA Model Rule that embraces the potential of the Internet to increase accessibility of legal services. Adoption of the ABA Model Rules of professional conduct is already widespread. To date, California is the only state not to adopt professional conduct rules that follow the format of the ABA Model Rule. To be sure, states will have legitimate concerns before they adopt relaxed regulations, especially given the speed and efficiency of the Internet and the potential for significant abuse. Advertising and advanced web design can create an impression of reliability, while masking unqualified and potentially harmful legal advice. For this reason, and to reduce likely resistance from certain sectors of the organized bar, relaxed regulation of ILPs must be accompanied by meaningful oversight through state licensing and accreditation requirements.

## B. ILPs Should Be Required to Comply with Reasonable State Licensing, Disclosure, and Accreditation Requirements

State licensure and regulation of ILPs is necessary to alleviate the most significant concerns of legal malpractice over the Internet. In order to receive a license, ILPs should be required to comply with reasonable regulations that include a variety of consumer protection standards. For example, disclosure rules could require ILPs to state when a service is not comprehensive. Such disclosure would inform clients about the limitations of ILPs up front, including a warning about the potential harm that often results from misapplied legal advice. For more complicated facts, ILPs should provide background information, while certain facts trigger attorney referrals and more information about ILP limitations. If personalized service by an ILP employee is required, the entity should be required to disclose these individuals to the client. Disclosure of whether lawyers or non-lawyers provided services, and other qualifications of these employees, also should be required. A system of accreditation would oversee compliance and issue licenses. Existing accreditation systems for web-based post-secondary schools, which operate in conjunction with the United States Department of Education, could serve as a potential framework for such Internet oversight.

Accreditation requirements also should include specific protections designed to prevent disclosure of confidential information. This would include advanced scanning systems to prevent malware, and network backup mechanisms. Governing bodies could mandate certain communication rules. For example, customer service agents could be restricted to helping individuals navigate their product, and prohibited from providing specific advice. Regulation also should also require ILP employment of a licensed supervising attorney in each jurisdiction in which the ILP sells its product—potentially resulting in numerous supervising attorneys. These individuals would be responsible for providing accurate and up-to-date legal information. Minimum competency requirements, similar to state continuing legal education standards for attorneys, also could also be required for non-attorney creators of legal content. ILPs should design these licensure and accreditation requirements to ensure a minimum level of accuracy and accountability.

There is legitimate apprehension that a majority of states may not adopt these proposals; for this reason, some advocate for a national rule to create the uniformity and clarity necessary to effectuate ILP advancement. A federal statute in particular would create much-needed nationwide uniformity for ILP regulations and promote investment in ILP innovation. But the regulation of lawyers for generations has been a state function, and federal legislation preempting state law in this arena is unlikely. State bar associations also would likely resist such federal legislation. Although a uniform standard is ideal for many reasons, state adoption of an ABA Model Rule establishes a more practical mechanism by which to facilitate much-needed change.

# G. LOOSENING THE REINS ON LEGAL ASSISTANTS

PAUL R. TREMBLAY, SHADOW LAWYERING: NONLAWYER
PRACTICE WITHIN LAW FIRMS

85 Ind. L. J. 653 (2010)

* * *

## C. The Nonlawyer Delegation Framework as an Alchemy of Risk Management, Informed Consent, and Unauthorized-Practice Prophylaxis

### 1. The Alchemy

Consideration of the[se] three factors ... establishes that lawyers ought to have discretion to delegate to nonlawyers any tasks which, in the lawyer's professional judgment and subject to the informed consent of the client, will provide the best and most efficient legal services to the client. Any substantive-law constraint depriving a lawyer of the discretion to delegate certain categories of activity would be inconsistent with the practice philosophies accepted within the legal profession. The lawyer-discretion model builds upon the trust that lawyers will recognize competence gaps and will manage risk responsibly, and will only delegate activities to nonlawyers if the lawyer's client has bought in to any significant risk taking. For reasons of economy and efficiency, a client is likely to buy in if the lawyer oversees the delegation and vouches for its soundness.

A lawyer who elects to use a nonlawyer assistant to complete some legal tasks frequently does so for the benefit of the client. Any task assigned to a nonlawyer assistant could, of course, be performed by the lawyer, but at a higher price. The use of nonlawyers provides a more efficient delivery of legal services at a lower price than if the lawyer acted alone; the resort to the use of nonlawyer services is thus financially adverse to the lawyer's interests, at least most of the time. A client might prefer that arrangement for the same reasons that a client might prefer to hire a lay advocate instead of a lawyer in order to save money; in this instance, contrary to the request for a lay advocate, the law permits a client to make that choice, because the client has a lawyer available to monitor the work. The lawyer will only choose to employ the nonlawyer assistance when it makes sense for the client's case, given the client's economic needs and the client's risk aversion. A client will only agree to nonlawyer assistance when he trusts the lawyer's judgment, accepts the risk, and welcomes the cost savings. The unauthorized-practice dogma has no complaint, both because the nonlawyer's work will be evaluated and monitored in accordance with the lawyer's professional judgment (which the dogma trusts), and because the scheme does not present anticompetitive threats to the legal profession.

I thus envision the following confluence: A lawyer who, against her economic interests perhaps, opts to generate a more efficient work product by the judicious delegation of tasks to a competent nonlawyer; and a client who, understanding the fiduciary responsibility of his lawyer to protect his interests and desirous to obtain the most inexpensive responsible legal services from the lawyer and her firm, accepts his lawyer's delegation of tasks to the supervised nonlawyer; and the legal profession which, trusting the lawyer's judgment and foreseeing little anticompetitive threat from the use of nonlawyers, sees no basis to ban the concept of delegation. Those collective actors with those overlapping interests ought to support a lawyer's delegation authority and discretion. Those actors would be challenged to justify a categorical ban preventing a lawyer from choosing to delegate certain selected tasks to nonlawyer assistants.

## 2. A Taxonomy: Drafting, Legal Research, Fact Investigation, Legal Counseling

A nonlawyer employed by a lawyer to assist in her practice performs important tasks which the lawyer, because of her delegation to the nonlawyer, will not perform herself. I refer to the tasks as important because they are essentially that-without those tasks, the lawyering would not achieve its ends, or would be incomplete. Someone must perform those tasks; in the settings we are exploring, it is the nonlawyer, and not the lawyer, who performs them. The lawyer, of course, must supervise the performance of the tasks by the nonlawyer, but supervision cannot mean, and does not mean, that the lawyer must accompany the nonlawyer and observe his performance of the tasks. No reasonable understanding of supervision contemplates such close monitoring, and any such proposal would be an absurd understanding of the use of legal assistants. Nor must the lawyer repeat the work of the nonlawyer to ensure its accuracy or soundness, for the same obvious reasons.

Supervision, then, will mean something different from constant monitoring or replicating the nonlawyer's work. If supervision has any substantive meaning, it must mean that the lawyer, who is the only person on the team who may orchestrate the lawyering work in its final form, must be confident, within the realm of reason, that the nonlawyer has gotten the task right. Consider four examples of tasks which a lawyer might choose to delegate to a nonlawyer: drafting documents; performing legal research; performing factual research; and advising clients about the state of the law and the options available to them. As we have seen above, the advisory authority regularly permits a lawyer's delegation of the first three of these, but often prohibits a lawyer from delegating the fourth, the offering of legal advice. A comparison of these four tasks will help us to understand the function and the limitations of the concept of "supervision." It will also show us that acceptance of the propriety of the first three activities' delegation requires acceptance of the propriety of the last activity's delegation.

### a.  Document Drafting

The first example-drafting a legal document such as a pleading-might serve as an easy beginning example. It is a task categorically permitted to be delegated to a nonlawyer by virtually all authorities, and its acceptability may be understood by reference to the risk-assessment heuristic. Consider a lawyer who delegates to a nonlawyer the task of drafting a standard motion using templates available within the law firm. The lawyer will be able to evaluate with a high degree of confidence whether the resulting product reads properly and includes the language, the clarity, and the elements necessary for the motion to achieve its purpose. The lawyer likely saves time by delegating the task to a nonlawyer, but the quality of the resulting work may be perfectly evaluated by the lawyer. The risk management by the lawyer is cabined and easily assessed.

For other documents, however, the risks of delegation may be more pronounced or unclear. A lawyer who delegates to a nonlawyer the task of choosing from among a selection of sample templates, or perhaps to create a first draft of a pleading without employing any template, may not be able to assess with the same level of confidence whether the resulting document achieves its purpose as well as if the lawyer had drafted the pleading herself. Nevertheless, some lawyers might ask a nonlawyer to create such a document in an exercise of her lawyering judgment, to save time for the lawyer and money for the client. The lawyer will accept some small possibility that the resulting work will fail to achieve its purposes, but that risk assumption is an ongoing enterprise for the lawyer.

### b. Legal Research

Contrast the pleading-drafting task with the next example-performing legal research, another task categorically permitted by the advisory authorities. For legal research, the lawyer's confidence in the resulting work product may be high (the results can fit comfortably within the lawyer's understanding of the substantive law as she has understood it), but it simply cannot be as high as in the first motion example above. If the lawyer's case requires legal research, a task for which the client will be charged and which the lawyering responsibilities require, the necessary assumption is that the lawyer does not know for sure what the law is without looking it up. Few lawyers know the law perfectly without looking it up, and, for those few lawyers, their knowledge is likely limited to narrow and frequently repeated contexts. When a nonlawyer performs legal research, then, the supervision by the lawyer means that the lawyer uses her best legal judgment-the legal judgment she has acquired by her membership in the profession and her practice experience-that the results of the research, as reported by the nonlawyer, are sufficiently reliable that the lawyer may use the results in moving ahead with her strategic development, advocacy, and negotiation. Like with the drafting task, the ultimate question for the lawyer is whether the quality of the work product is sufficiently high to permit her to use it in her ongoing work.

### c.  Fact Investigation

The next example—factual research—demonstrates a potentially higher level of risk, but risk whose magnitude the lawyer might reasonably assess and account for in her work. Once again, performing fact investigation and interviewing clients are responsibilities regularly understood as permissible activities for a lawyer to delegate to her nonlawyer colleagues. For fact investigation, the lawyer's confidence in the resulting product must necessarily be less than in either of the first two examples. While some of the nonlawyer's factual research may produce uncontrovertibly reliable results-a witness statement notarized by the witness, for instance, or a certified copy of a publicly recorded document-not all factual research permitted to be performed by nonlawyers would satisfy that description. The lawyer might reasonably rely, using her legal and professional judgment, on the reports of her investigators and other nonlawyer staff about events, accounts, observations, medical histories, and the like, when she develops her strategy and completes her final lawyering activity.

Like with each example discussed, the lawyer's performance herself of the tasks would decrease the risk of distortion or error or sloppiness, but her performance would increase, perhaps dramatically, the cost of her services. The lawyer, her clients, and the legal profession have opted to accept this minimal additional risk in return for the benefits of cost saving and efficiency. They do so, it is safe to assume, because the resulting risk from the delegation is extremely small due to the oversight and supervision of the experienced lawyer with judgment to guide her assessments.

In each of the examples described (drafting, legal research, and fact investigation), the nonlawyer's work could possibly be wrong. The nonlawyer's drafting of a motion might omit a critical element of the motion's argument, leaving it fatally flawed. The nonlawyer's legal research could overlook a critical new development eviscerating the strength of the authorities located and reported to the lawyer. The nonlawyer's factual research might be sloppy, incomplete, or distorted for any number of reasons. Of course, a lawyer's performance of any of those very same tasks could also be wrong, although the odds of that happening are seemingly lower than in the case of the nonlawyer's work, especially if we accept (as we do for the sake of this Article) the premises of the unauthorized-practice dogma. The lawyer's supervision of the nonlawyer's work decreases the risk of error, but it cannot eliminate it.

Clients, though, should, and in fact do, accept the just-described use of nonlawyers as a reasonable trade-off that will reduce the cost of legal services with minimal effect on the quality of the services rendered. In assessing the wisdom of a lawyer's use of nonlawyer services to assist in her work for clients, that matrix is the ultimate standard by which the profession ought to evaluate this scheme: Is a client sufficiently protected by the lawyer's delegation of some tasks to others? Put another way, should the profession permit a client to elect to retain a lawyer who will delegate some of her tasks to supervised nonlawyers? So long as the lawyer, exercising her judgment about the complicated practice world in which she operates and accepting the ultimate responsibility for the results of the risks involved, concludes that the work performed by the nonlawyer is reasonably close to what the lawyer would achieve at a significantly higher cost to the client, then the profession ought to permit an informed client to accept those minimal risks. It is, in other words, a sensible thing for the profession to allow and for an informed and understanding client to choose.

### d. Legal Advising and Counseling—A Categorical Exclusion?

We now reach our fourth example, that of providing legal advice to a client, the assignment most frequently identified by the advisory authorities as nondelegable. If the advisory authorities' description of the lawyer's duties is accurate, and if we accept a literal and not a nuanced interpretation of that description, then lawyers possess no discretion to delegate to a nonlawyer the task of providing to a client some legal advice, while possessing lawful discretion to delegate to the nonlawyer the responsibilities of drafting documents, performing legal research, and conducting fact investigation. We saw above that the literal reading of that prohibition was not supported by any fair interpretation of available substantive law. We see here why such a literal reading would be incoherent. Applying the same matrix of risk management, informed consent, and unauthorized-practice prophylaxis, we see lawyers must possess the same discretion to delegate to a supervised nonlawyer the assignment of providing some legal advice.

Lawyers who assign document-preparation, legal-research, and fact-investigation tasks to nonlawyers risk malpractice liability or other adverse consequences if the nonlawyers perform the tasks incompetently. Because any performer of legal services, lawyer or nonlawyer, risks committing malpractice if her work happens to be sloppy or in error, the question for the lawyer remains one of assessing the acceptable level of risk, and accepting responsibility to indemnify the harmed client if errors occur and result in malpractice damages.

The difficulty with applying a *categorical* test that would bar lawyers from delegating to a nonlawyer discrete lawyering activities like "counseling" is apparent. The underlying justifications for use of nonlawyers as part of an efficient, client-centered law practice apply equally as well to some forms of counseling as they do to some forms of document preparation, legal research, or fact development. To understand why, we return to the concept of supervision. All nonlawyer work must be properly supervised, whatever its nature. The critical question is what constitutes effective supervision.

As noted above, supervision of a subordinate, whether a lawyer or a nonlawyer, does not mean that the supervising lawyer must observe every action the supervisee takes. It does not mean that the supervising lawyer must reprise the work performed by the supervisee to ensure its accuracy. Instead, a practical understanding of supervision shows it to consist of measures by the lawyer which offer assurance that the delegated work will be performed competently. It is a risk-management concept-it cannot guarantee competent service any more than the lawyer's doing the work herself could guarantee that result.

A lawyer may delegate to a nonlawyer the responsibility to communicate legal advice to a client in the same manner, and employing the same risk-management and supervision skills, as the lawyer would delegate a legal research or document-drafting task. A lawyer who knows that her nonlawyer colleague-assume, for the moment, an experienced lateral who is not a member of the bar and is not practicing "temporarily" in the state-understands a client's legal issues with depth and sophistication and can discuss those issues with clarity and nuance can, consistent with the lawyer's fiduciary duties to her client, suggest that the nonlawyer meet with the client and advise the client about his rights. That delegation would be an essential part of the lawyer's representation of the client, for which the lawyer would remain ultimately responsible. The client would understand that the advice has been communicated by a nonlawyer and by implication (or perhaps expressly so) would consent to the use of a less-expensive device to further the client's case. No worry about unauthorized practice of law arises, both because the client is the beneficiary of the purported special skill of the lawyer and because the nonlawyer presents no threat to the lawyer's livelihood, since the lawyer has full control over the use of that practice option.

Recall that a nuanced reading of the apparent categorical ban on nonlawyers offering legal advice supports this conclusion. The authorities which repeat that generalized prohibition often qualify it with some version of the "conduit" notion, approving a nonlawyer's communication to the client of the lawyer's ideas. It is critical, however, not to read the conduit conception in too crabbed and narrow a fashion. The narrow conduit version would approve a nonlawyer's providing legal advice only as a script reader, one who has heard the lawyer's legal conclusions and transmits those ideas to the client by rote. By that understanding, a reasonably talented high-school intern could accomplish that task.

A more sensible, and in fact the only sensible, understanding of the conduit idea goes much farther than the script-reading function. The better understanding approves of the nonlawyer's engaging the client in a spirited dialogue about the client's legal rights and duties, so long as the lawyer is confident that the nonlawyer may perform that task competently and effectively. The assistant still serves as a "conduit" for the lawyer's judgment and for the lawyer's skill at reading complexity and nuance. Because the lawyer is certain that the nonlawyer has the ability to manage the interaction, that judgment (and that risk assessment) controls. The lawyer is using the nonlawyer as one useful component of her lawyering "toolkit."

This richer conduit conception, however, suggests some possible limits. Its trusting of the lawyer's assessment about the nonlawyer's skill might imply more liberty on the part of the lawyer than even an expansive reading of the unauthorized-practice-of-law dogma would tolerate. For instance, a lawyer might *accurately* trust her nonlawyer colleague's abilities so much (imagine, again, an experienced lateral associate) that the lawyer would confidently choose to assign the nonlawyer to handle a client's matter from beginning to end without any oversight by the lawyer at all-indeed, the lawyer may never even know of the client's existence, except perhaps to approve formally the creation of an attorney-client relationship with the law firm. By all of the criteria we have employed above-the risk-management responsibilities of the lawyer, the informed consent of the client (who, we may assume, has assented to the nonlawyer's role), and the unauthorized-practice prophylaxis-that arrangement should pass muster. Given the lawyer's ultimate responsibility and her judgment about the depth and breadth of the nonlawyer's talent, there is no *conceptual* difference between that delegation and the lawyer's assigning the nonlawyer to draft a pleading. Nevertheless, despite the logic of this proposition, a lawyer using her nonlawyer assistant in this way proceeds at her own peril. The critical problem with this setting is that the lawyer has not supervised the matters on which the nonlawyer has worked. Mere confidence in the talents of the nonlawyer would not suffice; the lawyer must oversee the actual work of the nonlawyer.

Thus, a categorical exclusion of "counseling" or "advice giving" from the activities permitted to be delegated to a nonlawyer would be hard to defend and difficult to apply. The only conceivable justification for categorical treatment of that activity would be a purely prophylactic one. A creator of guidelines governing nonlawyer practice supervised by a lawyer might claim that the risks of harm to a client are so great from a nonlawyer's advice giving that even a wise and experienced lawyer ought never be permitted to delegate a counseling activity to a nonlawyer colleague, regardless of the comfort level of the lawyer with the nature of the task and the qualifications of the nonlawyer. That argument, though, is a remarkably weak one. Risk abounds in assigning any task to a nonlawyer, just as risks abound (albeit presumably lower ones overall) in the lawyer's doing the work herself. Some advice-giving tasks will objectively carry far less risk than some legal-research tasks. The guideline creator's prophylactic arguments would perhaps support a categorical ban on the use of legal assistants entirely, but not to carve out categorical distinctions within the panoply of activities that a lawyer engages in while representing a client.

Similar arguments would apply to any attempt at a categorical exclusion of "negotiation" from the acceptable roles of nonlawyers in law firms. The concept of negotiation tends to refer to activity involving the resolution of differences through bargaining and compromise in an effort to come to a settlement of a dispute or to complete a transaction. Assuming for the sake of this argument that negotiation can, if performed within a legal setting, represent the practice of law that nonlawyers may not pursue, a lawyer may nevertheless delegate to a nonlawyer assistant certain parts of the negotiation process with proper supervision and with the lawyer's acceptance of responsibility for the activity. Such delegation, of course, would include negotiation meetings occurring outside of the presence of the lawyer.

We might wonder whether negotiation ought to be seen as qualitatively different from any of the previous categories, especially negotiation outside of the lawyer's observation. A critic might think of that process as too inevitably intertwined with legal judgment and deliberation such that a lawyer ought never-categorically-assign a nonlawyer to perform that role. While that worry has some plausible merit, it cannot justify a categorical ban on such delegation as a matter of professional ethics. As with all of the previous topics, the assessment of the propriety of the assignment rests on the lawyer's practical wisdom about the effectiveness of the nonlawyer's communication and implementation of the lawyer's judgments. Without doubt, some complex negotiations will never properly be assigned to a nonlawyer. But other less complex bargaining events, such as telephone calls to communicate and defend an offer or demand whose terms are easily understood by both parties, might sensibly and properly be delegated to an assistant. The question will always remain one of the lawyer's exercise of her professional judgment given the risks and benefits involved, with her assurance of satisfactory supervision of the nonlawyer.

Any of the other categories where some authority has precluded assignments to a nonlawyer may be understood using the same analysis. For instance, a nonlawyer could not independently establish an attorney-client relationship with a client. Because only a lawyer may represent a client, only a lawyer may create the relationship. But a nonlawyer, as the lawyer's conduit, may communicate the lawyer's agreement to accept an individual or an entity as a client. Similarly, only the lawyer may decide to terminate the relationship, but no authority would claim that the lawyer may not delegate to a nonlawyer assistant the communication of the closing of a matter. That kind of assistance is regularly accepted within the profession.

Therefore, once we exclude the distinctive context of the court appearance and proceedings auxiliary to that setting, not one of the categorical limitations on nonlawyer practice appearing in the literature is either accurate or valid. The only categorical limitation on nonlawyer delegation is, essentially, the substantive law of malpractice. * * *

## H.  IN-HOUSE CORPORATE
## LEGAL PROFESSIONALS

### DEBORAH L. RHODE, PROFESSIONAL INTEGRITY AND PROFESSIONAL REGULATION: NONLAWYER PRACTICE AND NONLAWYER INVESTMENT IN LAW FIRMS
39 Hastings Int'l & Comp. L. Rev. 111, 113–14 (2016)

[T]he demand for nonlawyer practice has considerably outstripped the bar's capacity to prevent it. As the chair of Tennessee's unauthorized practice committee put it,

> In recent years, it seems every Tom, Dick, and Harriet have gotten into . . . businesses that either constitute the practice of law or the law business or that are so close, the border is invisible. Tax consultants, document

production 'mills' such as 'We the People,' and numerous title insurance and closing companies have sprung up offering services or advice that cannot be differentiated from the services offered by licensed lawyers.

Often with no meaningful supervision by lawyers, nonlawyers play an increasingly important role within organizations in areas like contracts and compliance.

### THOMAS D. MORGAN, CALLING LAW A "PROFESSION" ONLY CONFUSES THINKING ABOUT THE CHALLENGES LAWYERS FACE
9 U. St. Thomas L.J. 542, 564 (2011)

Often, the non-lawyers will benefit from lawyer assistance, and current legal ethics rules require a lawyer in a private law firm to supervise and take responsibility for the non-lawyer's work; but within a corporation or other organizational client, lawyer supervision need only be provided if it is cost-effective to do so.

### SUSAN HACKETT, INSIDE OUT: AN EXAMINATION OF DEMOGRAPHIC TRENDS IN THE IN-HOUSE PROFESSION
44 Ariz. L. Rev. 609, 616 (2002)

In-house counsel are considered industry leaders in delegating traditional legal work to nonlegal departments/personnel, sometimes under the continued supervision of lawyers. Consider, for instance, the development of compliance programs under the purview of nonlegal compliance officers and the departments of the corporation they serve: environmental; health/safety; marketing-sales/antitrust; treasury functions; HR; etc.

This leads to a meshing of business and legal ethical standards in such a way that is potentially redefining the "laws" governing both legal and business behaviors. Questions that blur the line between legal services and other professional/managerial services as lawyers team with business people to solve multidisciplinary problems will dominate the agendas of professional regulators at the bar in coming years.

Lawyers' functions for their clients will change dramatically because of these practices, pioneered by in-house counsel. It will not be enough for law firms to fulfill the function of legal analysis. Law firms will be required, as their in-house counterparts are currently, to join a team of problem solvers that provide integrated solutions rather than mere assessments of problems.

# I.  HOW THE UK REGULATES LAWYERING

### GILLIAN K. HADFIELD & DEBORAH L. RHODE, HOW TO REGULATE LEGAL SERVICES TO PROMOTE ACCESS, INNOVATION, AND THE QUALITY OF LAWYERING
#### 67 Hastings L.J. 1191 (2016)

\* \* \*

Many current discussions of the need for reform of the American approach to legal professional regulation eventually circle around to the United Kingdom's alternative model. This model diverges substantially from the modern American approach, and it is because of the ways in which it diverges that it succeeds in promoting access and innovation without sacrificing the quality of lawyering. In this Part, after a quick summary of the American approach, we show how the U.K. model achieves these goals.

The modern American approach to regulating the practice of law dates to the late nineteenth and early twentieth centuries, led primarily by deliberate efforts in the American Bar Association to regulate admissions and practice and to wrest control from state legislatures and lodge it in state supreme courts. The resulting scheme, however, went far beyond the common law history of granting courts the power to determine who could appear before them. In effect, state courts delegated authority to bar associations to set rules (most of which followed the lead of the ABA Model Rules) that encompass all aspects of the practice of law. The power of these rules to exclude practitioners who did not meet bar standards or adhere to bar practice requirements (such as prohibitions on the corporate practice of law and fee-sharing) was often buttressed with legislation making it illegal to practice law without the authorization of the state supreme court. As many have recounted, the boundaries of this regulatory authority have always been expansive, with the definition of what constitutes the "practice of law" stretching to incorporate effectively everything done by lawyers: legal advice, drafting, negotiation, representation, and support in dispute resolution processes. Moreover, state supreme courts have claimed an inherent authority, grounded in the constitutional separation of powers, to regulate the legal profession in all of its activities.

The British approach to regulation of the legal profession has never followed the same path. From the earliest days, the United Kingdom has always had multiple legal professions—originally barristers, solicitors, attorneys, and scriveners. At no time has the provision of legal advice or the drafting of documents (other than those required to participate in a lawsuit or convey real estate) been subject to regulation. And since the passage of the Legal Services Act ("LSA") of 2007, the regulatory approach in the United Kingdom has diverged even further from the American model.

The current regulatory approach of the LSA begins with designation of regulatory objectives. These regulatory objectives are:

    (a)  protecting and promoting the public interest;

    (b)  supporting the constitutional principle of the rules of law;

    (c)  improving access to justice;

    (d)  protecting and promoting the interests of consumers;

    (e)  promoting competition in the provision of regulated services . . . ;

    (f)  encouraging an independent, strong, diverse and effective legal profession;

    (g)  increasing public understanding of the citizen's legal rights and duties;

    (h)  promoting and maintaining adherence to the professional principles.

The professional principles mentioned in (h) are set out in the Act:

(a) that authorised persons should act with independence and integrity,

(b) that authorised persons should maintain proper standards of work,

(c) that authorised persons should act in the best interests of clients,

(d) that persons who exercise before any court a right of audience, or conduct litigation in relation to proceedings in any court, by virtue of being authorised persons should comply with their duty to the court to act with independence in the interests of justice, and

(e) that the affairs of clients should be kept confidential.

Thus, the U.K. professional principles thus track all of the core values of the legal profession as articulated by the ABA—with the important difference that the LSA adds a commitment to promoting competition and does not elevate as a goal in itself the preservation of a single (self-regulated) profession.

The strategy of the LSA is to designate particular instances of legal work as reserved activities and then to require that those activities only be performed by "authorized persons." These reserved activities are:

(a) the exercise of a right of audience;

(b) the conduct of litigation;

(c) reserved instrument activities;

(d) probate activities;

(e) notarial activities;

(f) the administration of oaths.

This is where we see a major difference between the British and American approaches. The American bar associations and state courts effectively open the practice of law to bar-licensed attorneys only while reserving the right to add to the category of the practice of law down the line. This approach forces alternative providers to seek carve-outs for things like document assembly, supplying blank contracts (real estate agents), tax advice (accountants), non-profit assistance to immigrants in some hearings, and appearances before some federal administrative bodies such as the U.S. Tax Court, the Patent Office, and the Social Security Administration. The U.K. approach, in contrast, carves out specific activities for licensed lawyers, and leaves the residual open for competition from alternative nonlawyer providers.

A second major difference is that the category of "authorized person" in the United Kingdom includes multiple legal professions and licenses. Currently in the United Kingdom there are nine different professional licenses or designations for those performing reserved activities: solicitor, barrister, legal executive, notary, licensed conveyancer, patent attorney, trademark attorney, costs lawyer, and chartered accountant. Professionals practicing under these licenses have nonexclusive authorization to perform particular reserved activities and hence there is interprofessional competition. Barristers, solicitors, and legal executives can perform all reserved activities with the exception of notarial activities, which only notaries can perform. Notaries, however, can, alongside licensed conveyancers, also engage in reserved instrument and probate activities; neither can exercise a right of audience or conduct litigation. Patent and trademark attorneys can appear in court, conduct litigation, and engage in reserved instrument activities. Costs lawyers can appear in court and conduct litigation. Chartered accountants can engage in probate activities only; they are the only legal professionals who cannot administer oaths.

Regulation of each of these professions is carried out by a different *approved regulator*. The Law Society regulates solicitors and the Bar Council regulates barristers, for example. Approval and oversight of these front-line regulators is carried out by the Legal Services Board ("LSB"), an independent administrative body that is accountable to Parliament and operates out of the Ministry of Justice. With the exception of the Chief Executive (who is appointed by the Board), Board members are appointed by the Lord Chancellor. The Legal Services Act requires the LSB to have a lay chair and a majority of lay members. The Act also requires front-line regulators, which operate as trade associations promoting the interests of their members, to establish independent regulatory arms (the Solicitors Regulatory Authority and the Bar Standards Board, for example). Under the authority of the Act, the LSB has established internal governance rules requiring the regulatory bodies set up by approved regulators to be governed by a board with a nonlawyer chair and a majority composed of nonlawyer members.

This is an example of what we earlier called *competitive* or *meta-regulation*: a legal practitioner who wishes to conduct litigation, for example, can choose from which professional body authorized to regulate that particular activity she wants to secure a license. This means that not only are existing practitioners engaged in interprofessional competition across dimensions such as cost and quality, so too are the front-line regulators in competition in the design and implementation of their regulatory requirements.

Competition between regulators occurs under the umbrella of oversight by the LSB, which must approve regulators' rules and processes. Ultimately, the LSB is responsible for ensuring that regulators are fostering regulatory objectives. This involves reviewing, for example, proposed rule changes, monitoring the performance of the approved regulators, conducting research and investigation of the performance of legal services markets, and making recommendations to the Lord Chancellor about changes to the regulatory scheme implemented by the Legal Services Act. In carrying out its activities, the LSB is required to consult with the Lord Chief Justice (the head of the judiciary), the U.K. antitrust authority (the Office of Fair Trade), and a Consumer Panel.

The U.K. scheme also provides for the licensing of entities. These are known as *alternative business structures* ("ABS"), which supply an alternative to the law firm through which lawyers have traditionally offered their services. The LSB approves and oversees the bodies authorized to license ABSs. There are five licensing authorities: the Solicitors Regulatory Authority, the Bar Standards Board, the Council of Licensed Conveyancers, the Institute for Chartered Accountants, and the Intellectual

Property Regulation Board (which regulates both patent and trademark attorneys). Collectively, as of 2015, these five licensing authorities had licensed over 800 entities, including solo practitioner entities, law partnerships, for-profit corporations, entities owned by unions and other non-profit organizations, and cooperatives. Most are private, not publicly listed, companies and include such recognizable names for Americans as Ernst & Young, LegalZoom, KPMG, and PriceWaterhouseCoopers. Slater & Gordon LLP—an Australian firm with approximately twelve percent of the U.K. market in personal injury law in 2015—is one of the few publicly traded companies on the list.

The regulation of ABSs is two-pronged: the entity is regulated and the authorized persons within the entity are regulated. Both are subject to losing their license or authorization to practice in the event of a breach of the rules of a licensing authority (in the case of an entity) or an approved regulator (in the case of an authorized person). The licensing authority must approve anyone who holds a material or interest in an ABS. Approval is based on a determination that the holding of the restricted interest in the ABS will not interfere with the regulatory objectives of the LSA or the duties of the entity and any authorized person it employs to comply with their regulatory duties. Reserved activities must be carried on within the entity only through people authorized to perform those activities. There must be at least one manager who is authorized to engage in the reserved activities for which the ABS is licensed. Unauthorized persons—owners, managers, employees—are subject to the regulation of the licensing body and obligated to refrain from doing anything that might cause the licensed body or the authorized persons within it to violate their professional duties. An ABS is required to have a Head of Legal Practice, approved by the licensing authority. That individual serves as a compliance officer responsible for ensuring that only authorized persons carry out reserved activities and that unauthorized persons (including owners and managers) do not violate their duty under the Act not to cause the licensed body or its employees and managers to breach applicable regulations. The LSA also requires approved regulators to have systems in place to protect confidentiality. The traditional privilege against disclosure of confidential information covers any authorized provider or licensed entity.

The U.K. approach foregoes none of the traditional framework of professional regulation. It preserves all of the profession's long-held duties. And it preserves the capacity of the professional body to revoke individual lawyers' authorization to practice regardless of practice setting.

In terms of enforcement, the U.K. scheme relies on multiple strategies in addition to license revocation. It is a criminal offense punishable by fine or imprisonment for an entity to carry on a reserved activity through someone who is not an authorized provider. Approved regulators can also impose substantial fines: the maximum fines approved by the LSB are £ 250 million for an ABS and £ 50 million for a manager or employee of an ABS. Regulators can disqualify individuals from serving as owners or managers of an ABS. Licensing authorities are authorized to intervene and take over management of an ABS that has violated regulations when necessary to protect clients. Approved regulators carry out annual compliance surveys and spot checks. They can also impose supervision on individuals and entities, as well as conditions on licenses.

The U.K. regulatory approach also takes other steps to protect the interests of clients. The major approved regulators require individual lawyers and ABSs to hold indemnity, in essence malpractice, insurance. Those licensed by the Solicitors Regulatory Authority (the largest licensing authority) must have client compensation funds. The LSA establishes an Office of Legal Complaints ("OLC"), with which any consumer can lodge a grievance. The OLC operates a Legal Ombudsman scheme, consisting of a chief ombudsman (who must be a layperson) and an assistant ombudsmen. Ombudsmen are authorized to resolve complaints by remedies such as apologies, fee rebates, compensation, and rectification of errors.

The U.K. approach thus substantially relaxes or eliminates the traditional restrictions on the business models within which lawyers can practice and the financial and managerial relationships they can enter into with nonlawyers without sacrificing the professional values that have so worried American judges and bar associations.

These tradeoffs—between the benefits arising from greater competition and flexibility in business models and the risks to consumers of failures of the quality they expect or are entitled to—are in fact an overt part of the regulatory framework. The U.K. approach is self-consciously risk and outcome-based; it identifies the nature of risks and the outcomes that regulation seeks to achieve. For example, in its rules for determining whether to approve a regulator, the LSB has set out a chart that specifies the evidence it will be looking for to confirm that specific principles and risks are addressed. To gain approval, the regulators must "ensure that authorised persons must keep clients['] money separate from own . . . [and] must be able to compensate clients[;]" "demonstrate how regulated persons and entities are indemnified against losses arising from claims[;]" have a code of conduct that "enshrines the primacy of acting in the client interest and subjugates other pressures, be they commercial or otherwise to that principle[;]" and "ensure that definitions of appropriate skill and competence are proportionate in order to ensure both value and professionalism[.]"

The largest approved regulator, the Solicitors Regulation Authority ("SRA"), has defined four outcomes they expect to achieve and adopted an explicit risk framework to guide approvals for ABSs. They have expressly stated that their approach "is in contrast to our historical rules-based approach: we no longer focus on prescribing how those we regulate provide services, but instead focus on the outcomes for the public and consumers that result from their activities." They focus "attention and activity upon issues, firms and potential risks that pose the greatest threat to our regulatory outcomes." The SRA publishes annually a Risk Outlook that reports their ongoing assessment of where the risks lie.

How well is the U.K. approach working? As one of us has documented elsewhere, the evidence to date is promising. Both as a result of the longstanding acceptance of the idea that useful legal help can be provided by a variety of legal and lay professionals, and as a result of the licensing of ABSs, the U.K. framework includes many more options for English and Welsh consumers of legal services than the American model. Many of these options come in the form of unbundled services to support what in the United Kingdom is called "DIY" law and a wide range of advisory services to help people manage legal questions and issues that have not turned into lawsuits (yet). Total revenues in the legal sector increased eighteen percent between 2010 and 2014. There has been no loss of employment for lawyers. The number of practicing solicitors increased 2.3% from May 2014 to May 2015, and the number of vacancies advertised for law firms increased forty-eight percent in 2014. There has been substantial consolidation of practice, with the percentage of solo practitioners falling from forty-six to thirty-nine percent, and the percentage of firms with two to four partners growing from forty-one to forty-six percent between 2008 and 2011. As of 2013, ABSs were more likely than other practice entities to use technology: ninety-one percent reported having a website to deliver information and services, compared to fifty-two percent of solicitor firms using a website for advertising. Overall, ABSs showed higher productivity and innovation and were statistically more likely to have seen an increase in revenues (fifty-seven percent compared to forty-nine percent). A 2015 study found that ABSs were thirteen percent to fifteen percent more likely to introduce new legal services and that twenty-five percent of all legal services providers had introduced a new or improved service in the three years following the introduction of ABS licensing. In short, "the major effect of innovation in legal services has been to extend service range, improve quality and attract new clients."

Consumers are clearly benefitting from the U.K. changes. Although we lack systematic studies of the impact of changes on pricing, it is clear that the U.K. environment offers much more flat fee pricing than the U.S. environment—a pricing model that supports increased access by reducing uncertainty and risk and promoting transparent choices among providers. In 2014, 46% of consumers reported paying a fixed fee for services, up from 38% in 2012. Moreover, there are clear improvements in choice and perceptions of value, with the greatest gains in family law. The percentage of fixed fees in this area increased from 12% in 2012 to 45% in 2014. Between 2011 and 2014 the percentage of consumers saying they shopped around for services increased from 21% to 41%, and the perception that they had received value for their money increased from 50% to 62%.

There is no evidence of a flood of problems along lines that American commentators have raised. The SRA Risk Outlook for 2014/ 2015 indicates, for example, that dangers that the SRA in previous years had identified as possible risks—a lack of due diligence over outsourcing arrangements and a lack of transparency in complex alternative business structures—had failed to materialize. The rate of errors by unregulated will providers, while substantial, was equivalent to that of regulated solicitors, which led the government to reject a proposal to make will writing a reserved activity. Law firms with nonsolicitor managers and partners, known as Legal Disciplinary Partnerships ("LDPs"), generated fewer complaints on a revenue adjusted basis than solicitor-only firms from 2011 to 2013. ABSs resolved a higher percentage of complaints received than solicitor firms (93% compared to 83%). Although these are still early days, if anything the call has been for further loosening of restrictions to prompt even greater innovation and improvements for consumers.

### DEBORAH L. RHODE, PROFESSIONAL INTEGRITY AND PROFESSIONAL REGULATION: NONLAWYER PRACTICE AND NONLAWYER INVESTMENT IN LAW FIRMS
39 Hastings Int'l & Comp. L. Rev. 111, 114–15 (2016)

Although leaders of the organized Bar repeatedly insist that broad prohibitions on unauthorized practice serve the public's interest, there is little support for that claim. * * * In other nations that permit nonlawyers to provide legal advice and assist with routine documents, the evidence available suggests that their performance is adequate. In a study comparing outcomes for low-income clients in the United Kingdom, nonlawyers generally outperformed lawyers in terms of concrete results and client satisfaction on a variety of matters, including welfare benefits, housing, and employment. After reviewing their own and other empirical studies, the authors concluded that "it is specialization, not professional status, which appears to be the best predictor of quality."

In Ontario, Canada, which allows licensed paralegals to represent individuals in minor court cases and administrative tribunal proceedings, a five-year review concluded there were "solid levels of [public] satisfaction with the services received."

In the United States, studies show that lay specialists who provide legal representation in bankruptcy and administrative agency hearings generally perform as well or better than attorneys. Extensive formal training is less critical than daily experience for effective advocacy.

# TABLE OF CASES

The principal cases are in bold type.